Date: 1/24/23

Y0-CJF-687

PALM BEACH COUNTY
LIBRARY SYSTEM

3650 Summit Boulevard
West Palm Beach, FL 33406

Just One Backyard

Just One Backyard

One Man's Search for Food Sustainability

Dr. John Zahina-Ramos

Copyright © 2015 by John Zahina-Ramos
All rights reserved. In accordance with the U.S. Copyright Act of 1976, the scanning, uploading, electronic storage/retrieval and electronic sharing of any part of this book without prior written permission of the copyright owner is unlawful.

First print edition: January 2015

Library of Congress Control Number: 2015900583

CreateSpace Independent Publishing Platform, North Charleston, SC

ISBN-10: 1505834821
ISBN-13: 978-1505834826

The author or publisher is not responsible for websites (or their content) that are not owned by the author or publisher.

For more information, visit the Just One Backyard website at www.justonebackyard.com.

THIS BOOK IS DEDICATED:

To my maternal aunts and uncles, for showing me a long-gone era.
I will always appreciate having had that window into the past
And treasure the time I spent gazing through it in wonder.

To my parents, who never forgot where they came from
And who sacrificed more than I could ever understand
So their 15 children could be safe, properly fed, clothed and proud.
You were both exceptional.

Most of all, to my spouse Eddie,
This research would never have been done,
Nor would this book have been written,
Without your unwavering and profound love.
Te quiero siempre, mi vida.

CONTENTS

Preface	ix
1. On The Farm	1
2. Industrial Agriculture	6
3. Getting an Education	15
4. Yucateca	37
5. The Road Turns	47
6. Sustainable	60
7. Over the Rainbow	73
8. The Ancient World	88
9. Home Again	107
10. Garden City	125
11. Letting Go	141
12. The Circle of Life	151
13. Water, Water Everywhere and…	164
14. Of Saharan Proportions	172
15. The Green Stuff	189
16. Just One Backyard	205
17. What Has Been Lost	217
18. Back on the Farm	227
Afterword	232
Acknowledgments	235
Footnotes	237
About the Author	263

PREFACE

*W*hen I was a young child, my mother would buy eggs from a woman in town. She would drive up a steep hill, park the car with the wheels pointed towards the curb and set the emergency brake so that the car would not roll away on the near-vertical incline. She would get out of the car and warn us kids to mind ourselves until she got back. Then, Mom would disappear up the concrete stairs, which were embedded into a steep hillside, and enter a large Victorian-styled house that was perched on top. A few minutes later, she returned with several cartons of eggs. Sometimes, she took us up the long stairs to visit the woman who lived in the house above. I never knew who that woman was or from where she got the eggs. All I knew was that the eggs just seemed to be there when we needed them and we ate them. This is how most people feel about their food, whether it comes to them from a vegetable market, a grocery store or a restaurant. The story contained within this book will change all of that.

This book, like life, is a journey. No one can predict where life will take him or her. Sometimes the changes are subtle, sometimes, jarring. Sometimes life takes you to an unfamiliar place and introduces you to people you would otherwise not have known. Sometimes it forces you to look into your own past. Life always brings mistakes and missteps; these too are valuable experiences. Life always brings new insight from others who have thought about things in ways that no one else had before. It is because of all of these experiences that this book has been written.

This book is preoccupied with the subject of sustainability. Although scientists have created definitions for sustainability, popular culture is still struggling with the concept and its meaning. This struggle often leads to disagreements and arguments about what is sustainable. Most of these arguments arise because people view sustainability through the lens of their individual situation or they focus only on a local scale. What appears to be sustainable at the individual or local scale is often unsustainable at a regional or national scale. This leads to a curious paradox- a paradox where two opposite things seem to be true when they apparently cannot be. Recall the example of the elephant, where two blind men are each feeling and describing a different part of the animal. The man at the front will describe the elephant much differently than the man who is at a hind leg. Both interpretations are correct in the context of the particular location they are feeling. But, neither of these is adequate to describe the entire elephant. Only when many observations are taken together can a complete and accurate picture of the elephant be described, when a more comprehensive view is taken. The idea of sustainability is like this, it must include a full range of considerations rather than a single, local perspective. In this book, I usually talk about sustainability in the overall sense- at large scales and not individual scales. I also look at a much broader range of considerations than someone at the individual or local scale would. This is for good reason. If a practice is sustainable for an individual but causes negative impacts elsewhere (perhaps somewhere the individual never sees or knows about), then the cumulative effect of many individuals doing the same practice leads to an unsustainable condition. If this is not clear to you now, it will be by the end of this book.

 I wrote this book for the home food gardener, so they understand how their seemingly small efforts can have influence far beyond their own backyard. This book is for the agricultural researcher, so they can understand the ways that food growing is connected to the world far beyond the farm field. This is for civic leaders, so they can understand how seemingly small actions can create big change within their own communities. This is for the student of sustainability, so they can move beyond concepts and into the realm of quantifiable fact. I wrote this for the rancher, who can play a vital part in preserving our natural heritage. This is for the politician, so they can make more informed decisions about policies that will affect the generations to come. This is for the community gardeners, residents of large cities who have little greenspace, people living in developing countries, world leaders and people who want to know where their food comes from.

I wrote this book for both the academic and non-academic reader, which was a big challenge. During the process of doing research for this book, I discovered how differently these two groups of people interact and communicate. The academic audience most values facts and figures. In contrast, non-academic readers most value emotional connections and the human experience. After a career of writing scientific reports and technical documents, which must be scrubbed of all hints of feelings or humanity, writing a non-fiction book that includes personal experiences and emotional contexts has been refreshing. The challenge has been to represent scientific information in a way that is exciting, interesting and easy to understand without the liability of cold, clinical fact. By drawing upon both scientific facts *and* human stories, I hope that this book appeals to and empowers both kinds of readers- the analytic and the caring. More importantly, I hope it will bridge the great gap that exists in our society today- the gap between academia and popular culture. Each has its own language, which neither understands. Because of this, they seldom communicate. This has led to misconceptions, misunderstandings and misinformation on massive scales. But, academia and popular culture each have something terribly important to contribute to the subject I address in this book- our food systems- because there can be no other subject more grounded in both the sciences and the humanities.

I wrote this book as a warning. It is clear that humanity is heading towards a food crisis that will be more challenging than any that has ever been faced before. Many developed countries are only beginning to realize that their large-scale agricultural practices are becoming an expensive liability. The warning is also directed at developing countries that are headed towards the same mistakes that developed countries have made with regard to their food systems. Developing countries can change course now and end up much better in the future because they were able to adopt sustainable practices that preserved, rather than depleted, their precious natural resources. Once these natural resources (including native ecosystems) are gone, poverty will certainly follow. I believe that we can solve our food sustainability crisis and restore some of our ravaged ecosystems. By restoring these resources, we regain the benefits that they provide to humanity and ensure a sustainable future.

An important thing to remember while reading this book is that each reader will come from a different set of experiences. Because of this, no two people will connect with the information in the same way. Someone who lives in a small town in Australia's rural outback will have an entirely different perspective than someone who has lived in downtown Chicago all of their life. The rural Australian has grown up with a vast expanse of open, undeveloped land. To them, losing several hundred acres of natural land to agriculture is probably not a big deal and may be a real economic benefit to the community. For the Chicago native, who has lived without open space their entire life and where so little of the original ecosystem still exists, the loss of hundreds of acres of natural land is unthinkable. The rural Australian and urban Chicagoan will see water use and water conservation issues differently too, since the latter lives next to a seemingly endless body of freshwater that is as large as a sea. In spite of these different perspectives, they face the same issues. The long-term problems that come from environmental degradation are the same no matter where you live.

Many regions of the world still have large intact ecosystems that can be preserved, even as products can be sustainably harvested from them. For those regions, it's not too late to avoid the profound losses experienced by other areas of the world where native ecosystems were destroyed for the sake of agricultural or urban development. These losses can happen quickly. The extensive North American prairie lands, which once spanned half of the continent and were inhabited by great herds of wild beasts not unlike the Serengeti Plains of Africa, were destroyed in the span of a single generation. These losses can also happen slowly, with the native ecosystem slowly nibbled away over the span of centuries until almost nothing remains. We can preserve our biodiversity, have space for human settlements and grow enough food to feed our world's population; these do not have to compete against each other- so long as there is a commitment to sustainable practices. But, this can't happen without a sober assessment of the current problems.

First and foremost, scientific knowledge is built like a high-rise building- one cannot build the higher levels without the solid footing of the structure beneath it. The solid factual footing of this book is based in a large body of research studies, data and information that was collected by a lot of different people. In order to give credit where it is due, I have included a footnote at the end of a phrase or sentence (this appears as a small number); please refer to the Footnotes section at the back of this book for more information on that particular topic. I also have placed additional stories in the Footnotes, which would be a distraction if put into the book's main story, but are entertaining nonetheless. I hope you will refer to the footnotes as you read through. While writing this book, I was concerned that using footnotes would be distractive, as they can often be. On the other hand, it would be wrong to not acknowledge the source of ideas or information that are not mine or are not considered to be commonly known. I believe this adds to, rather than takes away from, the reader's experience.

I wish to thank you- the reader- who has taken an interest in this topic and in my book. I, and other researchers like me, can collect the best data that science could ever hope to have, discover exciting new things, uncover important new breakthroughs and write compelling prose but, if it isn't read and understood, if it does not provoke change for the better, it is worthless. Now, get yourself comfortable and let's begin this journey together. I promise, it will be worthwhile.

Dr. Z
December 12, 2014

Just One Backyard

1. ON THE FARM

I was seven. It was late November and this particular day was unseasonably warm for eastern Iowa. Temperatures were not cold enough to require a winter jacket and mittens. I was out in the backyard playing with whatever I could find to amuse myself: sticks, rocks and dirt. Next to the house was a flowerbed, an extension of the brick that formed the main structure of the building, which had been cleared of the season's flowers and was beckoning for a seven-year-old to play in. I sat on top of the cold low brick wall of the bed and dug into the loose sandy soil, pretending to look for precious stones or perhaps even gold! I had come to hope for such possibilities after being told fantastic children's stories where kids like myself stumbled upon buried treasures. To my surprise, I felt something buried in the soil...it didn't feel like a rock, it wasn't that hard. As I brushed the dirt away from it, I could see that it was orange. I pushed my fingers underneath it and pulled up a large carrot! Reaching down, I uncovered several more. It was clear that the carrots had not been growing there because they had been laying on their sides in a neat little row. I had seen carrots growing before and they grew upright, with their tops coming out of the ground. How very odd it seemed, but I was sure that I must have hit some kind of vegetable mine...what else could this possibly be? I thought about how wonderful it would be to have discovered a little magical place where you could dig up the food you needed right from your own backyard! This was all the mystery a seven year old could take and there was only one thing to do...dirty hands and all, I ran into the house to show Mom, who was standing over the stove cooking dinner. When I explained to her where I had found them, she smiled in an understanding way and explained to me that she had put them there. She was storing vegetables in the planter's sandy soil next to the south side of the house where they could be kept without refrigeration into winter. I didn't realize it then, but this was her way of root cellaring in the city, where space for true root cellars was limited. By this time the practice of root cellaring, which was a way to use the natural cold in the ground to store fresh fruits and vegetables without refrigeration, was becoming frowned upon as being uncivilized and outdated, especially for people living in cities who had modern appliances.

 Exactly 45 years later, I recalled that imagined childhood vegetable "mine" as I drove through the blighted neighborhood just north of the luxury high-rise condominiums of downtown West Palm Beach, Florida. I was in my vehicle following a retired gentleman, who everyone referred to as Boz. Most residents in this part of the city were unemployed or making less than poverty level wages. The neighborhood's small, dilapidated and boarded-up homes stood in stark contrast to the opulent seaside mansions in the town of Palm Beach, one mile to the east across the Intracoastal Waterway, which seemed to represent an economic divide as deep and as wide as the Grand Canyon. Boz told me that this neighborhood was one of 27 food deserts in Palm Beach County, places where residents have limited access to food markets or affordable healthy food, particularly fresh fruits and vegetables. Boz had been working unpaid for four years to create a non-profit urban farm on a 1.5-acre vacant lot along the railroad tracks. His dream was to feed this underserved and hungry community. We parked next to an abandoned building, across from an abandoned home, and stood in the street looking at the vacant lot, which once held apartment buildings. A few weeks later, this same spot where we stood would be the place of a senseless and brutal murder of a 22-year-old African American man. The vacant lot in front of us was as desolate as the Sahara, except for patches of resistant weeds, several cabbage palms and a decaying strip of asphalt driveway that led nowhere. The soil was dry, sterile sand. This really was a field of dreams; there was nothing else there.

Little more than a hundred years earlier, these same struggling neighborhoods north of downtown West Palm Beach were on the edge of a large and productive food plantation. Vast fields of pineapples greeted northern visitors destined for grand resort hotels as these same train tracks carried wealthy guests through West Palm Beach, then across the marshy Lake Worth to the island of Palm Beach. Henry Flagler, a founder of Standard Oil Company, had built the railroad to open up this region for tourism and development by connecting the northeastern United States to southern Florida with a relatively rapid and comfortable means of transportation. The railroad arrived here in 1894, with expansive winter resorts opening soon afterward. This area was one of the more desirable food growing areas in the country, with food being shipped from here to northern markets hungry for exotic tropical fruits during frigid winter months. It seemed beyond comprehension to visitors from "up north" that food could be grown here while the rest of the country was gripped in bitter cold. "Well," one could not help but brag, "it would be impossible for anyone to go hungry in a place where you could grow food all year!" The descendants of the plantation workers who had waved to the arriving vacationers still live in the blighted neighborhoods surrounding Boz's planned urban farm.

Boz unrolled the large-format drawing of his plans for the site. On it, he pointed at places for vegetable gardens, fruit trees, places to learn and to build community interaction. He believed this urban farm could produce enough food to make a real difference in the community. He told me about its strategic location, how residents from three of the city's neediest neighborhoods could access the farm's produce without having to own a car. He saw the future. Weary from the financial, regulatory and funding battles he had to fight to make this barren piece of land yield the food needed to feed these neighborhoods' residents, he was ready to plant. You could hear it in his voice. But, the site was not ready. Yet.

This vacant lot next to the railroad tracks holds a story about how an area that once produced abundant food became a place where fresh and affordable food is beyond the reach of this neighborhood's residents. It is a story repeated in countless cities across the United States and in other countries, developed and developing. The world's population is growing and migrating into cities from rural areas.[1] For the first time in history, more people live in urban areas than in the rural areas outside of cities. According to experts, the extent of human development worldwide is poised to triple between 2000 and 2030,[2] and with the expansion of cities comes the challenge of feeding the growing urban populations as prime farmland is paved over for development. Inadequate access to affordable and healthy food is a growing problem in some urban neighborhoods, the direct result of dependency on a precarious food market system that heavily relies on food grown on distant lands, the location of retail food markets only in areas where maximum profits can be realized and a wholesale loss of food growing skills by city residents.

The current industrialized agricultural food system is inadequate and is causing irreparable environmental damage. With additional uncertainties arising from climate change, today's agricultural system simply cannot meet the needs of the world's current population or that of the future. The problem is not that we are unable to produce enough food, it is that we are not producing it properly or in the places where it is most needed. It is ironic that we need government-imposed food price supports for farmers because we are overproducing some kinds of commercial crops, yet within some agricultural communities there are people who have inadequate access to food. It doesn't have to be that way and the current food system needs to be reconsidered at all levels. Our food can be produced in ways that enhance the environment and protect natural resources. Instead, our agricultural systems are assisting in the destruction of ecosystems and are depleting the natural resources that the next generations must have. Meeting our current and future food demands will require us to re-examine where we are, where we have come from, and how we can reasonably and sustainably feed ourselves from within our cities- the very place where most of the world's food is consumed. It is not a matter of conscience, it is not a matter of reason; it is a matter of survival.

2. INDUSTRIAL AGRICULTURE

I was eight. My brother-in-law lived in the city, but was raised on his family's farm and his farmer brothers still planted corn each year. This particular season, the weather was good and there was a bumper crop of sweet corn. Late one Saturday morning, my brother-in-law arrived at our house with a pickup truck, its bed filled to the brim with just-picked ears. This was piled in a large heap on our concrete carport floor and everyone in the family was recruited to help. The younger children shucked the corn and the older sisters helped Mom prepare it for preserving. Each ear, and there were hundreds, had its tender, sweet kernels cut off of the cob with a sharp knife. Dozens of canning jars were filled with creamed corn, along with dozens of freezer bags, until the carport floor was empty. We had preserved enough corn to last our family for the year. Besides an afternoon's work, there was little cost for the corn; the farmer took some money to cover his costs, but we received a delicious side dish for countless meals to come. In the cold of winter, when ice and snow covered streets and sidewalks, the steaming bowl of creamed sweet corn came to the table, making us giddy with anticipation and rekindling the warmth of summer.

    Small family-owned farms, like those that my uncles once owned and the one that provided my family with the truckload of sweet corn, had been the main food suppliers to America from the time this country was established until the 20th century. Then, small family farms found competition from an unlikely source...a new form of agriculture that grew out of the Industrial Revolution. This new agriculture grew and sold food in ways that were revolutionary, but untested. It also created problems that no one could have ever foreseen.

"Industrial agriculture" was born out of Industrial Revolution advances in the areas of mechanization, assembly-line production and transportation that began in the late 1800s and continued past the turn of the 20th century. As these advances were applied towards agriculture, food production shifted in significant and life-altering ways. The impacts of the industrial food system on local food production and food choices were profound. This new industrialized agriculture was radically different from what farming had been throughout most of history and in most of the world.[3] An experiment with an entirely new food system had begun.

One catalyst for the development of industrial agriculture was the creation and expansion of cross-continental railway and highway systems that allowed farms to transport their crops across long distances. Other important advances were the invention of refrigerated transport, the production of chemical pesticides and fertilizers, and the manufacture of industrial machinery. With all of these new technologies and infrastructures in place, the food production and delivery system could expand far beyond the boundaries it had previously known. The natural outcome was the development of truck farms.

Truck farming, which grew food that was intended to be transported to consumers in distant markets, emerged as the major type of agriculture in the 1950s. This gave rise to vast vegetable production operations in the northern Everglades, Midwestern states and California. Unlike the local farms and family gardens of a half-century earlier, truck farms were located long distances from consumers, and relied heavily on fossil fuels for growing and transporting products.

With transportation barriers dissolving, large-scale farms were developed in rural areas and in arid western states. These farms allowed economic development in areas where it would not have been possible before. But, these new ventures were not cheap. They were only possible because of the adoption of federal policies that encouraged large-scale rural food production and support by Federal subsidies.[4,5] These vast, new agricultural lands and the development of truck farming caused agricultural production to change from a mostly local and near-urban activity to a predominantly rural enterprise. This change also brought about the movement of land ownership away from family farms and towards large agri-businesses.[6]

With most food production in the hands of commercial operations, food became a market commodity, something that could only be obtained through retail outlets. In the quest to produce more profit per acre, vast swaths of land were planted using intensified growing methods and very few types of crops.[6,7] The development of a nationalized industrial agricultural system occurred at the same time that the supermarket, with purchasing power and high volume sales, began to spread across the United States.

By the early 1970s, the impacts from the new industrialized agriculture became visible in my working class Dubuque, Iowa neighborhood. They were called supermarkets; they were like large department stores, but for food, and had many different types of offerings consolidated under one roof. The housewife, who did most of the housekeeping and child rearing then, could save time and money by having everything she needed under one roof. This concept also gave rise to the enclosed shopping mall. Around the same time that supermarkets began to pop up in communities, shopping malls were spreading across this country and one was being planned for the cornfields at the western edge of our city. This was a radical shift away from how people had been shopping and purchasing until then. As outlying malls devastated the downtown shopping districts of cities, so supermarkets wiped out the small, family owned neighborhood stores. The argument in favor of these centralized shopping points was that consumers benefitted from competition and convenience. However, the costs of these benefits came with a great price elsewhere in society and the environment- costs that were not known at that time and were not considered in the calculations of benefits.

At the beginning of the 1970s, neighborhoods in my city still had their own small stores, but these were closing one-by-one. Most of these were located within a reasonable walking distance from anywhere in the neighborhood and we had known the families that owned them for generations. Our neighborhood still had home milk delivery from the milkman and a store that specialized in dairy products (the Milk House). There were also small neighborhood stores that specialized in the sale of quality meats (the butcher shop), fresh-baked breads (the bakery) and general goods (the market). Once a supermarket anchored itself in a part of town, nearby small stores, owned and operated by neighborhood families, went out of business. My parents owned such a store during the 1950s, which they ran out of the first floor of our house, the house in which all of us children were born and raised. Neighborhood stores like these were centers of neighborhood social interaction. Almost everyone in the store, from customers to workers, grew up with each other, grew old together, looked after each other, attended the same churches, had children in the same schools, ate at the same supper clubs and relaxed at the same taps (the local name for a neighborhood bar). My father had the foresight to see the impacts of supermarkets as they inevitably advanced toward our own neighborhood. To secure a stable income to support his family, he closed the store and took a job at a meat packing plant that supplied supermarkets.

When the first supermarket opened near our neighborhood, Mom continued to shop at the small specialty stores until they closed or the prices at the supermarket became too attractive to resist. Being a poor working-class family with so many children to feed, it became an issue of economic sense. But there were other reasons too and these were cultural, not economic. We, like so many others in the United States at that time, were beginning to drift away from our agricultural roots. My mother was born and raised on the family farm. My father, who grew up in the city, saw farming as a dirty and rural occupation. For him, vegetable gardening was a pastime but he was very proud to be among the city people who were keeping up with the times. By the late 1970s, my parents had made the full conversion to supermarket shopping and abandoned home food gardening. Locally grown fruits and vegetables almost entirely vanished from our diets. My parents constantly complained about the poor quality, lack of taste, and high prices of these commercialized fruits, vegetables and meats. Subsistence food growing was going out of style and was considered to be old fashioned. Who would want to bother with all of the work involved with growing food when you can go to the store and buy it? We were modern, evolving like the rest of the developed world. Those of us who lived in cities and worked good jobs had earned the right to not grow our own food. We were beginning to see ourselves as being freed from the burdens of gardening labors. But that freedom came with costs, many far greater than we could have ever dreamed. I could not have imagined then that, later in my life, I would dedicate years of research aimed at quantifying the true breadth of those costs.

The new industrial agricultural system allowed consumers to purchase many types of fresh fruits and vegetables that they would otherwise not have access to, especially when these were not available locally or were out of season. Of course, the trade-off for shipped or out-of-season produce was quality and price, but that was not all. Behind the produce stand display were other impacts that would not be fully realized for decades. This new form of agriculture relied heavily on natural resource consumption, particularly non-renewable energy and fertilizers. Industrial farming practices have polluted waterways, caused soil erosion, used natural resources in unsustainable ways and have had far-reaching negative ecological impacts.[8] Although industrialized farming has increased access to some kinds of foods, there have also been negative impacts on local economies and public health.[3]

Industrial agriculture relies on relatively new methods and products to increase commercial crop yields. One of the most important of these relatively new products is chemical fertilizer, which are fertilizers that have been manufactured or purified through a laboratory process. One type of fertilizer is nitrogen, an important plant nutrient needed to grow the green parts of plants, such as leaves. Another fertilizer is phosphorus. When these plant nutrients are not present in sufficient amounts, plant growth and food production are limited.

I use the term "relatively new" when referring to chemical fertilizers because these products were not widely used until well into the 20th century. The farms surrounding my family's Iowa homestead only began using chemical fertilizers during my lifetime. For millennia, farmers didn't use chemical fertilizers to grow crops, so the intensive application of them over the past half-century must be viewed as a new practice, as an experiment. Only now can we begin to assess the negative aspects of their long-term, widespread use and examine the viability of other alternatives before we can say if they should be a permanent addition to long-term agricultural practices. Chemical fertilizers have increased crop yields in some places and under some circumstances. But, in taking the broad view of their potential benefits, we also have to look at where these fertilizers come from, whether similar amounts of food can be grown without them and where agricultural fertilizers go after they have been applied to the land.

Nitrogen is the most abundant element in the earth's atmosphere. It is all around us, but is useless until it is changed into a form that can be taken up by plants. This is where synthesized nitrogen fertilizers come into the story. Certain nitrogen fertilizers are synthesized in factories, but the process requires a lot of energy, the use of non-renewable resources such as natural gas and high-pressure conditions that can be expensive to create. It has been estimated that the use of synthesized (chemical) nitrogen fertilizers has allowed food production on a single parcel of land to increase fourfold as compared to what could have been produced in 1900![9] However, the validity of this claim and the examples used in the comparisons are questionable. I will talk more about this misconception in a later chapter.

The story for phosphorus is somewhat different. Phosphorus is an element that is especially important for plants that produce flowers and fruit. It occurs naturally in certain kinds of rocks, but is often in low concentrations in the natural environment. Significant deposits of phosphorus-containing rocks are not common, so where they do occur they are usually mined. Phosphate mining is destructive to the environment because it destroys natural habitat and permanently alters the natural landscape. For example, phosphate mining in Florida has created large, deep pits that were turned into deep lakes after the rock was extracted. These deep pit lakes support little life and have far less ecological, environmental or economic value than the natural landscape that once occupied the site. Things are much worse for Nauru, which is a South Pacific island country in Micronesia. There, 80 percent of the 8.1 square mile island has been strip mined for phosphate. Now that the phosphate deposits have been exhausted, the island's economy and ecology have collapsed.[10]

Proponents of chemical fertilizers point out that if synthesized fertilizers were not used in commercial agriculture, up to four times more agricultural land would be needed to produce the same amount of food. This higher agricultural efficiency, they argue, saves natural lands from destruction by reducing the amount of space needed to produce food.[9] However, long-term studies of crop production using organic methods question the validity of these arguments in favor of chemical fertilizer use. By using the traditional practices of crop rotation, planting a mosaic of crop types and enriching farm soils with natural amendments (e.g., manure, compost, cover crops), food production can equal that of industrial agriculture while reducing the potential for pollution (pesticide and nutrient) runoff, maintaining soil quality, reducing soil erosion, reducing fossil fuel consumption and conserving water.[11] There are ecological benefits too. Studies that compared biodiversity on conventional and organic farmlands found that, on average, the fields that used organic methods had a 30 percent higher number of species such as birds, insects and plants.[12]

The use of nitrogen and phosphorus chemical fertilizers has come with a heavy price. Today, in some regions of the United States, it is difficult to find waterways that have not been polluted by farms. The United States Environmental Protection Agency estimated that half of the pollution in rivers and streams in the United States originated from farm runoff.[13] The natural ecology of these waterways is being altered, sometimes significantly and permanently, because of the way our food is being grown. The negative effects ripple throughout the food web, impacting fisheries and migratory bird habitat and other game and non-game wildlife species. At risk are the productive shellfish beds in Florida's Apalachicola Bay, the Chesapeake Bay fisheries and other important areas. These are also important food suppliers. Fertilizers in rainfall runoff in the American Midwest are partly responsible for the vast dead zone in the Gulf of Mexico along the Texas and Louisiana coasts,[14] which is larger than the state of Connecticut. I wonder how much of this damage was caused by farmers near my grandfather's homestead? How would they know? The Gulf of Mexico is a thousand miles away, out of mind, and each farmer believes his contribution is too small to be significant. Sadly, the farmers that use chemical fertilizers and pesticides believe that those products are required to produce an adequate crop. Long-term studies of alternative methods have demonstrated otherwise.

Industrial agriculture was invented to be a solution to an enormous problem, which was the issue of how to feed the world's growing population by producing more food on less space. This was an important and noble goal. By producing more from the same amount of land, there would (theoretically) be fewer hungry people in the world. The rapid growth of industrial agriculture in the mid-20th century was undoubtedly fanned by the memory of food shortages during the Great Depression. But, missing from this conversation was the broad view of the costs and impacts of industrial agriculture, especially compared to other agricultural methods.

During the early part of the 21st century, an estimated 98 percent of the United States' food supply came from industrial agriculture that used intensive farming practices.[15] As food production sites are located farther from the point of consumption, consumers are becoming more isolated from their connection with the land, knowledge about food production, food safety, the resources consumed and the environmental impacts resulting from agriculture. Through time, apathy towards resource conservation, responsible resource consumption, environmental protection, carbon dioxide emissions, the well being of agricultural workers, agricultural pollution, pesticide use and food safety issues is inevitable.[16] Consumers are also becoming distanced from agricultural production and seasonality. For many who had grown up with food gardens, this distance creates apathy about growing food for oneself. At no time in the past millennia have the skills of home food growing and preserving been abandoned so thoroughly and so rapidly. When I look at my own family, I can see the profound changes that have happened from the time of my grandfather to my generation; the impact of industrial agriculture is unmistakable.

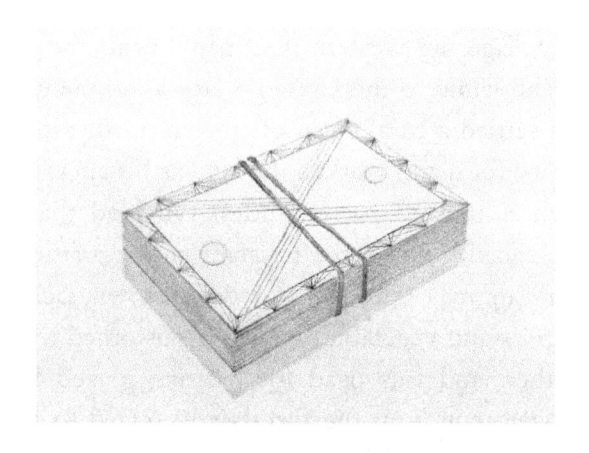

3. GETTING AN EDUCATION

On summer Sundays when I was a child, my parents would corral the younger children into the family sedan, those that wanted to go, for the 20 minute drive down to a very small town in eastern Iowa where Aunt Elizabeth lived. Of course, some of the children resisted; those who were teenagers wanted to hang out with friends or go shopping, but I loved to visit there. The town was small, quiet and modest, with so few homes that I could have walked through town and counted them all in a few minutes. My mother was the youngest of 12 siblings and Elizabeth was her oldest sister. Besides the big age difference between them, 21 years, there were also generational and cultural differences as well. Although both were raised "on the farm," on the same piece of land homesteaded by their German father and Luxembourger mother, they lived in entirely different worlds. Mom and our family lived in the city, in the thoroughly modern way; Elizabeth and some of her siblings lived in the same way people did in the "Old Country." Visiting Elizabeth's home was like spending time in another era, like being in a living history museum where you could see and feel how our ancestors had lived for an uncounted number of past generations.

My maternal grandfather, Ferdinand, was born in 1862 in a rural

Mosel River village in western Germany near the border with Luxembourg and came to the United States as a young man. By the 1890s, he had settled a rural piece of land in northeastern Iowa. My grandfather grew food and worked the land as his ancestors had done in his German homeland for centuries. On land that was fit for cultivation, he sliced through the resistant native prairie with a plow pulled by work animals. The soil was deep brown, rich, perfect for growing the fruits and vegetables he was accustomed to eating in his homeland. Other land was used for pasture, grazed by cattle and horses. Logs were cut from the forests and milled to build a home and barn, and the land yielded the materials they needed to live. When Ferdinand arrived in the United States, Iowa's native prairie still covered vast expanses. At that time, it was viewed as a wasteland. It seemed to be an endless and formidable obstacle for those who sought to live off of it. By the time my grandfather settled on his land, the prairie was already being decimated. The vast herds of bison that roamed the great plains of the Midwest had been exterminated, as well as other staples of the Native Americans who had lived on the land for thousands of years before these new immigrants arrived. Promotional materials told of reclaiming the land for agriculture and promised that it's soils were among the richest in the world. Use of the word "reclaiming" suggested that it was a resource that had been lost and only development would bring back its value. One by one, settlers fragmented the native prairie and within several decades, most of the area around my grandfather's property had been plowed for crops.

The first child born to Ferdinand and his wife Josephine (my Luxembourger grandmother) was Elizabeth, in 1896, followed by John in 1897, for whom I am named. John purchased additional land around the homestead, lived alone in a very small one-room cabin and farmed in the old style until he was no longer capable of physical labor. He lived a very modest life, without most modern conveniences, and was referred to as "Tarzan" by locals because of his enormous physical strength. John knew the land and knew how to feed himself from it. He knew which wild plants could be eaten and which wild mushrooms could be harvested from the woods. There were an abundance of wild fruits like gooseberries, strawberries, mulberries, blackberries and ground cherries. Hickory nuts, butternuts, black walnuts and hazelnuts grew wild in the nearby woods. His vegetable garden, cattle and wild game provided every type of food he could ever have wished to eat. John and his father understood their land's value and importance to their families. The land was used in such a way that its soils remained healthy, productive and intact. The meadows were lightly grazed by cattle, which maintained both the meadow's health and a steady food source for the browsing cattle. The woodlands provided building materials and food without being harmed or exhausted. Today, we call these agricultural methods "sustainable." Sustainable practices were necessary because the land owned by my grandfather and Uncle John was intended to be passed down through an indefinite number of successive generations.

In contrast to John, who was a lifelong bachelor, Elizabeth married and settled down in a nearby small town. Elizabeth's home had a functioning outhouse until the late 1960s, when an inside toilet was installed. She had wood-burning stoves for winter heating, a naturally cool basement for food storage and a kitchen at the back of the house with a door leading to the outhouse and the food garden. When visiting, I sat on the parlor floor and played with empty wooden spools from sewing machine thread, constructing buildings with them as though they were store-bought building blocks. I would also keep an open ear to the adults' conversation, which at any moment would carry them en masse to the upstairs to view the newly completed quilts Elizabeth had sewn. Although Elizabeth had lost her fingertips to frostbite as a young child, she would complete a dozen quilts in a winter, sewing them from salvaged fabrics or old clothes. No visit was complete without a trip down into the cellar (which had shelves loaded with canning jars full of vegetables, stewed tomatoes, canned meat and dried wild mushrooms) and out to the garden to see what was being grown. Home food gardens then were sometimes referred to as kitchen gardens because of their proximity to the kitchen itself.

Elizabeth's entire backyard was a kitchen garden. In so many ways, it was a wonder to behold. She knew every plant as though it were a special child and was quick to point out the medicinal uses of the weeds that grew between the vegetables. There were flowers, too, but these were relegated to the fringe areas; flowers were appreciated, but they were not given the same lofty positions within the garden as the vegetables. There were giant Mother Hubbard squash that grew to half my size, something that always made me a little nervous. There were many rows of potatoes (badaders, as they were referred to then), tomatoes (these were good for your blood, Elizabeth pointed out), tall onions, giant green cabbages, bulbous kohlrabies (a German vegetable), cucumbers and many other types of vegetables that eventually ended up in canning jars that sat on the shelves in the cellar. All around the garden bed were clusters of brilliant red and white poppies, irises that were as blue as the sky (one variety, she confided, had flowers that smelled like root beer and she was the only person who grew such a scented iris), orange geraniums, confetti-colored zinnias and cheerful yellow flowers with names I never remembered. The backyard perimeter fence kept out animals and served as an arbor for the best concord grapes one could ever hope to find. Compostable kitchen scraps were worked into the garden soil to enrich it. Wood planks were laid across the ground to allow one to tend to the plants and harvest without sinking shoes into the Iowa mud.

From this robust garden, Elizabeth grew enough vegetables to feed her household and more; she insisted that we take jars of her canned goods home with us after each visit. Meat and other food necessities came from her brothers' nearby farms. Dry goods and sundries were purchased from the small town store. Elizabeth's home and lifestyle were typical for 19th century rural immigrants to the upper Midwest, small towns in rural western Germany and

Luxembourger villages. But, for my siblings and me living in the city in the 1970s, it was something of a curiosity. My father's family was city people and prided themselves on being modern. My father always remarked that Elizabeth and her brother John were living more than a half century in the past, and it was not intended to be a compliment. If not for the modern plumbing and electricity, they were living the same way as their ancestors had. I did not realize it then, but in my aunt Elizabeth's home I was seeing into a way of life that had existed in my family and in most of the Western world for centuries- I was seeing into the Old World. That way of living was about to abruptly change, being abandoned so rapidly that the baby was thrown out with the bathwater.

During their lifetimes, my mother's siblings witnessed a profound change in the way food was produced, sold and obtained by city residents in the United States. Until the 1900s, most people lived in rural areas and grew their own food in the same way my aunts and uncles did. City residents had home food gardens too, but also relied on market farms that produced food on lands adjacent to cities. Most of the food produced in this country was consumed within the region where it had been produced and was often sold by the farmer who grew it. Nearly all of the money earned from food sales in that economy went to the local farmer and was respent within the community, a sort of monetary recycling.

A century ago, many urban residents grew fruits and vegetables in home food gardens; these gardens produced much needed fresh produce for the household regardless of income level, employment status or economic conditions. Food was much less of a market commodity then. It could be grown with little or no financial cost and traded for work or other goods. In many ways, it was an important type of currency whose market value was determined by those who could not grow it for themselves. My mother's siblings continued to live this way until they died in the 1980s. I was so very fortunate to have seen this kind of agriculture first-hand. It would be decades after the last of my ancestors died before I would discover the true worth of home food gardens.

As the fourteenth child in a family with fifteen children, the societal and career importance of education changed dramatically from the time when my mother went to high school (1930s), my oldest siblings were in high school (1950s) and the time when I was (1970s). It was never about intelligence. Anyone in our family, men and women alike, could take a gadget apart and reassemble it with uncanny intuition or understand complicated subjects. I have an older sister that when confronted with a flat tire or worn out brake shoes on a vehicle, you had better stand aside and let her fix it. When I would work on splitting apart an old tree stump in the yard, the remnant of a large oak that was cut down to provide more sun to the family vegetable garden, my 77-years-old father had no qualms shooing me away, taking the sledge hammer and wedge from me to split it himself. College was well beyond the reach of most of us, particularly because of college costs. The need to get a job as soon as you were of working age and the likelihood of men being drafted into the Vietnam War effort further discouraged higher education. Fortunately, this was beginning to change by the time I entered high school in 1975.

Education was not a priority in my family. My father had an 8th grade education and that was enough for men in his generation. Men were expected to get a good job in construction, a trade or in a factory- that was where the good money was. Women were expected to get married (to the previously-mentioned men) and tend to the home and children. Higher education and careers, in my father's thinking, were not necessary for anyone and especially not for women.

Although my mother had a high school education, she had to leave her home on the farm and live in the city (Dubuque, Iowa) to get it. In the 1930s, during the Great Depression, education beyond the 8th grade was not considered important- especially for a woman living in the country. Some of Mom's siblings were quite upset that she, a woman, would enroll in high school. Resistance to her

Getting an Education

attending high school was so great from her older brothers, she had to leave the farm and live with her sister in the city to do so. As my father once told me, her brothers would snipe "who does she think she is, a woman smarter than a man?" This move had a profound influence on my mother's life in two ways. First, it made her appreciate education and she was a quiet supporter of her children's education goals. Second, it was the reason she met my father. My mother attended a small girls-only Catholic high school that was a couple of blocks from her future husband's parent's house. Although my father saw the struggle my mother went through to obtain a high school education, he did not care if any of his children went to high school. In fact, whenever the chance arose, he encouraged us to drop out. Unfortunately my oldest sister and youngest brother did just that.

Perhaps because I was near the low end of the pecking order in my family, I went through school with a low self-esteem. It wasn't until well into my later teens that I discovered that I was at least as smart as my other high school classmates. I had always felt inferior to them and because of this, I kept to myself and had few friends. But as I entered my senior year, that changed. I had grown. I also had little to lose because I had completed nearly all of the required number of credits for graduation. Another point in my favor was that I turned 18 during the first half of my senior year and this made me a commodity (when something becomes a commodity, it takes on values it otherwise would not have). This made me a very important commodity, in fact, particularly with respect to the unique geographic characteristics of the region in which I resided. Here, the state of Iowa (on the west bank of the Mississippi River) met the borders of Wisconsin and Illinois on the east side of the Mississippi River. In Dubuque, Iowa, you could take the north bridge across the river into Wisconsin and the south bridge into the state of Illinois. It was no coincidence that there were taps conveniently located at the foot of each bridge. This setup was well understood by, and of particular interest to, high school students throughout this tri-state area.

Most of my classmates were 17 in their senior year of high school. It was legal for an 18-year-old to purchase and drink alcohol in the state of Wisconsin, but the legal age for alcohol purchases in Illinois and Iowa was 19. At that time, my family was living in rural East Dubuque, Illinois, a town on the east end of the ¾ mile long Mississippi River bridge from Dubuque. The winding, up-and-down country road in front of our rural house drifted northward through corn fields, cattle pastures and prairie meadows, then crossed the Illinois state line into Wisconsin less than two miles from our driveway. Sitting on the Illinois-Wisconsin border was the ever-popular State Line Market, which sold little more than seasonal vegetables, cheese, beer and wine. It was said that the state line ran right through the middle of the store and that the shopkeeper kept a watchful eye on which aisle its state-regulated products (alcohol and tobacco) were offered for sale. This was entirely believable. My best friend in high school lived across the street from the market and his family's house was in Illinois, but their backyard and barn were in Wisconsin. One local legend tells of shopkeepers who would drag displays of alcohol and tobacco products from the Wisconsin to the Illinois side of the store when Wisconsin regulatory inspectors would come to call. Once the items were under another state's jurisdiction, there could be no inspection nor could citations for violations be issued. The market had steady and robust sales to 18-year-olds from Iowa and Illinois who came to purchase beers with names like Blatz, Heileman's Old Style, Hamm's and Falstaff, and wines with tempting names like Apple and Tickle Pink. These were the market's most popular commodities. Besides the products of great interest to teenagers, they also carried some of the best local sweet corn that could be purchased in the area.

In the last half of my senior year, I began to bloom socially and academically. I joined the high school band, took a drama class and had a major part in the high school's first theatrical production. I played the part of the traveling salesman in Rodgers and Hammerstein's famous musical Oklahoma! At the end of the school year, I won the high school's Best Actor award. I was part of our high school's marching band that traveled to downtown Chicago and marched on State Street in the 1979 St. Patrick's Day parade (spot number 112), which we later watched on television from our hotel rooms. While watching The Loop shut down, come together to drink green beer along the dyed-green Chicago River and cheer for total strangers along the parade route, something inside of me changed that day. For the first time, I saw a horizon that stretched beyond my Upper Mississippi River Valley home.

The high school guidance counselor, seeing the changes in me, called me into her office one day and asked me to take an intelligence quota (IQ) test. I thought that would be an interesting thing to do, but didn't know why it was particularly important. She saw that my grades were average, but felt that I was as bright as her honor-role students. She wanted to confirm that my grades were a reflection of my lack of confidence and encouragement, rather than a lack of intelligence. I came away from the IQ test with a score of 139, which seemed to excite her; in fact, she insisted that I go to college and said that she would personally drive me to classes if necessary. Even though the validity and relevance of these IQ tests would later be challenged, this was the first time in my life that I felt encouraged about education. Milestones like these boosted my self-esteem and gave me the courage to think of better things for myself. They also gave me the freedom to reconsider the hometown life that I was expected to lead.

In Dubuque during this time, one was supposed to live according to long-held familial expectations, expectations that your parents had lived up to and that were accepted as the norm. Although my parents had cast these expectations as long-held traditions and part of the family's heritage, they really were not...these expectations were created during the 20th century and my grandparents lives, if closely examined, were certainly not the gold standard. The problem was not that all of these expectations were inherently bad, it was that some of them were no longer good and those that no longer worked needed to be replaced with something that worked better. The rigidity in my parent's thinking was that these expectations were universal and fundamental, unchangeable. The expectations for me were that I should remain in my hometown, become trapped in a mindless factory or trade job the rest of my life, a job that I would hate but would stay with to survive financially. Those were the jobs almost all of the men in my family had taken and they were told to be glad to have them. I was expected to work a good blue-collar job, get married to a nice local girl, have several children and settle down. With that, I would have fulfilled all of the expectations that life held for me. By my senior year, I saw many of my classmates moving well down that path with wives and children on the horizon. The thought made me feel nauseous and claustrophobic.

Late in my senior year, I made the decision to heed my guidance counselor's suggestion to pursue a college education. Although there were two colleges and a university in my hometown, all private and affiliated with religious denominations, I resigned myself to the fact that I could not afford them. The cost of attending those schools was on par with more prestigious institutions such as Duke University. Seeking other options, and at the urging of my high school guidance counselor, I found a book at the public library that contained a full listing of the colleges and universities in the United States and began to search for schools in areas where members of my family lived. I was pleased to find a community college in Lake Worth, a suburb of West Palm Beach, which was affordable and in the same town where one of my older sisters had moved to two years earlier. Later that same week, I made the long-distance call to ask if she knew where the school was at and how far it was from where she lived. As fate would have it, it was nearby, perhaps two or three miles away. Six weeks after I graduated from high school, I packed my belongings and moved to West Palm Beach, Florida to live with my sister and start college.

My father was flatly against any of his children attending college. "A waste of money," he chanted over and over again. Many years later, after my mother had died, he gave away most of his belongings and moved to Florida to live next to my sister and me. At that time, I was working on my bachelor's degree. At 82-years-old, even ill with terminal cancer, he insisted that I should stop going to college and that it was a waste of time and money. He literally went to his grave believing that. Needless to say, my family never supported my college education financially or otherwise. I had to work full-time and go to school part-time through nearly all of my college years, which made progress painstakingly slow. I simply could not afford college any other way. When I graduated, my achievement was acknowledged by few of my siblings- not because they didn't care about me but because they didn't value higher education.

I left my hometown on a warm summer morning, the 19th of July 1979, and arrived in West Palm Beach on the afternoon of the 21st. My oldest brother drove me from Dubuque to Union Station in downtown Chicago, where he left me to catch the train to Florida. It was a miserable 38-hour train ride. For the first time in my life, I was completely alone, without parents, family or friends. I had left everyone and everything I had ever known to live in a place I had never been to before. I had spent most of my savings on the train ticket and had only $35 in my pocket, all the money I owned, and two medium-sized cardboard boxes that contained my worldly possessions. Most of those possessions were clothes, which included hand-me-downs from my older brothers. I could not afford a sleeper bed on the train and was only able to get brief naps in my uncomfortable seat. The food was expensive and terrible; I purchased a hot dog for supper, which cost more than a full-course meal back in my hometown. The hot dog was burned on the outside and nearly frozen on the inside. It was inedible and I threw most of it away. In my pocket was a deck of cards my mother gave to me the morning I left home. At that time, she was barely able to walk, the victim of a progressive and insidious Parkinson's-like disease that robbed her of any sense of balance and left her with slurred speech. She was only able to walk by holding on to furniture and edges of tables to steady herself. The morning I left home, she fell and broke her wrist. She had tears in her eyes as she literally crawled to the dining room table to get the cards that we used to play together. She told me that I would need them to pass the time during my train ride. They were my only companions on that trip to Florida, to my new world. It would be the last physical thing she would ever give to me. Later in life, I thought back on that day. Playing cards was a way for my mother and I to spend time together. Food gardening was too. But, with the advent of electronic games and supermarkets, card games and home food gardens were beginning to fade into the past. As my mom (and those in her generation) became aged and crippled, society ran away towards new things. Card games and food gardening were abandoned. But, that deck of cards was a gift to me from my mom, as was the knowledge of how to grow food for myself. I still have that deck of cards, locked away in a safe-box.

Only in my older years have I been able to grasp the emotional and physical hardships that my immigrant ancestors endured to come to this country. They came to the New World because they could have no future other than their parents' and grandparents' past. I had left my birthplace for the same reason. As I thought about my own move to Florida, which permanently severed the physical connection I had with everything I had ever known, I began to think about how difficult it must have been for my grandfather to leave everything he knew behind. Although we were born nearly 100 years apart and on different continents, we shared many similarities and had many differences. In my case, I was moving to a different part of the same country and when finances would permit, I could talk with my family by long-distance telephone calls or return for visits. But, when my grandfather came to this country, it was with the full knowledge that he likely would never see his parents, grandparents, aunts, uncles, cousins, village or homeland again. His language, with all of its quips and quirky phrases used by loved ones and words of comforting familiarity, would only partially be known by his children because he spoke it in his home. Some of his grandchildren would come to despise immigrants who spoke a language other than English. My grandfather's children would speak an entirely different language from that which had been spoken by every person in his family for centuries. The only possible lifeline to his roots, letters, did travel between Europe and the midwestern United States, but these could take months to arrive. News of an illness or death back home would not be known until well after the deceased had been mourned. The emotional pain must have been profound. One can understand why my grandfather, and other immigrants like him, clung tenaciously to the practices, food preferences and gardening styles of his ancestors. They were among the few tangible things from his distant homeland that he could draw close. They were what sustained him.

Stepping off the train in West Palm Beach, the sun was hot, the humidity high and the air was heavy. I had never been to south Florida and did not know what to expect. Storm clouds loomed to the west. "It's the rainy season," my sister informed me when I asked if it was like this all year. I came to find out that there was also a dry season and that neither of these seasons resembled anything I was accustomed to experiencing "up north," as everyone says down in south Florida. Weeks later, I experienced another aspect of this tropical climate that I had never known in the Midwest- a category 2 hurricane named David.

For the next 20 years, I would live in apartment buildings and townhouses with no private land ownership, just tiny patios that had scarcely enough room for patio furniture. This was how people in larger cities lived. One of the touted benefits was that residents were liberated from the burdens of cutting grass, pruning landscaping and maintaining gardens, allowing more time for leisure activities (and second jobs to pay for it all). Inside, I was still Iowan and the love of the land remained with me although I could no longer see a forest or farm field. Something inside of me longed to have my hands in soil and to grow food, it was an inherent part of my being. For years, I grew one or two potted vegetables, mostly tomatoes, on patios. These were never productive enough to be worthwhile, either in expense or labor. Instead, the potted plants served as desperate and lasting connections with my childhood experiences and heritage. As my aunts and uncles and mother, those who had known the world in another era, grew sick and died, I saw something slip away as I watched helplessly from 1500 miles away. When the last of them was gone, the final threads that tethered me to the Old World were broken. Although I was encouraged to celebrate the fact that I had moved beyond the old-fashioned and outdated, I mourned the loss of what they had known and how they had lived. This made me feel empty.

During my first years in West Palm Beach, I worked at a fruit and vegetable stand that was owned by a local family. The store's owners (three brothers who inherited the business from their father) were not growers, but purchased produce directly from groves and farms in the region. The store only offered local produce for sale and the store's owners personally knew the farmers they purchased from. Because of the quality of the fruits and vegetables, seasonal residents and tourists flocked to the store to enjoy their fresh selection and to mail fruit to northern family members enduring the cold winter weather.

As a sales person at the fruit and vegetable stand, I met many people from New York City and other large metropolitan areas in the northeast United States who had moved to south Florida to retire. When I talked, they knew I wasn't from south Florida. When they talked, I knew they weren't either. Although we were from the same country, we were from vastly different cultures and had very little in common. I found the heavy regional accents and mannerisms of those retirees startling. I responded the same way to Southerners, too. Up to this point, my whole world had been populated by rural or small city Midwesterners. I had only seen and heard New Yorkers (and Southerners) on television and now that they were standing in front of me, they seemed to be curiosities. I was a curiosity to them too. The New Yorkers were genuinely surprised to meet someone from Iowa. In fact, many said that they had never met anyone from

Iowa before. When I described the area I was from, most of them would chuckle and shoot back callous comments, indicating that Iowa was unsophisticated, rural and uncivilized. Usually, I had to endure farm jokes...did I have manure on the bottom of my shoes? Did I know how to call the cattle in? Did I grow corn? They could not imagine being from a place where there was no high culture, no world-class theater and no affluence- at least, not to their lofty standards. How sheltered a life I had led, some consoled me with pitying voices and assurances that they understood why I had left. In turn, I was bewildered at their sympathetic gestures; I certainly didn't feel like I had been freed from some outer wasteland. But, those remarks made me feel ashamed of where I had come from. I also became ashamed to admit that I liked to grow my own food and that shame was something I carried with me well into my middle-aged years.

The retirees from the metropolitan northeast told me about the places they had lived most of their lives. I was shocked. Sure, there were renowned museums and professional theaters and world-class restaurants, but there were also thefts, muggings, rapes, murders, the blatant distrust of strangers, abrasiveness and unkindness to others. I never experienced any of that growing up and it seemed unimaginable that anyone could live in a place like that. These people were business savvy and very selective when shopping at the produce market, but they knew nothing about the farms that provided their food. Few had ever seen the plants or animals that produced the food they had been eating their entire lives.

Many years later, I came to understand the aversion these retirees had to food gardens. They had come through the Great Depression as children and saw what food insecurity looked like. Living in crowded cities, where little food could be grown, the only way out of starvation was to rely on food handouts, to live off of the charity of others, to grow your own food (which many city dwellers did not know how to do) or work hard. These retirees had chosen the latter, dedicating themselves to careers that had paid off and it was their time in life to take it easy. The idea of people growing their own food recalled the desperate times they knew during the Depression. For these retirees, having a food garden was a sign that you had not been successful, you were in financial need or that you were of a lower social class (falsely associating the practice of home food growing with poverty). They lived in gated communities and formed homeowner associations that required manicured lawns and banned the growing of food gardens, perhaps in an attempt to surround themselves with people who had been successful and were of an equal (or better) social class. Decades later, as times changed and city residents began to embrace urban food growing again, these community restrictions against food gardens were challenged as archaic and shortsighted.

During my first two decades in Florida, it was rare for me to eat a piece of food that had not been purchased from a grocery store. This was new for me and it took a long time to get used to. It seemed strange to be entirely dependent on a commercial supermarket for all of my food. During this time, I noticed how locally produced foods had vanished from our grocery store shelves, particularly fresh fruits and vegetables. Some of the food that used to be raised and sold locally was now being grown in distant places and transported to where I lived. This transition occurred during the same time when my parents, aunts and uncles died. It was as though their way of life, their custom of growing food for themselves, had become an old thing that was no longer wanted. When that generation passed away, it marked the end of an era. The successive generations became more distanced from where their food was grown, became less knowledgeable about how their food was grown, were ignorant of the environmental impacts of large-scale food production and were disconnected from the land. And, I had become one of them. I had become fully urbanized. Later I found that it wasn't just me, but people who lived in other places- even in places such as the Midwest and Iowa itself, one of the most productive agricultural areas in the world. From my aging siblings and down to their children and grandchildren, people were becoming increasingly dependent on food that had been grown by large commercial agribusinesses and had been transported across the continent. They seemed oblivious to what that might mean to them, to their local economy, to the environment and to the quality of the food they consumed. How could they know? The food appeared in the store, dressed in the best of displays, packaging and slick marketing. There was no way to know the rest of the story.

The stories created by my ancestors did persist though. Their memories and stories about how things used to be are, paradoxically, both powerful and precariously fragile linkages to a great reservoir of knowledge and experiences. The importance of ancestral agricultural heritage cuts across all cultures and countries. A friend of mine from India, Ramesh, talked with me one day about his family's food growing heritage. "My grandfather had a large food garden and loved it. He would care for the garden each day and it gave the family food as we needed it," he told me. Ramesh's father grew food for the household, but Ramesh has never grown a single food plant himself. "I tried growing pots of herbs, but these died," he lamented. "Since I moved to the United States, I have lived in apartment buildings and there isn't any land for me to grow food on, but if I had access to garden space, I would definitely grow vegetables." I asked him about the importance of home food gardens in India. "Agriculture and farming and urban areas are very separated in the United States, but this is not so in other countries," Ramesh explained. "In India, many people grow their own food. A couple of times each week, a truck loaded with fresh fruits and vegetables drives through neighborhoods and past apartment buildings to sell food, like ice cream trucks do in the United States, except it is produce for the household and not sweets for the children." Ramesh explained that he would like to grow vegetables but he didn't know how; he had left his parent's home before it could be taught to him.

One couple I knew was very concerned about the ever-widening distance between them and agriculture. They lived in an upscale development with no space for growing their own food garden and even if space were available, the community's restrictions would have prohibited it. On weekends, the couple would take their two young boys to local farms and community gardens to show them how food was grown and where their food came from. The mother was of Italian heritage, but had been born in a rural town in Brazil; her grandparents had family farms, which she used to visit every weekend. This was a woman who deeply valued homegrown, fresh produce. These Brazilian parents spoke gravely about how people are losing their connection to agriculture and to the land. They were doing everything they could to pass those values to their children.

Many people in my generation had parents who grew food for themselves, especially during the Great Depression or World War II when Victory Gardens were promoted as a way to support the war effort. An acquaintance of mine, who was born and raised in Allentown, Pennsylvania, told me about how food growing declined in his family through the generations. He explained, "My grandparents used to have a home vegetable garden all the time, but they lived through the Great Depression and that was what carried people through back then." He felt that younger generations were not growing food for themselves because it wasn't as necessary today as it was years ago and that people have less time to tend gardens than they used to. Those were sentiments echoed by my friend Ramesh and the Brazilian couple.

I began college in January 1980, attending Palm Beach Junior College (now Palm Beach State College) in Lake Worth, Florida. I purchased a bicycle, which would be my main form of transportation for many years, and headed to class each day. I had decided to major in music, although my first college career choice had been astronomy. I had read that there were simply too few jobs for astronomers and that I would need an advanced degree to get any permanent position in that career. Besides, reference guides and student advisors warned in ominous tones, astronomy majors needed to take *a lot* of physics and mathematics courses. That generated enough fear to help steer my ship of future career choices away from the cruel rocks of certain failure. So, I fell back on something I knew I could do. Besides, music was in my family. My parents both played instruments and my father's brother was a regionally famous musician. In fourth grade, I had been pulled from classes by the nuns at my grade school and told that I would be learning guitar. And, I did learn how to play guitar. I also began playing the organ, which we had in our living room at home and, at the age of fifteen, I started writing melodramatic teenage love songs.

One September afternoon in 1980, our music class took a trip to the Glades Campus to meet with other students there. The Glades Campus ("Glades" being a local shorthand for Everglades) was about an hour drive west of West Palm Beach in the city of Belle Glade (translation: "Beautiful Glade"). Belle Glade was situated on the southern shore of Lake Okeechobee, the second largest freshwater lake entirely within the borders of the United States, so I had been told. I looked forward to seeing the lake! They told me that it was so large that you could look out over its waters and not see the other shoreline. This was my first excursion outside of West Palm Beach since I had arrived in Florida over a year earlier.

I had been told what it was like "out by the lake," but no description would adequately capture it. I recall one person telling me that the soil was black and that it was called muck. They described it as soft, oily and if you got it on your clothes, it left a permanent stain. How strange that sounded to me, being from a land of loamy prairie soils. A stain from the soil back home would wither away when faced with the strength of homemade lye soap. As the school bus headed west on State Road 80, the urbanized area quickly fell away as we entered a natural world of saw palmetto and whispering pinelands. The road was perfectly straight as far as the eye could see. We passed through the Village of Royal Palm Beach, then farther west through Loxahatchee, an unincorporated area with unpaved roads, large lots and very few homes. Then, we came upon a landmark that every local person knew- Twenty Mile Bend, so called because it was the first place along the road's route where there was a curve. This bend on State Road 80 occurred exactly twenty miles west of the Atlantic shoreline.

The entire character of the landscape changed at Twenty Mile Bend, where a sign welcomed travelers to the Everglades Agricultural Area. We suddenly left the piney woodlands and entered into an open world that was expansively, profoundly flat. Painfully flat, in fact. Grant Wood, who made eastern Iowa's rolling hills famous in his paintings, would have thrown down his brushes in frustration if he had come to this place. One could see all the way to the horizon without the slightest bump or rise obstructing the view. There were no trees, nothing but agricultural fields tightly packed with sugar cane (which vaguely resembled corn plants) and a few vegetable crops springing from the blackest soil I had ever seen. This soil was muck and it looked like coal. It was said then that in these muck soils, one-fourth to one-fifth of the winter vegetables consumed by the United States were grown.

The road jolted a hard left at Twenty Mile Bend, then eventually twisted westward again. The asphalt road through the vast agricultural fields was difficult to travel, wavy and buckled in places due to subsidence of the organic soils beneath it. The road was not banked along curves and was dangerously narrow, with no guardrails, and shoulders that plunged into the adjacent canals that kept the farmland dry enough to grow crops. During harvest season, the roads were swarmed with tall, speeding trucks loaded to the top with sugar cane that had been hand-cut by seasonal workers brought in from the Caribbean Islands. Fatal accidents were common along the stretch of highway from Twenty Mile Bend to Belle Glade. It was a harrowing journey. That stretch of State Road 80 would eventually be recognized as one of the most dangerous roads in the state, gaining the moniker of "Bloody 80."

Belle Glade, established in 1925, exists only because of the vast federal wetlands drainage project initiated in the early 1900s, which drastically lowered the stage of nearby Lake Okeechobee and successfully drained hundreds of thousands of acres of Everglades marsh and swamp for agriculture. As our bus entered the city, a cheerful sign greeted visitors with the slogan "Her Soil Is Her Fortune." This is no doubt an acknowledgement that the fields surrounding Belle Glade produced a substantial part of the sugar cane consumed in the United States. We passed a run-down shopping center and housing that resembled barracks and slums. The sights jarred me. There were bars on windows and rags for curtains, when there were curtains. Residents were poor farmworkers, or their families, evidently imprisoned in a cycle of poverty and starved of opportunities. It was hard for me to believe that I was still in the United States. I recalled this memory of Belle Glade many years later when I passed through poor rural villages in Mexico and Puerto Rico. The resemblances between them were striking. Only a few years after this visit, Belle Glade would become known as the city with the highest HIV infection rate in the United States.

Twenty years before my visit, Edward R. Murrow's legendary documentary about the treatment and living conditions of migrant agricultural workers aired on national television on Thanksgiving Day. Belle Glade was featured in this documentary entitled "The Harvest of Shame." The living, working and economic conditions of agricultural workers were described as a modern-day form of slavery. Many workers could not earn enough money to pay rent for their own rooms, which cost from $6 to $15 per week. When they moved, some were only able to take with them whatever belongings they could carry. As an example of the dire conditions these people faced, one woman with fourteen children described picking beans from 6 am to 4 pm and making only $1. I thought about my own mother, who had 15 children, and was horrified to think of her (and us children) in that kind of situation. Workers typically earned less money than what they needed to feed their families. As the documentary pointed out, federal regulations requiring rest, water and food for cattle being taken to market were better than those for agricultural workers at that time. These dismal and demoralizing conditions condemned these people to an inescapable cycle of poverty and hopelessness. After more unfavorable press in the 1970s, large agribusinesses began to make changes, but there was so much more that needed to be done when I first came to Belle Glade. The plight of agricultural workers here was a profound irony, similar to the man who finds himself on a raft adrift upon the sea, surrounded by water but not a drop to drink.

When we pulled into the parking lot of the college campus, I was stunned. It consisted of a single small two-story building with few classrooms. This was nothing like the campus I attended, which sprawled for acres and had entire buildings dedicated to individual areas of study such as science, art and athletics. Nor was it anything like the clean Neo-Gothic stone campuses of the colleges and university in my hometown. It occurred to me that this school was perhaps the only means the children of this community had to escape the isolation and financial desolation of this community. If they could find a way to afford it.

4. YUCATECA

*U*nder an intermittently warming sun, I stood and gazed in wonder at the restored buildings of Uxmal, one of the ancient Maya's great cities situated almost 40 miles south of Mérida in Mexico's Yucatán Peninsula. Its elegant beauty was captivating, unlike anything I had ever seen. Although I had studied two semesters of art history in college and understood urban American, traditional European and Middle-Eastern architectural styles through thousands of years of history, none of that fit into this indigenous Native American architectural style that I was seeing for the first time. For me, a citizen of the United States, born and raised in North America, this indigenous architecture seemed foreign and completely new only because the relatively young cities I came from were based on imported ideals.

Uxmal is one of very few other places on Earth where rigid stone has been transformed into something so fluid and graceful. The United Nations has christened this stone city as a World Heritage Site, recognizing its importance in history, art and architectural style. Its monumental buildings reflect the classical period of the Maya's culture and many of these structures, built more than a thousand years ago, are a perfect expression of high art. But, by the year 1000, around the time of the Maya civilization's great collapse, the city was abandoned. There were few residents in the area by the time the first European explorers arrived.

Climbing up the precariously tiny steps and severe incline of the enormous Pyramid of the Magician, I looked out on the surrounding landscape from the summit temple. The pyramid itself is a marvel. Built over a period of 400 years and reaching up to 115 feet, it is considered to be the most distinctive and recognizable structure on the Yucatán Peninsula. Although this pyramid was one of the more austere buildings in the complex, the summit temple had carefully carved stone decorations and moldings that required a great deal of artistry and skill to execute. Other buildings adjacent to the pyramid were lavished with carved stone figures and intricately interwoven geometric designs throughout. It was clear that this was once a socially advanced city with a sophisticated culture.

From the pyramid's summit I surveyed the landscape. As I looked across the horizon, the land spread out in a mildly undulating rhythm with occasional bumps interrupting the monotony. Incomplete restorations hinted at a once larger city than what I could see immediately around me. The restored Uxmal was certainly much smaller than it had been during its high point, when its estimated population grew to as much as 25,000 people. As with our modern cities in the 20th century, food had to be grown in other areas and transported into the city to feed the expanding urban population. For Uxmal's residents, this city must have seemed immortal, being so grand and so finely crafted from the most durable of building materials. Great temples and grand religious ceremonies offered assurances that divine powers would protect their well-being. For centuries, generations of families lived and died here; it was their home and their heritage. Then, things changed. This was the first time I had seen an abandoned city of this size and grandeur. I could not help but wonder what might have caused this great city of carved stone to become silent.

By mid-afternoon, I had finished exploring Uxmal. The partly sunny weather had turned cloudy and a cold breeze cut through my light clothing. Under graying skies, my travel companions and I left Uxmal by car and set out for other lesser-known ruins in the region. We navigated along a narrow and twisting unimproved road toward Oxkintok, an abandoned Mayan city that had undergone little restoration. The landscape was dry, rocky, with no streams or lakes or wetlands- no water visible anywhere. We passed an empty sisal hemp factory that once processed the native agave plant's stiff fibers into rope, twine and other products. Some rural houses were made from wooden posts and mud, with thatched roofs. Gazing out the car window at the scrubby landscape, I was startled by something I saw. I recognized one, then another, corn stalk in the brush as we carefully drove forward on the bumpy road. To me, these seemed terribly misplaced; up until now, I had only seen corn growing in fields or packed into the corner of a vegetable garden. Looking at the rural Yucatecan landscape, I saw sparsely scattered corn stalks, not in the neat rows created by industrial machines but growing out of more-or-less random holes created by a stick pushed into the dry soil. Even though the native brush and trees ruled the landscape, hand-planted corn was being grown and harvested in its midst. This was how corn had been grown here for millennia and I was seeing indigenous, sustainable agriculture for the first time. How very different this was from the densely packed cornfields back in Iowa, where all vestiges of the local ecology had been cleared away to grow commercial crops.

Nearing our destination, we passed oddly shaped rocky hills with trees and shrubs growing from them in erratic angles. Those strange hills rose abruptly from the flat land around them. We turned a final sharp corner around one of these steep hills and immediately entered a dusty, barren parking area. The only thing there was a local Mayan, who had been sitting in a chair. As we exited the vehicle, he stood up, approached us and held out his hand for payment. This was the sign that we had arrived at Oxkintok.

The ancient Mayan city of Oxkintok looked very different from

Uxmal. It was much older, by as much as 500 years, and lacked the intricate stonework. There were many ruined buildings in the complex, some loosely arranged around a plaza, but very few had any significant restoration. Most of the unrestored buildings were nothing more than tall, rocky lumps overgrown with a jungle-like growth of trees and shrubs. A single face of the great central pyramid had been only partially restored. Climbing to the top, which took considerable effort and nerve, I was able to see all the way to the horizon. Under the cold, cloudy sky, there was more of the monotonous brushy vegetation I had seen as we approached Oxkintok, broken only by uncountable numbers of scattered lumps and bumps on the rolling landscape. These lumps seemed out of place, as though they were not a natural part of the land, and they appeared to be more of the same oddly shaped rocky hills I had passed on the way to Oxkintok. Looking at the ruins around Oxkintok's main plaza, I realized that these lumps were not hills at all. Each was a ruined building from the ancient metropolis. Five centuries after being abandoned, the city had been reduced to a loose collection of crumbing stone piles. Like Uxmal, Oxkintok had once been a thriving urban center.

Many of the great Mayan cities, particularly those in the south, were abandoned in the 9th and 10th centuries. Scientists who study the Maya civilization's collapse have suggested that it may have been caused, at least in part, by environmental and ecological changes brought on by urbanization and large-scale agricultural development. Some research has suggested that the Mayan population grew to be larger than the land's natural resources could support, leading to agricultural land depletion and overhunting. There is significant evidence to support this theory. Other research has uncovered evidence that a long-term drought, lasting up to 200 years, was at least partially to blame. More recent studies have indicated that the conversion of native forest to cropland may have altered natural weather patterns, exacerbating the impacts from drought. Although there may have been several different factors that contributed to the collapse of the Maya civilization, those that are based in environmental degradation are the most concerning. Oxkintok, Uxmal and the other abandoned Mayan cities in Central America are a warning to us today- the destruction of the natural environment for agriculture and urban development cannot continue indefinitely without causing a ruinous and widespread human disaster.

Sometimes a society embraces a course of action that seems to be the right thing at the time, but is later reviled as shortsighted and ruinous. Sometimes, these ill-fated practices are venerated as heritage or as cultural norms when they are neither. This was the case for the ancient Maya and humanity today is no less susceptible to the same course of action. Humanity needs to periodically re-examine where it is going, how it is getting there and what the wide-reaching costs of unsustainable practices are. If sense prevails, problems are identified early and corrected so the damage that has occurred can be reversed. But, this is often not the case because financial investment, emotional attachment and inertia tend to preserve the status quo regardless of whatever evidence to the contrary surfaces.

Few people in the United States would say that this country has experienced a large-scale ecological catastrophe. Certainly, there were the chestnut blight and Dutch elm disease disasters, but we still have thriving forests and younger generations may know nothing about them. There were the Three Mile Island and Love Canal crises, but those have been confined to a limited area. There were also the Exxon Valdez and Deepwater Horizon oil spills, but those impacts occurred in places most people never see. Driving around neighborhoods or the countryside, there are still woodlands and free-flowing brooks and butterfly-filled meadows. In fact, most people would point to these as evidence that things are really not that bad. For many, the environment is possibly harmed only when a large tract of land is entirely cleared for development. I use the word "possibly" here, because there is a perception that there is still so much healthy natural environment, that the loss of a few more acres could not possibly be a problem. Even in cases where all remnants of the local ecology have been wiped from a site, well-designed landscape and lawn cover tends to soften the perception of ecological destruction. A neighbor of mine once pointed to the abundance of little anole lizards on the side of her house as proof that the bimonthly applications of atrazine and fertilizers to her verdant lawn over the past three decades were not polluting the groundwater, which was only seven feet below her house- the same groundwater that my household well was drawing from. I certainly desired more assurances than the lizard test.

When, as a child, I passed the pastoral cornfields of Iowa on the way to the old homestead, I saw a tranquil and beautiful landscape filled with farm fields as far as the eye could see. I had no idea what had been there before or what that might have meant. I did not even know that there had been anything else there before the cornfields. To me, they were eternal. When I saw the Everglades Agricultural Area for the first time, I saw food being grown in the blackest soil I had ever seen. I saw workers gathering the harvest and large mills on the horizon busily converting the raw cane to sugar and molasses and other food products. The land held a certain beauty in its vastness and neatness. The rows of food crops were reassuring in a comforting way- this was a place that was feeding American's cities. What I could not see was what had happened before I had arrived- that this place had been the site of an ecological disaster of such magnitude, that international outcry would have been raised if it were to occur today.

The northern and eastern portions of the Everglades were entirely drained and converted to agriculture. This was not done by the current landowners. Everglades drainage was the result of government initiatives to develop new lands for human settlement and was widely supported by residents at the time it occurred. In fact, a politician by the name of Napoleon Bonaparte Broward ran for and won governorship of Florida on the platform of draining the Everglades for agricultural development. By cutting miles of major drainage canals from Lake Okeechobee through the Everglades, the government had achieved its goal of "reclaiming" what was viewed as wasteland. People at that time did not appreciate or understand the Everglades ecology, its uniqueness in the world, its value and its connection to the water that residents of south Florida depend on. Concerns about environmental damage were almost absent; the extent of wet prairie, marshes and swampland in southern Florida was so vast that it seemed inexhaustible. Besides, it was a place where lethal diseases bred and dangerous wildlife roamed. Draining it was considered to be to mankind's benefit. The vast region, which once teemed with abundant wildlife, great flocks of birds so numerous that they could darken the midday sky and uncountable numbers of fish, was transformed from a wondrous watery prairie to a bleak landscape of black, decaying muck. These are the agricultural fields that Bloody 80 traversed and the land upon which the town of Belle Glade was founded.

Once the natural organic soils in the Everglades were drained, they began to decompose and shrink. These marsh soils, which promised abundant food production during the cold of winter, soon began to decay and disappear beneath the subtropical sun. Soil loss happened faster on farmed land because the nutrients that were applied as fertilizer for the crops also stimulated the decay of the soil itself. In some parts of the Everglades Agricultural Area, soil loss has been as much as 12 feet. In areas to the east, where there is a sand layer underneath, all of the organic matter has decomposed, leaving nothing behind but pure, sterile sand. These eastern areas eventually became agricultural fields and rangeland, then housing developments. Although thousands of acres of constructed marshes have been created on farmland that was once Everglades, and these have proved to be havens for wildlife, it will never be possible to return the farmed areas of the Everglades to their original state. But, drainage of the Everglades is minute in comparison to the great North American ecological disaster that occurred from the 1800s through the early 1900s- the destruction of the vast prairie and bison herds in North America's Midwest.

It has been estimated that the American bison numbered over 60 million when the first Europeans arrived in North America. These large, stoic beasts roamed from northwest Canada to central Mexico, from Florida to Maine and westward to Oregon and northern California. Weighing up to one ton each (or more), they were surprising agile and swift. But, the bison could not resist government policies set on destroying the indigenous people's freedom nor could they outrun the shot of a well-aimed gun. By 1890, there were only an estimated 750 bison left in small, scattered herds. The destruction of this iconic species was mostly because of commercial hunting and indiscriminate slaughter, which was actively encouraged by the United States government as a means to clear land for cattle ranching and to deprive the Native Americans of a vital food source.[17] So many were the rotting carcasses of slaughtered bison, that for many years settlers to the West collected bones and skulls for supplemental income- these were ground up and sold for fertilizer.[18] Although conservation and ranching have raised numbers over the past decades, the total number of bison today is still less than a half-million. Another reason for the decline of the American bison was the wholesale destruction of their native habitat- the great prairie lands of North America.

The enormous North American prairie once stretched from Canada to Mexico, from the Rocky Mountains to the state of Indiana- covering an area of nearly 545 million acres.[19] This prairie was not homogeneous, rather it changed along an east-west rainfall gradient. Parallel to the Rocky Mountains, a band of shortgrass prairie once ran along the eastern areas of Montana, Wyoming, Colorado and Arizona. A contiguous swath of tallgrass prairie once existed throughout the states of Minnesota, Iowa, Illinois and Missouri. The land between the tallgrass and shortgrass prairie, the mixed prairie, had characteristics of both.

After the Native Americans were driven from their ancestral lands and the bison herds exterminated, the United States government opened the empty prairie to European settlers in the late 1800s and early 1900s. Among them was my grandfather. Year after year, acre after acre of prairie was plowed under for agriculture- at first to grow food for the homestead and then later for commercial markets. Two-thirds of North America's native grasslands fell to the plow.[19] Because of the tallgrass prairie soil's richness, these lands were some of the first to adopt industrial agricultural practices. Land that was once tallgrass prairie is now among the most intensively farmed areas of North America, producing mostly corn and soybeans. It is estimated that only 0.3 percent of the original tallgrass prairie land has been protected. As compared to other states, my Iowa homeland has the least area of uncultivated land remaining, a true heritage of shame.

The mixed prairie lands were also plowed under for agriculture. Today, these lands produce wheat and other grains that require less water than corn and soybeans. Shortgrass prairie seems to have fared better than either the tallgrass or mixed prairies, but it too is threatened. Originally, shortgrass prairie was too dry to support many commercial crops and was used for grazing cattle. Later, particularly during the 1920s and 1930s, unsustainable farming practices destroyed the native, deeply rooted vegetation that maintained soil stability and moisture. Settlers with imported ideas about agriculture ignored the limitations of local soil and climate. Government agricultural subsidies and the newly available industrial agricultural methods that used plows, tractors and mechanical harvesters encouraged landowners to convert shortgrass prairie to cropland. During a series of droughts, agricultural crops died and the exposed soil turned to dust. Strong winds blowing across the plains carried soil dust in great storms that blanketed homes, roads and cities. Referred to as the "Black Blizzards," visibility was sometimes less than three feet. [19] In some places, up to 75 percent of the valuable topsoil was lost- topsoil that was required to grow crops. The effects of the drought and soil loss, covering an extent of more than 156,000 square miles, affected areas of New Mexico, Colorado, Texas, Oklahoma and Kansas. This ecological disaster left a half million people homeless, forced tens of thousands of people to abandon their family farms and caused an exodus of some 3.5 million people from the region.[20] The impacts of the "Dust Bowl," as it would be referred to later, intensified the economic woes of the Great Depression.

To put the destruction of the North American prairie in perspective, the Food and Agriculture Organization of the United Nations estimated that between 1990 and 2005, almost 11,500 square miles of Brazil's tropical rainforest was cleared for agriculture. That rate of loss raised international concerns and conservation groups worldwide raised money to help preserve parts of that resource. Throngs of scientists descended on the rainforest to study it and document its ecological and economic importance. The native peoples and their ancestral lands have been the focus of cultural preservation efforts. National and international discussions about preserving that important ecosystem continue today. However, using that same rate of rainforest loss, it would take more than a half-century to begin to approach the extent of North American prairie that had been lost to agriculture. North America's greatest ecosystem was destroyed with barely a whisper of complaint.

In America today, little thought is given to the bison, the prairie chicken or the species extinctions that came from the prairie's demise. When I drive past the cornfields of my birthplace today, I see more than the tranquil and beautiful landscape. I also see what was lost and knowing this has changed my perspective in two very unsettling ways. First, I see the land's vulnerability, not just in scattered small parcels but also on regional scales. If millions of acres of prairie could be obliterated in the span of decades, then the agricultural landscape in front of me may not be as permanent as it seems. Second, we really do not know how this conversion to unsustainable agriculture might become a liability later. Recalling the collapse of the Mayan civilization should be a warning to us today. There will, no doubt, be other chapters written for this land. Depending on the decisions that people make today, this future may not be so desirable.

5. THE ROAD TURNS

I was nine. It was late September. My dad and mom piled the younger children into the car and we headed out to the old homestead to work in the vegetable garden. Although my mother grew up on the farm, my father's family lived in town, being laborers and tradesmen by occupation. My father's parents grew food in their backyard and purchased food that was grown on farms that were in their part of the country, as did other city dwellers at that time. With so much food growing experience in my parents' families, it was unthinkable that they would not have a food garden too. Because they needed access to more space than our yard could provide, we had a plot for growing vegetables in the country. The drive out to the homestead was about thirty-five minutes but seemed a whole world away. We passed corn fields, dotted with upright bundles of straw-colored corn stalks and blazing fall colors draped over roadside trees; the scene looked like it had been taken from a picturesque autumn painting. We grew vegetables in a fenced-in plot beside the gravel road that dead-ended next to my uncle John's cabin. The fencing kept deer and rabbits out, but the weeds thrived and weekend trips were necessary to fight back the prairie grasses and wildflowers that wanted to return to the rich soil of their ancestors. After harvesting most of what was ready, we met up with Uncle John. This day, he was taking us out to pick apples. We were herded into his pickup truck and my parents' four-door sedan and drove across the bumpy pasture edged with relic native hardwood forests and scattered prairie patches. After passing through several fence gates, we arrived at an ancient, ungroomed apple orchard. I was amazed at what I saw. Out here, away from everything and everyone, was a grove of apple trees that seemed to have been planted by someone who was just traveling through. At that moment, every story that I had ever been told about Johnny Appleseed, stories that I had been hearing for years in my grade school classes, was confirmed! They were *really* true and I was seeing it for myself! How else could it be possible that these old trees out in a remote meadow came to be? I kept asking my uncle who planted these trees, but his replies were vague. We walked from tree to tree as he explained the types and uses of each apple variety there. The small ones were best for canning, the yellow-red ones were best for storing in the root cellar, the very large apples were for cooking and the medium red apples were for eating fresh. I looked at them all in wonder. On the way back to town, I sat on Mom's lap, clutching a large, pink cooking apple as though it were a trophy.

Six months after I moved to Florida, at the age of 19, I began college. I took a full schedule of courses for one year. But, I could not afford to pay the tuition required for a full-time student while working a part-time job. I left life as a full-time student in order to take a full-time job. I did take several classes over the next few years, but had lost my interest in music as my major after I realized what the life of a musician was really like...low pay, working nights and working weekends, none of which appealed to me. At the age of 25, without any real commitment to a major area of study, I completely dropped out of college.

Over the next three years, I found myself frustrated with my long-term employment prospects. I came from a culture that valued the idea that you should be happy with what you have, even if it wasn't enough. That outlook worked for my grandparents who had little and for my parents who raised their children on poverty-level wages without charity or government assistance. Unfortunately, that outlook wasn't going to work for me, especially when I saw others my age prospering and moving ahead in their careers. I could see myself as a 30-year-old with the same job prospects and qualifications that I had when I was 18 and newly graduated from high school. When I thought about my long-term career prospects, the feelings of nausea and claustrophobia flared up in the same way they had when I was 18. I knew I could do good things, I felt it in my gut. I also knew that I could spend my whole life waiting for opportunities that may never come. I was young enough to still make a change in my life, but change had to come as a result of focused work and not through sheer luck. I knew that I had neither the knowledge of how to make a good career happen nor the education credentials to open the doors of opportunity I longed to pass through.

In the fall of 1989, at the age of 28, I returned to college. I had to make it work this time because the opportunities available to me without a college education were unacceptable. What precipitated this more serious and determined effort was a seemingly innocuous event that happened one day on my job. At that time, I was working as a painter of artistic finishes for a very small company with very notable clients. The artistic finishes included painting objects, such as furniture, lamps, picture frames, vases, baseboards and crown moldings, to look like they were made of marble, wood or a fine limestone. These were ordinary household pieces, but finished by an artist's hand. I took great pride in my work. Sometimes, an antique chair or table would be copied and the unfinished piece would be sent for me to finish so that it would look as though it were two hundred years old. I would beat it with chains to make it look worn, stab it with an awl to simulate termite damage, spatter it with black-brown dots of paint to simulate fly excrement and scrape the finished surface to make it look distressed and old. In one instance, a cabinetmaker constructed a mirror frame out of maple wood and sent it to me to be painted to look like it had been made out of knotty pine. Sometimes, I worked in the client's home. In at least two residences of rather famous individuals, I worked for a month painting wood baseboards and moldings to resemble the imported Italian marble used in the floor. This was truly art and each job was exciting in its own way. I threw myself into the work, trying to create results that made the clients happy and would be something I could be proud of.

One day in late April 1989, a truck pulled into the shop I was working from. It unloaded lamps, a table, a few assorted items and an ice cream cart (which was usually parked next to the client's swimming pool and stocked with frozen confections). These belonged to a famous movie star from the Golden Age of film who was enjoying retirement seasonally in Palm Beach. I called the interior designer to find out what was wrong with the pieces. I recognized each of them- I had hand painted them the year before! Nothing was wrong with the pieces, the designer assured me. They were redecorating and they needed to be repainted to match the new style and color palette. The designer explained that the client was only in their south Florida home for a couple of months each year, usually in January and February. While they were gone over the summer, the house was redecorated. It wasn't anything personal, he explained. The items just didn't fit the new design scheme.

For whatever reason, I was deeply struck by the futility of my job. All of my co-workers spent their lives partying, taking drugs and living a nightlife filled with bars and booze. I refused to be involved with any of it. It seemed to me to be repetitious, boring and tedious. I did not envy these people; in fact I saw them as listless and unfulfilled, wasting the precious days that life had given them. Around this same time, I became involved with outdoor groups and meeting people who were raising concerns about Florida's disappearing natural areas. These people were passionate, dedicated, had enthusiasm for what they were doing and were working for a cause that would better the world for generations to come. The contrast between my co-workers and new friends was striking.

At this time, Everglades protection and restoration had become a heated topic of debate and concern. Severe droughts had left the Everglades parched and vast wildfires raged for months, burning so hot as to catch the soil on fire, which smoldered like hot coals. Acrid smoke enveloped the metropolitan areas of southern Florida and ash rained down upon affluent developments. Towering clouds of smoke, reminiscent of the great Dust Bowl dust storms captured in old photographs, rose up menacingly on the western horizon and overshadowed busy urban expressways and suburban neighborhoods. As the community became concerned about the burning Everglades, I discovered Marjory Stoneman Douglas' 1947 landmark book entitled "The Everglades: River of Grass," which was a masterpiece of environmental literature. Ms. Douglas' book described the enormous value of that natural ecosystem to the average person and provoked an entire movement to save the remaining Everglades. Reading this book, I was struck at how much environmental damage had occurred in southern Florida. I, like nearly all residents of this region, were unaware of how profoundly changed the land had been. How could we know? Everglades drainage happened before we were born and there was no one to teach us what it used to be like, except for Ms. Douglas. At that time, Ms. Douglas was nearly 100 years old. She had seen the changes so many of us were ignorant of. She was still active and being recognized for her hand in tearing down the perception that the Everglades were a worthless wetland that should be drained and developed.

Back on my job, looking at pieces of furniture that once again needed my painting expertise, I saw how it contributed nothing meaningful to the world. This thought made me feel empty. My work might make the client happy for a short while, but with the next season, it would be taken away and replaced by something else to make the client happy for a short time. At this realization, I knew that I wanted my life to count for more and this was no longer the career for me. I needed a way out and a college education was the only thing that offered me worthwhile options. Since I had little savings, I would have to work full-time to put myself through college. It would be difficult for many years, but the price of doing nothing was worse.

After much thought, I made the decision to be a biologist! I had loved nature since childhood and the idea of having a job that involved being out in nature was like a dream. I thought about how much I loved to roam the meadows and woods back home and how I liked to grow plants; I knew that botany would be my major field of study. After beginning classes in the spring of 1990, I began looking for a biology-related job. The community college had a career center on campus, which had a lot of wonderful resources and dispensed much-needed hope to the students. I stopped in each week to look through job listings. Several weeks into my job search, I found a posting for a part-time field technician position with the Duke University Wetlands Center, a unit of the Duke School of the Environment in Durham, North Carolina. The job was local, sort of. It was in Loxahatchee, which was a 35-minute drive from my house. Back then a half-hour drive was a lot, especially when my sole means of transportation was a bicycle, a city bus or borrowed vehicle. But, I could buy an old car and make it work if I had to. It was too important for me to let go. I called the number and, after talking with the field station manager, was offered an interview.

On the day of my interview, I arrived a little early and was filled with anxiety. The field station was actually a rented house with no identifying features. I knocked on the home's garage door and was soon greeted by the field station manager. He led me through an improvised office area, a kitchen, a dining room and into a modern living room. Field sampling equipment sat in corners and plant samples were heaped on tables. I sat on a lumpy couch that had been purchased from a thrift store and talked with the post-doctoral researcher who was the hiring manager. He was impressed with my knowledge of Florida's natural areas. I walked him through the landscape around the building and told him the common names and scientific names of plants. I told him about the remote areas of southern Florida I had hiked and camped in. I clearly had zeal for the outdoors and wasn't afraid of fieldwork. I was hired! But, he told me, he had intended to hire two part-time students. Instead, he offered me a full-time job with full university benefits. He was also prepared to be flexible, as much as possible, with my schedule to allow me to continue my studies. I was dizzy with excitement. At last, I had achieved my dream!

I worked for the Duke School of the Environment for seven years. During that time, I would spend two to three days a week driving through the Everglades in an airboat, collecting water, soil, bug and plant samples. Sometimes, I would stay overnight in an island camp or on a remote levee many miles from the nearest human settlement. Moving through that watery world, I saw its different moods. The winter sun passed through the sky quickly and fell below the horizon with such speed that you could be caught in the dark unprepared. Violent summer thunderstorms that flashed and shook would grow and die in the span of an hour. Restless whirlwinds, detached from the dust of dry land, would tussle and rustle through the sawgrass like mischievous ghosts. I saw its rare beauty, too. Brilliant white-flowered water lilies lay spattered across sloughs, floating on contiguous ribbons of dark green leaves. Starlight reflecting off of its still, black water. Moonlight, sublime and stark, on the vast expanse of its savannas. I also knew how the Everglades felt- its scalding waters under the summer afternoon sun and the cool, soft peat between my toes as I walked barefoot through its marsh. Although I felt that the Everglades had become a part of me, the truth is that *it absorbed me*. It also sharpened my understanding of just how profoundly changed south Florida had been. To this day, my mind still struggles to believe that this teeming watery expanse of sawgrass and sloughs is what once occupied that place where much of Miami, Fort Lauderdale and the Everglades Agricultural Area are today.

As a biologist, I was involved in every experiment and study that was conducted during that time (I was the only field technician for several years, except for help from graduate students that worked over the summer). I learned a lot about ecology, weather, water, how nutrients affected plant growth and how fragile natural ecosystems can be. I learned about how the Everglades' plants were used by the Native Americans that lived there and the first settlers that arrived after the Native Americans had been driven away. I learned how to conduct ecological research, how to write results and how academia worked. By the time I left my job at Duke, I had finished my bachelor's degree in Biology and looked forward to a seamless transition into graduate school.

In 1999, after living in Florida for 20 years, I gathered up my courage and life savings and called the phone number of a realtor who had a "For Sale" sign in front of a run-down house near the neighborhood in which I lived. She was clearly hesitant about showing me the property..."I have others I would like to show you, if you have time," she quickly said during our initial conversation. I declined and assured her that I was interested in that particular property. She told me that there were people currently renting it but they would be gone in a few weeks and, after the house had a thorough cleaning, she would call me to arrange a time to see it. As promised, she called me several weeks later and I met her at the property early one Saturday afternoon. The outside of the house badly needed new paint and repairs. She opened the door of the home and I walked inside, finding myself in a property that had not been properly remodeled since it had been built in 1942. The living room's white painted pine paneling had resinous stains bleeding through from the knotholes underneath, making it look dirty and dingy. The small rooms felt claustrophobic. The septic tank was not functioning properly, as evidenced by the upwelling in the backyard. City water needed to be connected to the house and both the kitchen and bathroom needed complete renovations. Although this house had a lot of problems, it had exactly what I was looking for- character. I looked beyond what it was and saw what it could be. I quickly glanced about the rooms and, after less than 5 minutes in the house, I told her I wanted to place an offer on it- it was exactly what

The Road Turns

I was looking for. She cautioned me about taking the first place that I saw and handed me a sheet with five more property listings she wanted me to see. I assured her that I wanted this property, but resigned myself to the fact that I needed to be open to other possibilities. I also felt that she would not let me go until I saw the others. We spent the rest of the afternoon visiting bland properties in the area and all of them had issues for me. We returned back to the first property and I put in an offer to the sellers. By the end of the day, I was under contract.

The modest house sat on a one-quarter acre sandy lot, which felt spacious compared to the tiny spaces I had lived with for so long. Originally, the neighborhood development had been marketed to personnel stationed at the nearby World War II military airfield that later became Palm Beach International Airport. Back then, this development was in the country, miles from West Palm Beach. Today, it was in the heart of the metropolitan area. The house was originally 850 square feet, but previous owners enclosed the carport to add interior space. I was purchasing approximately 1000 square feet, just perfect for a single man. Although the house needed substantial renovations, I was eager to make it my own. As renovations progressed inside the house, I began to think about the outside and pondered the possibilities. Soon, I drew up plans for the landscape, which included a sunken garden, berry bushes, a private patio and, most importantly, a vegetable garden. At last, I felt, I had enough land to plant a decent vegetable garden! My suppressed, but persistent, need to grow food had found tinder and fuel.

I have always had the gnawing desire to grow a vegetable garden. Actually, it went beyond desire to need. Something inside of me seemed incomplete unless I was growing food. I think it was the activity that most linked me to my parents and ancestors, it was a bond that I could continue to share with them even after they were gone. I knew I was not the only one who felt this way. A friend of mine, Ian (a contracted version of his true Hawaiian name, Hinano) feels that way too. Hinano is in his mid-50s and has an advanced college degree. He left Hawaii to pursue a career on the Mainland, but the roots of his ancestral land are still strong within him. He grew up with a home garden. His parents and grandparents grew their own food in the dark volcanic soil and the warm, moist trade winds on the Hilo side of the Big Island. "There is a strong food growing ethic in my family," he told me. "My mother is an avid gardener and my father grew up on a farm; at 84-years-old my father still grows fruits and vegetables." Today, Hinano lives in an apartment building on the mainland. But, he points out, "I grow fruits and vegetables in pots on my patio; this makes me feel happy and growing things relaxes me." In some way, growing food also connects him with his parents and Hawaiian heritage. I completely understand.

Until I purchased my first house, I had little space to grow my own food. When I lived at home with my parents, I had my own corner in the vegetable garden. After moving to Florida, I lived on the 3rd floor of an apartment building and could only grow a couple of potted tomato plants, which seldom bore fruit. The townhouse courtyard was a small improvement. What little I was able to grow in the hot, dry gray-white sand was treasured in spite of its normally poor quality. But, I soon found that my ambitions and horizons exceeded the confines of the townhouse patio's wooden stockade fence. It didn't matter if the tomatoes were dry and filled with pithy core, they were mine and I had grown them. They were like beloved children.

Growing food is not always about growing the best produce, although that is one good reason. Sometimes growing your own food is about other things. This became clearer to me during a conversation I had with Marya, an acquaintance of mine who was born in Lebanon. Although we were from vastly different cultures, growing food was a value that we shared. "I grew up in a small Lebanese village," she told me, "and all of my family grew food- my parents, my grandparents and all of our relatives. My brothers have farms. The importance of food growing to us has not changed through the generations. Food growing is part of our culture. People in Lebanon never plant trees for show, for aesthetics, they only plant trees that produce food or have other uses." Marya has a husband and three children, and insists on buying only locally grown fruits and vegetables. "I want to support the local producers," she said. Marya was clear on the reasons she grew food- it made her feel connected to her heritage and growing food made her feel good. She grows more than 15 different kinds of fruits, vegetables and herbs, many of which are varieties that are essential ingredients in her ethnic cooking but are not easy to find for sale locally.

Living in my first home with more land than I could fill up, I could breathe great drafts of space. I could now plant a real vegetable garden! The new garden was appropriately sized to the lot and typical for an urban home- it was much smaller than the area of lawn and hidden away in the backyard. The total food growing area was about 25 square feet and would never be able to produce enough to contribute to my household in any meaningful way even if it did flourish. The first year, I purchased several packages of vegetable seeds, mostly varieties I remembered growing in the Midwest, and set about planting them in the sandy soil. In my mind I envisioned a bed of robust tomato plants laden with fruit, cabbages the size of bushel baskets and man-high corn stalks overflowing from the garden plot. These are what I remembered from Iowa vegetable gardens. What came up in my West Palm Beach garden were weeds and a few stray seedlings of this or that type of vegetable. The sand refused to absorb water, which beaded up as though it had been splashed onto waxed paper. My corn grew knee high, tasseled and died. Tomato plants grew for a month or so, then withered from unknown diseases. The cabbage never grew large enough to form heads. I was able to produce nice batches of string beans next to the house, but they refused to grow in the vegetable garden.

During the second year in my house, I ordered several pallets of sod and laid down Floratam grass, the type of grass everyone grew in southern Florida at that time. Floratam is a coarse grass, somewhat resembling the crabgrass that people in temperate climates are familiar with as a noxious lawn weed. When I lived up north, I loved walking through the grass in bare feet, especially when it was cool with dew in the morning. Floratam was unpleasant to walk on without shoes; it was bumpy and had thick, tough runners that could trip you. It was also a thirsty and needy grass, requiring frequent watering and fertilizers and treatment for controlling the pests that loved to destroy it. With the new sod, a carpet of lush green instantly surrounded the small vegetable garden. Both the vegetable garden and sod were dead by the end of that year. By then, I had figured out that my problems with growing grass and vegetables were the result of trying to grow in pure sand. All of my experience with growing gardens had been with the rich soil of Iowa. I had no idea how to remedy it.

The next year, I ordered another load of sod and it too died within a year. During this time, I was working full-time and finishing my master's degree in biology, which was focused on plant ecology. Between school responsibilities and ongoing home renovations, I had little time to devote to the luxury of vegetable gardening. I planted only a few vegetables to somewhat appease my gnawing desire to grow my own food.

The fourth year in the house, I purchased a more drought-resistant type of grass and installed a sprinkler system. I did have some success, but some areas of the lawn died anyway. I also came to understand why homeowners pay others to maintain their lawns. I resigned myself to what most homeowners already knew- frequent irrigation and fertilizing were required to grow a decent lawn in this part of the country. With my new lawn and irrigation system installed, some of my neighbors sighed with relief (so they told me)- at last my yard was looking like theirs, like it fit into the neighborhood and the rest of the city's ubiquitous green lawnscape. I had achieved equality with my peers. I also had to water the grass more frequently than I was comfortable with, which made me wonder if it was worth the expense of time and electricity to run the irrigation system. Although I was watering from my household well, I was concerned about my water usage. South Florida had come through a severe drought a few years earlier and the competition between landscape irrigation water and drinking water had become a topic of heated community discussion and concern. Memories of the burning Everglades were still in my mind. Residents in the region began to question if there was enough water for everyone and if there had already been too much development...was the amount of water used by all of this development unsustainable? Each time I turned on the well pump to water grass, I could not put these concerns out of my mind. What was my part in forcing a decision between green lawn and drinking water and the environment? After all, it was just one backyard; how much difference could it really make?

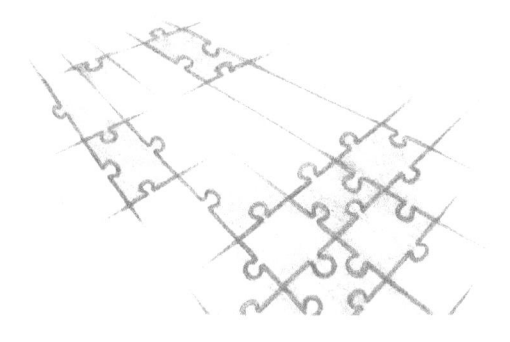

6. SUSTAINABLE

One fine autumn day, while back in the Midwest to visit family, I went for an afternoon drive through the countryside of southwestern Wisconsin. The air was cool, but the sun was warm and comforting when it burst forth between the scattered clouds. I stopped at one of my favorite hiking trails and climbed to the summit of Platte Mound, a natural landmark that defiantly rose hundreds of feet above the undulating landscape, to take in the panoramic view of the countryside. Looking down, I noticed that farmers were working in their fields, preparing them for winter. To one side of my view, there was an industrial farmer driving a tractor and large bin through his field. The equipment cut the dry corn stalks level to the ground, shredded them and blew them into the large bin. Clouds of exhaust from the machines and dust from the shredder blew hundreds of feet away, out of the field, carried along on the breeze. The shredded corn stalks would go elsewhere for other purposes. To my other side, there was an Amish farmer who had a team of horses pulling a shallow plow. He had harvested his corn, but was mixing the dead stalks back into the soil so that their nutrients and organic matter could be used to grow next year's crop. The industrial farmer took the nutrients and organic matter locked up in the corn plants away from his soil and instead depended on purchased concentrated chemical fertilizers to grow his crops. The Amish farmer conserved his soil's organic matter and nutrients, applying manure from his livestock to replace what had been lost through his harvest. Because the Amish farmer's soil's organic matter is continually replaced, it is better at retaining nutrients and holding water during droughts than the depleted soils of his neighbor's farm. The differences between unsustainable industrial and sustainable traditional agricultural practices could not have been clearer.

Over the past several decades researchers, community leaders and residents have become concerned about how urban areas are using the natural resources they depend on. This has led to the development of new fields of study which look at the needs of cities- the things they consume and the natural resources that keep them running. These natural resources include clean water, clean air, unpolluted soil, energy (from both renewable and non-renewable sources) and the raw materials used to make the goods we rely on. One main concern is how to make cities more sustainable. But, what is sustainability and what does it mean to be sustainable?

One widely accepted definition of sustainability says that it is the ability to meet today's needs without impacting the ability of future generations to meet their needs.[21] To live sustainably, we must pass along our natural resources in at least the same quantity and quality they exist in today. To do so requires us to protect the resources and use them properly. For example, the Amish farmer's soil will continue to be productive as it passes through generations because each year it retains its fertility and quality. Since the Amish neighbor's soil continues to lose organic matter and is on chemical fertilizer life support, the soil will eventually become exhausted.

Long-lived ancient cultures can offer us examples of sustainable living because their practices have withstood the test of time.[22] In these cultures, humans and their agricultural practices are highly interconnected with the natural environment. Examples of successful ancient agricultural practices can be found among the native peoples of South American rainforests, nomads on the Tibetan plains, Inuit peoples of Canada, Kogi tribes in Nigeria and, more recently, the Amish in North America. The people within these cultures share space with their food sources- it is a part of their day-to-day lives. This is in contrast to modern settlements that seem to banish food production from their midsts. Long-lived cultures understand that there are limits to the resources they depend on and they practice resource stewardship, which is an important value that is passed on to successive generations. Because resource limitations are respected in long-lived cultures, any efforts to achieve sustainability must include environmental preservation and the responsible use of resources. Since we are all dependent on the natural environment, healthy ecosystems are essential for our survival.

A main concern about urban sustainability is the continued expansion of cities and urban sprawl. Urban sprawl usually has fewer buildings and less people per acre as compared to the city core and has undeveloped tracts that are interspersed among it.[23] This is not a good thing because there are fewer people living on more land. Worse yet, urban sprawl is often built on land that was once local farmland or local natural habitat. One type of urban sprawl is large-lot development, which typically has lot sizes greater than one acre and occurs in rural areas. Many of these developments contain expansive areas of lawn and little of the original natural environment remaining. Both large-lot developments and urban sprawl have reduced local agricultural productivity and certain crop types in some areas are particularly at risk for being lost to development.

Recognizing the problems with expanding urban development, new planning and design trends have emerged. These new trends have focused on development that uses fewer resources, less space and is more efficient with respect to resource consumption.[24] This type of development is patterned after pre-20th Century cities that were built on a human scale. One example, New Urbanism, creates higher-density development to reduce energy and resource consumption. Unfortunately, local and urban food production is nowhere in the design even though it was a staple of pre-20th century cities. Another form of urban design is called Smart Growth. Smart Growth seeks to make existing development more compact by increasing residential densities in both new and existing neighborhoods.[25] Unfortunately, this practice also competes with potential food growing sites within cities. In spite of the trend toward making development more compact, there are questions about whether compact cities are a desirable planning goal, since low-density settlement is the overwhelming choice for residential living and high-density development within the city further distances residents from agriculture.[22] In both New Urbanism and Smart Growth design models, the dependency on food that has been grown in distant places and transported to residential areas is exacerbated.

All urban residents need food to survive- it is as essential to life as shelter, clean water and clean air. The quality of the food is also important, which includes freshness and variety. When urban planners and architects design cities and neighborhoods, drinking water supply is carefully considered. Hooking the new homes up to foul-tasting or polluted water is a fast way for the developer to go bankrupt. It is often true of air quality too. Neighborhoods that are planned downwind from belching smokestacks, a stinking landfill or a foul smelling high-density cattle operation will have a difficult time selling units once a prospective buyer draws their first breath of air. Curiously, though, neighborhoods are always planned without accommodations for food production. The expectation is that those who purchase homes in these new neighborhoods will have clean water and clean air, two essential needs for human life, but residents are expected to be completely dependent on purchased food that has been imported from distant places and grown under unknown conditions. Not surprisingly, food is one of the largest imports into cities and this comes with enormous energy and environmental costs. For this reason, sustainability initiatives seek to expand the practice of urban and local agriculture so that the consumption of energy and natural resources is reduced.

Whether food is grown on acres of farmland or in a home vegetable garden, there are limits to how much food can be grown in a particular amount of space. An urban resident who grows food in their home garden is primarily interested in the question of whether they can grow *enough* for their household, not the question of what is the maximum they can produce. These are very different questions. Those who want to feed themselves are preoccupied with the first question. Someone who wants to make a profit from growing food is preoccupied with the second question. The answers to these questions are very different too and can be the difference between sustainable and unsustainable practices. Most agriculturalists focus on the maximum amount that can be produced- the maximum limits of production. But, these are not the only limits that must be considered.

Natural lands have a limit on how much of their resources can be taken away before they are harmed. Sometimes this harm is ignored because it doesn't directly affect humans, at least not in the short-term. You will see how humans are indirectly affected in ways that are often unexpected and unwanted through the following example. There is a hypothetical forest that is full of many different types of trees, including those that produce a valuable hardwood that is prized by furniture makers. This hardwood-producing tree has a special root system that holds the forest's soils in place, retains moisture and prevents erosion. The forest also has a kind of tree that produces nuts that command high prices in food markets. Besides these two tree species, there are other kinds of trees that have different uses and roles in maintaining the forest. Many animals live in the forest too, including one that is considered to be prize game that hides seeds of the nut tree in the soil to eat later. Some of these seeds sprout and make new nut trees. There is also a bird species that only nests in the cavities of the hardwood-producing trees. This bird's diet is made up of mostly insects, such as gnats and disease-transmitting mosquitoes, and the birds eat a lot of them. In this forest, the trees and birds and wildlife and insects and soil are intricately connected...the animal depends on the nut tree's seeds for food, the bird depends on the hardwood trees to nest and the bird keeps disease-transmitting insect populations under control. The nut tree depends on the game animal to plant its seeds and the hardwood-producing tree maintains the soil quality, benefitting everyone. A few local (human) residents come to the forest to gather the dead wood of the hardwood-producing tree to make furniture, to collect nuts and, occasionally, to hunt the game animal. They use these products and sell what they don't want to make extra income.

This forest has a limit on how many hardwood trees, nuts or game animals can be taken before the balance of life changes. Taking away too many hardwood-producing trees for lumber will cause several things to happen. First, the forest soil will change, harming the other trees in the forest and reducing the number of nuts produced. Second, there will be fewer game animals because they depend on the nuts for food. Third, the number of insect eating birds will decline because they have fewer nesting trees, causing insect populations to rise. So, through this example you can see how harvesting more hardwood-producing trees than the forest can produce can have the unintended impacts of reducing the amount of goods (game animals, tree nuts) and services (natural control of disease-causing insects) that the environment can provide to humans. There are other negative effects that show up much later. For example, when the forest's soil becomes less able to hold water after a rainfall, the risk for downstream flooding goes up- some of these downstream areas may have residential developments that will be damaged. The problems of over-harvest are not limited to just the hardwood trees. If you take too many nuts or game animals from the forest, there will be ripple effects beyond the immediate impacts.

Sustainable use of the forest by the local residents allows them to indefinitely harvest modest amounts of hardwood, nuts and game, and to enjoy the benefits of less flooding, fewer pesky insects and less risk of contracting insect-born diseases. By protecting the forest, they are also protecting their health, their welfare, the financial benefits they receive from the many different kinds of forest products they sell and their food sources. By harvesting sustainably, they are also preserving the food supply (and income) of their children, their grandchildren and uncounted generations afterward. This is a sustainable heritage and it is the principle upon which the successful agricultural practices of long-lived cultures are founded. These peoples understand and respect the natural limits of the land upon which they depend.

This example shows how it is possible to take some of the hardwood trees, nuts and game animals while leaving the forest ecology intact. This is because most organisms produce more than the environment needs or can usually support. This extra amount is what can occasionally be taken without affecting the natural ecology of the forest. The beautiful thing about taking some, but not too much from this forest, is that the resource can continue to provide for you indefinitely- as long as the limits are respected. The same is true for other natural systems, such as oceans, lakes, wetlands and prairies. When too much is taken, the ecology becomes unbalanced and begins to collapse, eventually leaving little left to take. At that point, numerous other secondary and unintended problems appear that usually affect many other people.

Modern cropland has usually had all remnants of the native ecosystem removed. However, this does not have to be the case. There are some forms of agriculture that can work with, instead of against, nature. But this can only work when the land's natural limits are respected. For example, a natural prairie or grassland has a limit to how many cattle can graze on it. The land also has limits on how much pollution it can absorb without significantly altering its ecology or before there is too much to absorb and the excess drains into downstream rivers or lakes. This is referred to as the land's natural carrying capacity. When the carrying capacity is not exceeded, the land can continue being whatever it is indefinitely. This is a sustainable condition. When the carrying capacity is exceeded, this is an unsustainable condition and the land will be harmed in some way.

For example, Farmer A owns a parcel of land, which is covered with prairie or meadow, that has fewer cattle living on it than the natural environment can support. In this scenario, the cattle can graze the land enough to feed themselves but their grazing is not enough to damage the meadow upon which they depend. The cattle's manure benefits the meadow by recycling nutrients back to the soil. The meadow's native wildlife and plants and other organisms continue to live on the parcel of land because the meadow remains intact and healthy. The cattle and meadow live together in the same space in a sustainable way and this can continue indefinitely without harming or depleting the land's resources. By living together in this way, Farmer A can enjoy continual, modest harvests of cattle and natural products from the meadow, such as edible wild plants and wild game. The meadow also produces clean water and clean air.

   However, Farmer B has placed many more cattle on his parcel of land than Farmer A, exceeding its natural carrying capacity. This was done to increase yields and profits from his cattle. Soon, the meadow is overgrazed, damaged and exhausted. Game and other wild foods that the meadow once produced vanish. Manure, which in smaller quantities is a valuable addition to the meadow, builds up on the land because more waste is produced than the natural environment can safely assimilate. The excess manure stinks and the odor travels to neighbor's homes. Water runoff from the parcel becomes polluted and harms streams and rivers far away from Farmer B's land. Unless something is done, the cattle living there will die because of poor living conditions, pollution and a lack of food. To allow more cattle to live on the parcel than the land can naturally support, food must be brought in and the land must be regularly cleared of waste to maintain sanitary conditions and the spread of diseases. This works in some respects but the meadow is unable to recover because of the constant excessive grazing by the cattle. As a result, species that once lived in the meadow or depended on it at some point during their lives are lost. Because of the agricultural practices on Farmer B's parcel, the environment suffers in several ways: the parcel itself is degraded, areas far from the parcel are affected by its pollution and there is a loss of wildlife habitat. In Farmer B's parcel, food has to be transported to and waste products have to be carried away from the parcel in order for more cattle to live in the space than normally could.

Because there is not enough cattle food being produced in Farmer B's parcel to support the additional cattle the farmer wishes to raise, it must be grown elsewhere and transported to his land. If the food is grown in an unsustainable way or natural land has been lost to accommodate the additional agriculture required to feed the cattle, then two parcels of land have been environmentally damaged to raise the cattle- the land the cattle are on and the land that grows the cattle food. Also, the cattle's manure waste must be removed and disposed of elsewhere, potentially impacting a third parcel of land. Growing the cattle food and transporting it requires the use of energy, which is usually obtained from fossil fuel that also carries environmental costs with them. As you can see in this example, one can try to mitigate the negative effects of living beyond the land's natural carrying capacity by bringing food in from somewhere else and carrying away wastes to be disposed of elsewhere, but the negative environmental impacts (loss of natural habitat, energy consumption and carbon dioxide emissions) spread far beyond that of Farmer B's land. Simply put, it is cheaper, easier and better to respect the carrying capacity of the land.

Cities are places where the land's carrying capacity has been exceeded and resources (food, water, building materials, etc.) have to be imported to allow greater numbers of people to live there than naturally could. City residents, city managers and city planners are confronted with all of the same issues faced by Farmer B because food must be imported into cities and wastes exported. The negative environmental impacts, both in the loss of natural lands to urban sprawl and the environmental damage associated with unsustainable practices, are profound. Urban agriculture offers a way to decrease the amount of food that needs to be imported into cities and to reduce stress on the natural environment caused by unsustainably

Sustainable

practiced rural agriculture.

Although city dwellers today rely heavily on food that has been grown on farms that are great distances from where they live, several examples from around the world and throughout history suggest that this doesn't have to be so. Urban farms, community gardens and urban backyard food gardens can significantly contribute to local and regional food production. The World War II Victory Gardens in the United States and Great Britain met nearly half of the food needs of these countries. In England and Wales, community gardening is being considered as an important part of resource conservation and urban renewal.[26] In Cuba, severe economic conditions have been the driving force behind the nation-wide implementation of home and state-sponsored organic food gardening.[27] Today, nearly all of Havana's (a city of some 2.5 million people) vegetables and most of its fruit come from within a 30-mile radius of the city, and Cuba produces its food using organic agricultural methods. In these examples, backyard gardens were a primary contributor to urban agriculture and met a substantial portion of the total urban food demand.

The benefits of urban agriculture extend far beyond food growing. Private and public vegetable gardens can support a more sustainable urban environment that recycles compostable wastes, lowers carbon dioxide emissions to the atmosphere, conserves water and conserves energy.[28] Fruit trees in gardens can reduce carbon dioxide emissions, store carbon, offer wildlife habitat and provide other environmental benefits.[29]

Because the combined space of lawns, yards and empty lots is collectively the largest land area in cities, the potential production on these lands is huge. Residential gardens may represent the best places for local food production in most metropolitan areas because of the development pressure on large tracts of land within cities and on urban and near-urban farms. Acre for acre, small-scale farming is generally more productive and efficient than large-scale agriculture. For example, farm production in India was found to decline 20 percent as the farm size doubled.[30] This means that small-scale agriculture can produce more from the same space than could be achieved through large-scale commercial agricultural operations.[31] The higher efficiency of small-scale agriculture may be attributed to lower operating costs and a better use of resources.[32] From my experience, it is just plain easier to tend a garden plot than a 500-acre farm field.

Urban food gardens, unlike farms, can adopt creative solutions to grow food in places that are unconventional and support sustainable activities at the local level. One especially fun example can be found in Edinburgh, Scotland. Instead of viewing urban gardens as permanent fixtures that are at odds with developers and local government, The Grove Community Garden is a mobile garden that temporary uses two sites in the heart of Edinburgh. Temporary garden sites have been developed on two parcels of unused land, one owned by a land development company and a second owned by the Edinburgh City Council. The two gardens are a three-minute walk from each other. Instead of growing food in garden beds, it is grown in large mobile containers that sit upon a standard sized pallet that can be moved around with a forklift. When the temporary site is no longer available for use, the mobile plots can be loaded onto a truck with a forklift and taken to a new location! The temporary gardens are also set up to accommodate social, cultural and environmental activities for the surrounding neighborhood. Mobile gardens such as these can be quickly adjusted for size, location and need. They may also be taken to festivals, events and farmers markets for display and education.

Looking beyond Edinburgh's unique mobile garden solution, there is a much greater issue that must be addressed. Over the coming decades, the world is going to face a food crisis. This crisis will look very much like the one humanity faced early in the 20th century. At that time, large increases in population sparked profound changes in agricultural practices, practices that were founded on the new technologies of industrialism. The urban population of the 20th century was mostly fed from rural lands that had been converted from natural habitat to farm field. The extent of urban land area doubled between 1960 and 2000, raising concerns about how new development impacts local agricultural lands, production of local food and natural resource consumption.[23] This trend will continue.

Our planet is experiencing the largest and fastest period of urban expansion that has ever occurred. Over the next several decades, the area of land impacted by urbanization is expected to equal the size of the continent of Africa, more than triple what it was in 2000.[2] That is a lot of new people to feed and a lot of land lost to development under any urban design scenario. This urban expansion is occurring and will occur in areas that are hotspots of biological diversity, in countries that are limited in their ability to preserve their natural resources.[2] As human populations continue to grow during the 21st century, food will have to be produced in ways that avoid both social and environmental crises. More than 60 percent of the United States' vegetable farms (which is one-third of all farms in the United States) are located between urban development and rural areas, making these locally producing agricultural lands particularly vulnerable to urban expansion.[23] The loss of local agricultural lands to development has been recognized as a problem for urban planners and sustainability researchers, who increasingly face the challenge of maintaining farms in areas of rapid and often uncontrolled urban growth.[33] Given the known drawbacks and limitations of the industrial agricultural system, providing enough food to feed current and future populations sustainably is going to be a monumental problem.

Things are different this time around. The problems with industrial agriculture are so large, that it cannot continue to be practiced on the scales that it currently is. Foremost, it is an unsustainable practice that is currently unable to meet humanity's food demand. The second problem is that prime productive local farmland is being lost to urban development.[34] Unless more farmland is created, there will not be enough land in production to feed the world's new residents. Each acre of farmland that is being paved over for new settlements is one more acre of land that must be taken from the natural environment to meet the food demands of city residents. Then, additional agricultural land must be created to feed the additional urban residents that will result from future population increases. But, we cannot continue to create new farmland indefinitely. In some regions of the world, we are running out of natural lands to develop into agriculture. Humanity depends on healthy natural ecosystems for survival and these cannot be wiped away to accommodate human settlement. In addition, many of the world's large animal species and many endangered plant species are threatened with extinction because of habitat loss and degradation. We have reached a threshold where the continued conversion of natural lands to agricultural lands is unsustainable. The current industrial agricultural system cannot sustainably produce adequate food for the world's population today or in the coming century. Clearly, in many places, the situation is dire.

7. OVER THE RAINBOW

By summer 2004, I had graduated with my master's degree in Biology, was nearing completion of my home's major renovations, and was looking for another run-down house to fix up as an investment property. This was delayed by several very significant events that occurred during the next eight months.

The eye of Hurricane Frances struck the West Palm Beach area on September 5th, 2004. The storm was enormous, wide enough to cover the area from Florida's west coast to the Bahamas' eastern shores, from the Florida Keys to the state of Georgia. As hurricane watches were posted, I went to the local home improvement store and shuffled through a 1-½ hour-long line to purchase plywood to secure my home. Although I had some already, I needed a couple of extra pieces to be complete. Wood sales were rationed as delivery trucks were diverted from stores around the eastern United States to supply the insatiable demand in Florida. Food vanished off of supermarket shelves and gas stations ran out of fuel well in advance of the storm's arrival. I boarded up my windows with plywood and rode out category 2-strength hurricane Frances alone in my house. The hurricane moved slowly over a period of several days, prolonging anxiety and worsening the damage. Just before the center of the storm hit, the power went out and remained out for several more days after the winds had subsided. Cell phone service was lost early, too. Sustained winds of 105 miles per hour ripped at landscaping and damaged urban infrastructure. A few times, I was able to look out a peephole in the front door and watch 100 mile per hour winds rip apart the neighbor's mature oak trees. I had never seen anything like this before.

Around that time, I worked for one of Florida's water management districts and was required to staff the Emergency Operations Center (EOC) shift when the "all clear" was called after the storm. Making the two-mile drive to the EOC only a few hours after the worst winds had subsided, I passed downed trees and navigated around fractured concrete utility poles littering the street. Leaves were stripped from hedges and trees. Shredded roofing materials were everywhere. Stoplights at intersections were gone or without electricity and street signs were missing. Intersections that I had been driving through daily for twenty-five years were unrecognizable. Bands of rain continued to sweep in from the coast, dropping curtains of rain and rocking my vehicle. A ripping gust of wind sheared the driver's side windshield wiper from my car. Clearly, it would be some time before things would be back to normal.

Except for the inconvenience, all seemed to fare well at my house. The yard was littered with branches and debris, trees were bent over and the landscape was damaged, but nothing serious. Scattered pieces of roofing materials from less fortunate neighbors, which were in the lawn and embedded in shrubs, indicated that I was among the lucky- I wondered who they were? My vegetable garden, which had not been tended in months, stood there looking much like it did before the storm- empty. I should have planted it; at least I would have had fresh food to eat. Although electrical power would not be restored to my house for several days, water service was never lost. However, gas stations, grocery stores and other essential services were closed for days, unable to open without power or deliveries. I had enough stored food to get through a few days and, along with the neighbors, we pooled resources until things were up and running again. After several weeks, life began to return to normal, but only briefly.

Three weeks after Hurricane Frances struck, another large and powerful hurricane moved into the Bahamas, just east of West Palm Beach. Hurricane Jeanne drifted slowly northwestward, slowed, then moved toward the northeast, southeast, then westward- settling into the same path Hurricane Frances had taken earlier in the month. This was unprecedented and people listened to storm warnings in disbelief. Clearly, these back-to-back hurricanes would be one for the history books.

It was easy to retrieve and reattach the few protective wood panels that I had taken down after the previous storm; there had not been enough time to take most of them off the house since the last hurricane. The day before Jeanne made landfall, September 25th, 2004, I could hear explosions coming from power lines in my neighbor's backyard, the same power lines that fed electricity to my house. The lines were arcing great sparks into a small tree as the gathering winds blew the two together. I called to report the issue, but the electric company was powerless to do anything about it- they were struggling to rush protective measures for their own infrastructure. More than a day before Jeanne hit, before the storm's outermost bands moved onshore and into metropolitan West Palm Beach, I lost power to my house.

Before hurricane warnings had been posted, I had been selected to work the "lockdown" shift at the EOC. This meant that I would report to the EOC before Jeanne hit and would work during the storm sealed in a building that was constructed to withstand winds in excess of 200 mph. There was some comfort in knowing that I would be riding out the storm in a safe place. My 24-hour (minimum) shift lasted until the "all clear" was called, which was when the next shift was able to safely report for duty. I slept in a sleeping bag I had brought from home, rolled out on the floor of a small conference room where I had attended meetings only the week before. The world seemed upside down as business offices became living space.

My sister spent the storm with a neighbor who lived across the street from my house. Neither wanted to be alone during the storm. Category 3 hurricane strength winds gouged the same areas that were struggling to recover from the previous damage. Safe within the thick reinforced concrete walls of the EOC, I watched on radar as devastating storm bands slowly tore into southeast Florida. I read EOC briefings about reported damage and flooding to find any clues to how my own neighborhood was faring. Relying on radar images and live reports, this storm seemed worse than the last one. Miraculously, I had good cell phone reception throughout the storm and called my neighbor for regular updates. She and my sister were fine, but they felt that this storm seemed stronger than Frances. As the winds peaked, then began to subside, my neighbor assured me that she could see my house and that everything was fine, except for some debris in the yard that had blown in from someone else's house. That was reassuring and I breathed a sigh of relief, although I again wondered which of my neighbors had been so unfortunately impacted.

Storm weary and ready to be back in my home and in my own bed, I made my way through the windy, gray landscape after my EOC shift ended, once again avoiding downed trees and power lines and navigating familiar intersections that had been stripped of any identifying features. I was relieved the storm was over; it had been a long and difficult month. With two back-to-back storms, that should be it for this hurricane season and I was glad that I could return to a more normal life. As I drove home, swirls of dark clouds rushed ominously overhead, with gauzelike patches of blue peering through the mist before the next sweeping rains made the world look like it was in a blinding snowstorm. The downpour subsided as I turned the corner onto my street and saw a strip of brown metal roof flashing that I recognized- it was one I had painted on my own house the previous year. Large pieces of my roof lie in the street and neighbors' front lawns 500 feet from my house. It occurred to me that the debris my neighbor saw in my yard did not come from a neighbor's roof- it had come from mine. This was not going to be good.

I parked my truck on the street in front of my house. Before I could pull into my driveway, I had to pull tree limbs aside, wrestle twisted metal roof drip edging and drag away asphalt shingles, careful to pick up nails and other sharp objects that could puncture tires on my truck. A flat tire now could not be repaired for many weeks. Outside, my house looked fairly normal. It appeared as tranquil and welcoming as it always had, except for the missing trim around the flat roof. My home had two roofs: a pitched roof over one half of the house and a flat roof over the rest. One half of the pitched roof drained rainwater onto the flat roof, which then shuttled it off the side of the house. There were shingles missing from the pitched roof, but nothing catastrophic. Sheets of flat roofing in the street and nearby yards told me that I was going to face significant damage. The part of the house covered by the flat roof included a storage/electrical closet, the laundry closet, kitchen, dining area and part of the living room- rooms that I had completed, or almost completed, renovations on.

I unlocked the door to the house, turned the doorknob and peered into the dark living room. With boarded up windows, I had to wait for my eyes to adjust to the dim ambient light. The house was damp, musty and the sound of water dripping inside the building was an indication of what I should expect. Debris was scattered on the living room floor and furniture. I went back to my truck to retrieve a flashlight and returned to the house. I stepped through the front door and could hear water draining off of the roof and into the next rooms, the area under the flat roof. I made my way to the kitchen doorway and moved the flashlight across the room. The kitchen, dining room and utility rooms had been destroyed. The ceiling was collapsing under the weight of soaked drywall, dripping water and wet insulation. Kitchen cabinets were warped from the moisture and I could see daylight through the ceiling. Everything in the adjacent storage/electrical closet was soaked and unsalvageable. My herbarium collection, the culmination of a 6-year study of Everglades plants that

I was working on publishing, was a heap of sticky, molding, wet pages. Without the plant collection, the study was lost. I also lost my original artwork, drawings and photographs that I had exhibited in exclusive shows a few years earlier. There were other irreplaceable possessions as well. The appliances in the laundry closet were soaked and likely damaged, along with the stove and refrigerator. The electrical panel was under one of the worst leaks and it would be dangerous for electrical service to be returned to the house. As I tried to grasp the reality of the situation, I sat on the doorway steps leading into the damaged rooms and tears welled up in my eyes. A passing shower, part of the outermost bands from Jeanne, moved overhead and the rain started to fall again. As it picked up in intensity, water poured from the pitched roof onto the flat roof and drained into my house, falling on kitchen cabinets and appliances and polished Mexican floor tiles. The trickles and drips turned into a waterfall.

After Jeanne passed, my neighborhood was without power for 12 days. This was the longest I had lived without electricity. I was not alone. Most of our metropolitan area was without power and some residents lived without utility-generated electricity for more than a month. At night, we got along with candles, reserving flashlight use for only necessary activities since batteries were a hard-to-get commodity. The first thing we noticed was the night sky; without the diffusive glare of urban lights, it had been profoundly changed. It had been *restored*. The veil of glowing haze that obscured the dark sky had disappeared. The Milky Way shown in brilliant arcs across the heavens and my neighbors remarked how they could see so many stars. No longer distracted by electronic devices and technology, people lifted their eyes upward and saw our home galaxy and the universe beyond. Nearly every human being had known these same stars since humans first appeared on earth. Only a few generations ago, these stars guided our ancestors across oceans and deserts, they told us when to plant and harvest, and they were given fantastic legends that memorialized long-forgotten historical events. For many urban residents in my area today, it was the first time they *really* saw the stars.

Several days after Jeanne passed, an inspector from my municipality came by and pronounced my house unfit for human habitation. I was now legally homeless. Fortunately, my brother owned a home in the same neighborhood and his house escaped major damage. His sofa became my makeshift bed. My neighbors and I relied on our stored resources to get by, but these were gone after several days. Thawing meats and other food from our warming freezers were first put into coolers, then cooked on propane grills before they could spoil. Grocery stores and other food outlets were without power and, with many roads impassable, supplies were slow to arrive. Our municipal water had been contaminated and we could not use it to drink or cook without treatment. After stored supplies were exhausted, residents of our city were supported by water and food that had been donated and shipped in by emergency crews working around the clock. It was weeks before most grocery stores could get back into service and receive deliveries. We lived on what we could get. Co-workers cooked meals for me and came by to help me clear debris from my property. Through this, my vegetable garden sat unused in the backyard but would have provided a much-welcomed supply of fresh produce- if only I had planted it!

The flat roof had been peeled off of my house during the storm. The house was so water and wind damaged, that it was more than seven months until enough repairs could be completed to allow legal occupancy. I was desperate and moved in after five. It wasn't that I was slow in doing repairs, it was that building materials were scarce and only people who could afford premium prices could hire labor. Renovations that I had just completed before the hurricanes were destroyed and roofs, ceilings, walls and kitchen cabinets had to be replaced. During that period of homelessness, I stayed at four different residences. The first consisted of sleeping on my brother's sofa, which ended when a neighbor's one-room garage apartment became available for rent. I lost the apartment weeks later to a renter who was willing to sign a long-term lease. After a few more days on my brother's sofa, I then moved into a spare bedroom at a friend's house, which I left after a month when I found a small cottage rented by a neighbor of a long-time friend. It wasn't that I could not afford a place to live, it was that so many people were looking for places to live that there weren't any other options.

To say the cottage was drafty would have understated the reality to the point of absurdity. Many nights that winter were cold, at least by south Florida standards and the standards of anyone who has to brave them without an adequate heating system. The uninsulated cottage had a window air conditioner unit that had a heat setting, but this did not work. Overnight temperatures fell to near 40 degrees several nights in a row and down to a low of 37 on one particularly cold night. The biting north wind blew through the ancient and porous jalousie windows, waving curtains in its wake. With no heater, it was unbearable. The cottage was also infested with bugs; the worst were two types of cockroaches- the very large and almost bird-sized palmetto bug and the smaller German cockroach that seemed to infiltrate everything. There were other bugs that I could not identify. I would find them in dresser drawers, in my bed and throughout the kitchen cabinets that held my food and eating utensils. I set off bug bombs to fumigate the cottage every two weeks, but the insects returned after a week. It became unmanageable and I rushed temporary fixes at my damaged house just to get out of the rental. One Saturday morning, a swarm of bees invaded the cottage's attic, entering the living space through ceiling light fixtures and filling the rooms. Soon, dozens of bees became hundreds. After rushing the last of my personal items out of the cottage, I closed the door hoping never to return.

A couple of months after I moved back into my home, I met (or, more correctly, re-met) the man who would later become my spouse. I had met Eddie two years earlier at a local church service. I was a regular attendee and he was a guest, brought by a friend of mine. I took one look at him and was captivated. He was cute, shy and sweet, and I was love-struck. I thought to myself, "Gosh! I would marry *him!*" Two weeks before, I had been in Puerto Rico for vacation and had toured much of the island. I was still basking in warm memories of my experience. Eddie was identifiably Puerto Rican and I immediately moved to catch him for conversation about the island and his culture. We spoke for perhaps ten minutes before our mutual friend lassoed him and they left. I saw him again at a church event a few weeks later, but we had little time to speak. We parted without trading any kind of contact information. As the months passed I wondered about him. I wondered if I would ever see him again and how I could contact him...and what excuse I could fabricate as a reason to contact him. All I did know was that he lived in the south side of Fort Lauderdale, almost an hour away, and there was no way for a chance encounter within our different social circles. I literally abandoned all hope of ever meeting him again. Exactly two years later, in spring 2005, we met again purely by chance. We immediately set our first date night and have been together ever since.

By the time Eddie and I had been together for six months, we both knew we were in this for the long-term and talked about the prospects of moving in together. It would take some time to happen and we were content to let it work out by itself. In September of 2005, I decided to move forward with buying a second house. This home needed to be larger than my first one, to allow enough room for Eddie and I to eventually move in together. It would also have to be a run-down house that needed a lot of work. Then, we were at the height of the housing market bubble just before the Great Recession of the latter 2000s. I could only afford the lowest end of the market and was content to build value through "sweat equity."

Two weeks after I closed on the house, category 2-strength Hurricane Wilma struck, further damaging my newly purchased home. Before the hurricane, the house had no plumbing that worked, no heating or air conditioning, missing windows and kitchen cabinets falling off of the walls. I had purchased this second house in much the same way and for many of the same reasons I had purchased my first house- I saw what it could be and not what it was. Hurricane

Wilma blew out windows, tore asphalt shingles off of the roof, poured water into the home and tore down the roof over the carport. I rode out Hurricane Wilma closed up in the tiny bathroom of my first house. As my home shook under the storm's fierce winds, I sat on the floor next to the tub surrounded with cushions from the living room furniture for protection in the event the roof failed again. As I sat there, I wondered what it would have been like to ride out Hurricane Jeanne in my home as that storm tore the roof from the building. Fortunately, Wilma did no significant damage to my house. Over the next year, basic renovations to the interior of my second home were completed, both Eddie and I moved in, and my first home was rented.

As it is with all new relationships, there are surprises as you start to learn about each other. In the beginning, you have all sorts of ideas about your new love- they usually appear to be exactly what you want them to be. Then, later, you find out what they are really like and you begin to see the flaws (and they find those things out about you, too). Sometimes things work the other way around. You meet and there is no immediate attraction because that person doesn't fit the stereotype you have in your mind. But, when you get to know them, you find they are exactly what you need in your life! Only when you get past the initial stage of newness can you assess the real merits of the relationship.

On some level, I had both of these experiences with respect to Eddie. He did turn out to be everything I could ever hope to have in a loving spouse. But, I had to let go of my fantasy relationship first. To begin with, Eddie was not really Puerto Rican. He was Newyorican, meaning someone of Puerto Rican descent who was born and raised in New York City. The prospects of having long, reminiscences with him about my favorite places on the island of Puerto Rico, *La Isla del Encanto* ("The Island of Charm"), were never to be realized. He had only been there once for a couple of days and never left his family's house in San Juan. I had spent more than six weeks there over the span of four trips and had seen most of the island. I loved salsa music, which he did to, and loved to dance salsa and merengue. He didn't know how to dance either. Abandoned too was my fantasy of speaking a foreign language at home and becoming fluent in Spanish. I spoke it better than he did, having learned to speak it properly (and flawlessly, I like to tease him) in college. In fact, I was never really sure that he spoke Spanish at all; Newyorican is a language unto itself both in terms of content and pronunciation. I like to tell our friends, jokingly, that there is no known translation between the Newyorican language and English. I grew and loved vegetables. When Eddie was growing up, his mother would put vegetables on his dinner plate and he would throw them behind a radiator when she wasn't looking. Eddie did not like vegetables, not one of them. Growing up in The City, he had been fed only canned vegetables from the grocery store. I couldn't blame him.

These differences notwithstanding, the biggest contrast between Eddie and me was our backgrounds. I was from a small Iowa city with strong agricultural ties. Eddie was from Brooklyn and had never really been outside of a big city. After having two children while he was young and living in Queens, then raising them as a single parent in Miami, rural life was unknown to him. Raising children alone as a young adult, he could not afford the luxury of travel. When we met, he was living in the Miami-Fort Lauderdale area, about 50 miles south of West Palm Beach. People there often smirked when they found out that I lived in West Palm Beach. "How can anyone live in Palm Beach (county)? There's nothing there!" was told to me on more occasions than I can remember. These particular residents of Miami-Dade and Broward counties felt that Palm Beach was little more than some distant outpost. I knew that I had to overcome this preconception to convince Eddie to move north to be with me or, at least, to convince him that there was more to life than what big cities had to offer. I decided on the latter.

In the spring of 2007, I convinced Eddie that it was time for him to come with me to Iowa for a visit. In 2000, I had made the decision to return home twice each year to visit my family. My older siblings in Iowa were approaching their 70s and I was determined to spend time with them before they became sick and passed away. It also allowed me to get to know the many nieces and nephews (and great nieces and great nephews) I barely knew, many of whom were born after I left the area almost thirty years earlier. Eddie agreed to come along.

I had tried to explain to Eddie what the Midwest was like, how the people were and what the landscape looked like. I knew he could relate to big cities, so I decided that it would be best to begin by explaining Chicago to him. I told him how it had many of the same things that New York had (renowned museums, professional theaters and world-class restaurants), but was filled with Midwesterners instead of New Yorkers. Knowing that he had no concept of Midwestern values, I explained how during my last trip there, while walking to the El station in The Loop, I had lost the dollar bill I was going to use to pay the train fare. As I searched my pocket in vain for the money, a man far behind me yelled to get my attention...."Sir! Sir!" he shouted, "You dropped your dollar bill!" as he returned the lost money to me. To this, Eddie replied, "Hell no- nobody in New York would do that!" I had hoped he would be impressed by this Chicagoan's honesty but instead I suspected he thought the man was a fool. Maybe that wasn't the best story to lead with. So, I moved the conversation away from Chicago and into the country. I tried my best to tell him what Iowa was like. This was going to be a stretch. I showed him pictures of my hometown and of the Mississippi River along which it stood. I explained how you don't need to lock your car and roll your windows up when you go into the store (I was talking to a man who put the Death Claw on his steering wheel whenever he left his car). And, people you pass on the street say hello. But, as we all know, there is nothing like experiencing the real thing.

We arrived at O'Hare International Airport on a mid-June weekday. The weather was clear and pleasant. We got our luggage and boarded the El for downtown. We transferred from the Blue Line to the Red Line underground in The Loop, which I knew made

Eddie feel quite like he was in his hometown New York. Score! After a short ride, we exited the train and emerged from the underground State Street Station and into the canyon of high-rise buildings in downtown. As we walked toward our hotel, Eddie stopped, looked up and shouted, "This is just like New York!" I lunged to cover his mouth. Any Chicagoan would understand why.

We walked through The Loop, surrounded by metal and glass and concrete and asphalt. The only plants we encountered were street trees, strips of grass and flowers in planters standing guard in front of high-rise buildings. Passing world-renowned restaurants, there was not a single food plant to feed the enormous population that lived there. The urban landscape didn't change whether we exited the El in Wrigleyville, South Loop, Near West Side or Oak Park. Curiously, there were grand parks and the elegant conservatory at Garfield Park. An exquisite glass edifice covering 4.5 acres, Garfield Park Conservatory is a wonder and a place of refuge for city dwellers that long to escape the colorless, severe angles of urban design. Although the conservatory was built to shelter a large collection of botanically important and beautiful plants, it too held few food plants; those that were there were museum specimens and only intended for display. The city's disproportionate amount of investment in urban plant displays as compared to urban food gardens was stark.

A few days later, we boarded the Blue Line in The Loop and returned to O'Hare to get our rental car. I loved spending time in the city, but I was ready to get out of it and back to Iowa. There is something about large cities, a certain background noise and tension that wears on me after a while. When I am in the country, it is absent and I feel like I can breathe freely. I couldn't wait to feel that again. We piled our luggage into the back seat of the rental car and I drove us onto Interstate 90, the Northwest Tollway, heading toward northwestern Illinois. After a half-hour, Chicago's western suburban sprawl subsided and farm fields filled the landscape all the way to the horizon. I was nearing home. Calm was returning.

Eddie was stirring in the way that people do when they find

themselves in an unfamiliar environment. Puzzled at what he saw outside the windows, he asked, "What's that stuff in the fields?" "That is corn..." I pointed to the field north of the highway, "and over there are soybeans," I said gesturing another direction a minute later. "Oh," Eddie said, "this is really beautiful!" He paused to think and then asked, "Well, who owns all of this land?" "Well," I started slowly, pointing toward the northern horizon, "over there is a farmhouse and they own maybe 80 or 160 or more acres. They own the fields around their house." "But, where are their neighbors," Eddie pondered, "don't they have any neighbors?" For the first time, Eddie realized that you could live somewhere and not have neighbors just outside your window or clinging to the edge of your property line. "Well, over there...that other farmhouse, a few miles away, they are neighbors," I replied. How could things be so far apart? He was amazed.

As we approached Rockford, Illinois, we left the tollway and exited onto U.S. Route 20 West. Past Freeport, the road narrowed and the landscape changed. Here, we began to enter the Driftless Area, a land that was not flattened by the continental glaciers during the last Great Ice Age. Because of this, the landscape is ancient and hilly; towering bluffs rise steeply from river valleys with rocky pinnacles covered with forests and bald-like prairies. With the change in landscape came a change in agriculture. Neat flat fields gave way to contour farming, which is beautiful for its patterning and visual rhythms. Because of the rugged landscape, rangelands and forests dominate. In contrast to the tollway, U.S. 20 is a pastoral drive through the countryside with roadside markets selling locally grown produce and open barns selling antiques.

"What are those?" Eddie asked as he pointed to cattle grazing a meadow. "Beef cows, probably Herefords," I said. As we got closer to my hometown, I pointed out Holsteins and explained that these were different than Herefords; these cows were for milk production.

We passed through small towns with tidy homes that had small lawns in the front yards and large vegetable gardens in the backyards.

Handmade roadside signs advertised local farmers markets that were held on Saturday mornings in town plazas and church parking lots. At 45 years old, Eddie saw open space for the first time. Up until this moment, he had never seen how the food he had been eating his entire life had been grown or what it looked like before it arrived on the grocery stores shelves he purchased it from. A whole new world opened itself up and enveloped Eddie that day. I knew this trip to Iowa would be a landmark event in his life.

8. THE ANCIENT WORLD

*E*ddie, my niece and I walked down the wide, dusty trail that cut through the treeless prairie. The dense growth of grasses and wildflowers were waist tall and bending in the hot breeze. This uneven road, which was intended to be traversed by horse-drawn carriages as they travelled between villages, seemed an unforgiving place to be under the burden of cloudless skies and 92-degree heat. The quarter-mile walk into the rural Crossroads Village seemed much longer than it should have been, but soon the tidy one-room St. Peter's Church came into view and, upon reaching its threshold, we hurried inside to get out of the sun.

   A kindly, middle-aged woman greeted us cheerfully. Besides her, we were the only ones there. It was late on a Saturday morning, after all, and one would not expect the church to be occupied until the next day. I marveled at how she could keep cool with so many layers of clothing over her. She was dressed in her Sunday best, the best according to 1870s styles, and a fine purple velvet hat covered her head. The church was Spartan- white inside and out, except for the few altarpieces that had gold ornamentation and wooden pews. In stark contrast to the whitewash and summer heat, an imposing black chimney pipe appeared to defy gravity and rose up from a wood burning stove and flew through the roof in an odd angle. Our hostess told us about the church services as she sat to play us a traditional hymn at the pedal-driven organ.

Leaving the church, we walked the block or so to the village store, which was housed in a cut limestone block building with a door wide enough to accommodate deliveries by horse and buggy. A stout Welsh storekeeper was discussing corsets with two lady visitors. The storekeeper was dressed similarly to the church organ player, with a purple hand-crocheted collar and layers of print fabric cascading outward from her waist. She also had on a blue apron with deep pockets, which immediately identified her utilitarian role in the village. The store shelves were filled with dozens of bolts of colorful fabrics, both solids and prints, and notions, spools of thread and other sewing necessities. To the side of the counter, which was cleared for cloth cutting and the completion of sales, were wooden barrels containing various contents. Woven blankets and carpets hung from the ceiling rafters. Other cabinets held gunpowder, imported luxury soaps, scrub brushes, kiln-fired jugs and crocks, mason jars, cooking utensils, pots, pans and spools of twine. A small nearby table held a scale for weighing sales. The other side of room was stacked with barrels and manufactured shovels and various gauges of chain on spools. This village store, which was the main source of provisions for residents in this village and beyond, was interesting in what it did not carry- food.

While Eddie and my niece were occupied with the storekeeper's conversation, I walked to the other side of the store and peered out the wide rear door. I spied an outhouse behind the building, next to a fence where two horses grazed on prairie grasses. The outhouse was curious to me; I remembered using them when I was a child and I wondered if this one was functional- I could have used one at that moment. Checking to be sure the others were distracted, I walked over to the outhouse's wooden door and opened it, initially thankful it was neither occupied nor locked so that my curiosity could be quenched. Surprised by what I saw inside, I thoughtfully closed the door and smiled. It was a true outhouse, well crafted and authentic, except that under the hand-made (and very finely crafted) wooden stool was bare ground instead of a pit. Well, I thought, I should not have expected a fully functioning outhouse in a living history museum- although a part of me did.

Old World Wisconsin is the world's largest museum dedicated to the history of rural life.[35] This museum allows visitors to see, hear and experience how the first European settlers to this part of North America lived. More than 60 authentic historic structures ranging from farmsteads, houses and rural outbuildings have been moved here from their original locations throughout the state of Wisconsin, restored and assembled into a collection of ethnic villages. Here, one could see the unique building styles, gardens, food plants and food traditions that were transplanted to American soil with these immigrants. This reconstruction from America's past was also an accurate picture of European traditions from that same era. The immigrants built, planted and lived as they had in the Old Country, but adapted their styles to accommodate local conditions and available materials. Although Europe continued forward along a different path in history, what is on display here did not. Here are the food foundations upon which much of America was built. I knew that my own heritage was connected to this place…it was the world of my grandfather and aunts and uncles.

We walked through different ethnic villages, looking at the varied architecture and styles of fences and ways food was being grown. Meat and dairy came from livestock in nearby pastures. Each home's yard had a large food garden; there were no lawns. In fact, more yard space was dedicated to food production than to anything else. The vegetable garden's contents reflected the culinary preferences of the particular ethnic group. Although garden styles varied, many were carefully planned in rigid geometric patterns. What was most striking is that all of the food gardens were prominently displayed within the community. They were not hidden away in invisible corners of homeowners' properties, but were front and center. Many residential homes had their food gardens in their front yards. Residents of these communities did not think that growing food should be something to be ashamed of, it was not something to be conducted in secret nor was food growing something that should be treated with anything less than respect. In fact, food gardens were a source of pride both in their size and in their contents. When we arrived at the German village and I saw the kitchen garden next to the house, I immediately recognized it. Its placement on the land, the layout and most of its contents were identical to that of my aunt Elizabeth. I had a vague feeling of having returned home.

The importance of home food gardens to today's immigrants may be fundamentally different than it was to immigrants in the 1800s (few people in cities must grow their own food today), but the similarities are hard to deny. Besides representing an important connection with their heritage, home food gardens are a way to obtain better quality food than can be purchased, offer a broader range of food choices and provide opportunities for exercise and relaxation.[36] Today's urban gardens create spaces for social engagement and are a way for individuals, especially those not native to an area, to maintain parts of their culture by recreating familiar landscapes and cultivating culturally important foods. Sometimes these values are passed to children and grandchildren.

A couple of years ago I struck up a conversation with a woman who was involved with a community garden in her city. Amanda, a middle-aged woman from upstate New York, explained to me how her immigrant grandparents instilled a love for gardening in her. "I have vivid memories of planting carrot and tomato seeds in my grandparent's vegetable garden when I was a child. It seemed magical, planting seeds and watching them come out of the ground by themselves. My parents did not grow food for themselves, but my grandparents did. My grandparents were German immigrants and had gone through the Great Depression; food growing was something that was important for them- they understood the value of fresh food." Amanda talked about her fond childhood memories- playing in her grandparent's garden and how much she loved the fresh vegetables it gave them. Today, Amanda lives in an apartment complex that has no space for her to grow a garden, but does have four pots of herbs on her patio. Instead of a home vegetable garden, she frequents the local farmers market ("I LOVE farmers markets!"), belongs to a co-op and participates in a community garden. When I asked Amanda why she enjoyed being involved with the local food markets and growers, she enthusiastically replied, "I think that people who grow vegetable gardens are cool!"

Christine, an acquaintance who lived in England most of her life, is a thirty-something with a husband and two young children. They now live in the United States. Christine comes from a culture that is steeped in tradition; she was born and raised in a small English town where all of the residents grew food for themselves. "My family, brothers, sisters, parents and grandparents have grown food their whole lives," she told me one day while we were talking about our vegetable gardens at a church festival. Her, her husband and children live in a single-family home with a backyard and a "nice" garden in which she grows fruits, vegetables and herbs. "I spend as much time in the garden as I can, it makes me feel good," she explained. I asked her how she benefitted from her food garden and she replied, "Well, the fresh, high quality food is important; but, gardening makes me feel fulfilled and that means more to me than the food itself. Gardening, growing my own food, connects me with my culture. It is a part of my heritage and it is something that defines what it means to be a part of my family." For Christine and her family, food gardening was about cultivating connections with their culture and not about finances.

Veliko, a friend and recent immigrant to the United States, told me how the practice of food growing has been changing in his home country. Veliko is in his late-50s and was born and raised in Serbia. He has a wife and two children, but all of their extended family still lives in the regions that were formerly Yugoslavia. He explained to me, "Everyone in Yugoslavia that was born before 1970 has a great respect for food growing. After the mid-1970s, more rural people moved into cities and abandoned farming. Food shortages during the wars made people recognize how important it was to grow food." Living in a single-family home with a backyard, his family does grow some of their own food. "I don't mind seeing vegetable gardens in front yards or in developments," Veliko told me, "these can look nice and interesting." Most of the herbs that Veliko's family grows are varieties that cannot be easily purchased locally, but are important ingredients in their ethnic cooking.

The gardens of immigrants are founded on memories. Memories of gardens, particularly those of loved ones, can be powerful images that are passed through generations.[37] I know that the gardens of my aunts and uncles remain with me today as both practical references and emotional comfort. But, the practice of gardening is not always passed through generations. Around the world, elders in communities are concerned that younger generations will abandon the practice of food growing and lose that valuable connection to their heritage.[38] A look at the state of food growing in my generation as compared to those who came before me, as reconstructed here at Old World Wisconsin, demonstrates how justifiable that fear is.

The absence of food in Old World Wisconsin's village store was not an oversight by the stock manager; it was because there was no need for it. All of the townspeople and farmers knew how to grow food for themselves. It was plentiful, all around the community and produced by every home. Even if you did not have enough food, there would be surplus from a neighbor that could be shared or you could forage in the natural environment for herbs, greens, berries, fruits, nuts and meat. Absent from the store too were fertilizers. Natural sources of fertilizer were abundant in the forms of compost and manure. People then knew how to obtain them in sufficient quantities and because they understood the value of fertilizers, they recycled nutrients.

Besides being a cultural and historical museum, Old World Wisconsin is also a place for students of sustainability and resiliency to come to study. How did people feed themselves sustainably? How much land did they need? How can these practices be adapted for modern rural farms and urban food gardens? How can human settlement be integrated with its local ecology so both can thrive? I am not suggesting that today's urban residents should adopt the lifestyle depicted in this museum, but the agricultural models demonstrated here worked for millennia and have been only recently discarded as though they no longer have value.

The complete abandonment of traditional and ancient agricultural practices seems to be a phenomenon that occurs only in developed countries where governments have made a high investment in commercial market systems. These commercial market systems have systematically stripped away all vestiges of the pre-industrialized agricultural practices as though they were valueless. However, in other parts of the world, the indigenous peoples' ancient agricultural systems remain intact and are highly visible to urban and rural residents alike. The reason that these ancient agricultural systems still exist is because they have proven themselves to be sustainable. As I left Old World Wisconsin, I thought about how visitors to this place view the 19th century food-growing practices as a curiosity and as something that needed to be relegated to a museum. How strange, because I saw many of these practices first-hand when I was growing up…and I wasn't *that* old.

A decade before I stepped into the world of Old World Wisconsin, I traveled to South America to spend a couple of weeks in Peru. As much as people in the United States feel that 19th century practices are considered old enough to be enshrined in a museum, that is but yesterday in the timeline of the Andes. The mountain range's lofty heights and isolation have preserved and protected the indigenous way of life, including their agricultural systems. The Andes is a place that is unique in the world and, with its close proximity to the Amazon Rainforest Basin, it is also a place of botanical paradox and surprise. As I climbed arid mountainsides, I found tropical orchids growing next to cactus. On mountain summits there were lupines, which are known from alpine meadows, growing next to iris- a species of which is found in Florida's swamps. Where I was from, these plants would never be found together. But, here, the rigid rules of botanical order that I had learned and seen my entire life had been unraveled. As I explored and learned about the Peruvian Andes, other rigid rules of life soon fell apart too.

One day, my travel companions and I hired a taxi to take us to some of the more remote ancient ruins. After a long ride through the remote countryside, we exited the taxi at the foot of a trail and began to climb the mountainside towards an ancient ruined city. Soon a young, local guide that spoke English joined us- after we agreed on a reasonable fee for his services. The chilly, thin air made it difficult to walk at even a moderate pace and I had to frequently stop to catch my breath. I felt slightly light-headed and somewhat tired, as though I was mildly hung-over. I wasn't. The night before, I had suffered a bout of soroche, altitude sickness that had flu-like symptoms. It did not persist, perhaps because I had taken the advice of the local natives and consumed cups of mate de coca (a tea made from the leaves of the coca plant) with every meal. This was the recommended cure for soroche. The views from this precipitous trail were breathtaking, making me forget any physical discomfort. High on the mountain above the Urubamba River valley, a headwater to the Amazon River and known locally as El Valle Sagrado de Los Incas (The Sacred Valley of the Incas), I was walking on what was once part of an ancient road that linked the Inca Empire with the tropical rainforest jungles of eastern Peru. Not far ahead, perched on the mountain's crest at almost 11,000 ft. above sea level, I could see the ruins of Inca Písac just beyond the city's stone entry gates. The first sector of the ruins we would explore was Inti Watana, a sector that contained royal baths, religious altars, a ceremonial platform and the imposing Temple of the Sun. My travel companions, our fourteen-year-old guide and I would arrive there after another ten-minute slow walk.

Inca Písac, which was built in the mid-15th century, is believed to have been a royal estate that was constructed to commemorate a military victory. Other such royal estates in the Peruvian Andes included Ollantaytambo and Machu Picchu. The mountain upon which Inca Písac sits has been sculpted into extensive bands of agricultural terraces. Using a system of gravity-driven aqueducts, water flowed through the village's fountains, baths and then to the agricultural terraces to irrigate crops. These terraces once produced much more food than this village could consume and surplus was shipped 20 miles downstream to Cuzco, the Incan capital. Large stone buildings along the mountain's steep slopes may have been used to store harvested crops. Less than a century after its founding, Inca Písac was destroyed by the Spanish conquistadores. Because Inca Písac was designed to include sustainable agricultural production, the village and its residents survived their municipality's destruction and relocated to a nearby site in the valley. This new Písac, which is a vibrant village today, owes its existence to the wise agricultural planning of its ancestors. For all of its remarkable features, Inca Písac is not unique to the region.

After touring Písac, my travel companions and I returned to our hostel on Cuzco's main plaza. There were striking differences between the countryside and Cuzco's urban core. Most of the houses in the rural areas and at the outskirts of Andean towns were constructed of dried mud bricks and thatch, but finely fitted stone was the preferred building material in the city itself. The Inca's urban builders were masterful engineers and stoneworkers, designing for durability and sustainability. On Cuzco's main plaza, the ancient Spanish colonial-era cathedral was clothed in scaffolding. Church workers were repairing the extensive damage caused by a severe earthquake that had occurred several years earlier. Walking through the narrow passages of Cuzco, the tightly fitted stone walls of Inca craftsmanship were topped with colonial-era construction built during the time of the Spanish occupation. Although these Incan walls were more than seven centuries old and had ridden out numerous strong earthquakes, it was impossible to slip a piece of paper between the fitted stones. It was customary for the Spanish to tear down the upper part of an Inca stone structure and construct a new building on top of its foundation. By doing so, it asserted the superiority of the conquerors over the indigenous people. This newer construction was carried out according to imported European standards and styles, rather than local knowledge (which was considered to be inferior). Local residents love to tell how, during the 1950 earthquake that destroyed more than one-third of the city's buildings, the Inca stonework remained intact while the European-styled construction crumbled to the ground.

I traveled to other ancient Inca villages within the Cuzco district of the Peruvian Andes; these included Ollantaytambo, Chinchero, Puka Pukara, Tampu Mach'ay, Saksaywaman and the world-famous Machu Picchu, one of the more remote and beautiful of Incan settlements. Each of these villages had been carefully planned with and had invested much into their local agricultural systems, recognizing its vital role in their residents' health and welfare. If you doubt that, then look at pictures or maps of these places. Most surprising to me were the extensive networks of agricultural terraces that stretched for miles along the Urubamba River valley. The hillsides' rocky slopes had been transformed into productive agricultural terraces that worked with the local environment. Rich topsoil had been carried up to the terraces from the river valley below, bringing with it much-needed nutrients to grow crops. Because growing conditions at the base and summit of these hills were different, a variety of crops were grown during different times of the year. Although these terraces were constructed more than six centuries earlier, many were still in use. Each village along the Urubamba River produced an abundance of food, more than the local residents needed. This was evident at the local markets where piles of fresh produce sat waiting for shopping tourists. I wondered if our industrial agricultural systems in the United States would still be productive six centuries from now; I was certain that they would not.

After a week in the Cuzco district, I left for another town farther into the backcountry. This time, I was headed towards the Bolivian border. My travel companions and I took a long day train ride past high-elevation pastures where alpaca, llama and vicuña herds grazed on native grasslands. Even though the land was treeless, cold and dry, local agriculture thrived because it was a natural part of the local environment. The train stopped in remote Andean villages to collect and drop off mail, giving time for throngs of local residents to sell trinkets, handmade items and food to tourists through the train's windows. Some villagers offered ears of boiled or roasted indigenous corn that was creamy white, but with kernels that were many times larger than any other I had ever seen before. It was delicious and I wondered why North American farmers were not growing this. There were also granadillas, a large native passion fruit with a sweet and slightly aromatic flavor that was addicting. These too were delicious. I purchased a bag of them to eat later. Again, I wondered why I had never seen this fruit before.

At one particular stop, a native woman boarded the train and walked the aisles to sell sweaters that she had knitted from the very desirable local alpaca wool. These were much more comfortable, and much better quality, than the manufactured sweaters I had in my clothes drawer at home. Usually the sweater seller that boarded at a village exited before the train departed. But this time, she did not. A couple that sat two rows ahead of me liked one of the sweaters that the seller had, but they wanted two (a his and hers) for a matching set. Unfortunately, the seller had only one sweater of that style. Rather than pass on the sale, she told them that she would make a second, matching one. The sweater seller remained on the train as it departed the station. Standing to one side of the aisle as we lurched forward and continued down the uneven tracks, the sweater seller pulled out knitting needles and yarn, and began to knit with a speed I had never known possible. By the time we reached the next village forty minutes later, the second sweater was knit, approved by the customers and the sale completed. The sweater seller exited the train and, counting her money, sat to wait for her return train to arrive.

The sweater that cost the tourists twenty American dollars would have sold for several hundred back in the United States, but its intangible value was priceless.

The train bounced along its route through the Andean highlands. In spite of our high altitude, there were still mountains that pushed yet higher into the sky. At one point, the train arrived at La Raya pass and paused. We had reached an unfathomable altitude of 14,150 feet above sea level, just a few hundred feet lower than the highest mountaintops in the continental United States. Breathing was fine, so long as you did not get into a heated discussion. As daylight faded, I looked at the passing scene through the windows. This was a seemingly harsh land to grow food from, but people were doing it without fertilizers, pesticides, modern machinery, hybrid crops or anything else I had come to associate with agriculture. That was because they understood the land and worked with it, rather than against it. The countryside was pastoral and peaceful in the glow of the setting sun. Glaciers on mountainsides and peaks glistened and sparkled in the orange light. Occasionally, I could see plumes of steam billowing up from cracks in the earth's surface, the places where hot springs and geysers upwelled from the volcanically active subsurface. It seemed so contradictory, hot springs and glaciers co-existing, but here it was. Late at night, under a cover of deep darkness and stillness, we reached our destination of Puno on Lake Titicaca, a large lake that straddled the border between Peru and Bolivia that lies more than 12,500 feet above sea level- higher than many of the world's mountain ranges. Looking up into the moonless sky, I recognized only a few of the stars. Some of my familiar northern hemisphere constellations were unknown here. We made our way past the vacant marketplace and up the hillside towards our hotel. My next adventure was beginning.

After breakfast and two cups of mate de coca tea for good measure, my travel companions and I walked downhill (thankfully) to the market. At this altitude, the sun was surprisingly hot even though the air was chilly. With the thin atmosphere, few clouds and brisk cold winds, and you could get both a sunburn and windburn. It was common to sweat from the heat and shiver from the cold at the same time. One tourist brochure described the feeling this way, "…one feels as though they are a badly cooked hotdog- burnt on the outside and freezing on the inside." I recalled the hotdog that I had purchased during my train ride to Florida when I was 18 and could understand what that meant…that was exactly how I felt!

Although it was a weekday, most of the market stalls were filled with vendors. Some sold handcrafted items. Others were brimming with fresh fruits and vegetables. Native women with brimmed hats and long black braids and young children sat on top of piles of brightly colored hand-woven textiles, passing time by knitting, weaving or crocheting. As I walked along and looked into a vendor's stall, the attendant woman smiled, lowered her eyes and said "hello" as she pointed out something for me to consider purchasing. I was good up until the purchasing part; after that, I became uneasy. Coming to Peru, I was inexperienced with the custom of bartering. Bartering was the normal custom when purchasing anything outside of a modern commercial store. It made me feel uncomfortable and somewhat guilty to ask someone to take less than the asking price for a product or service. In the commercialized culture I had come from, you either paid the stated price or did without. This was because there were minimum profits that had to be realized along with insurance premiums, advertising costs, paychecks, taxes, building rent, stock, accountants and other overhead that needed to be paid for. But, I was told, that was a mindset I had to get over. Here, you were considered to be foolish if you didn't barter. That was a language I had never been able to become versed in.

I recalled purchasing a couple of items in a Yucatán village store the year before. Not one of the store's items had a price tag or sign to indicate what it cost. I soon learned that the price of any item depended on who did the asking. At the checkout, the cashier paused at each item as he seemed to ponder how much he should charge. I noticed that the local, elderly woman ahead of me at the checkout got a steep discount on the same soft drink I was purchasing. Apparently, a young male tourist was expected to pay more for something, perhaps to subsidize the local elderly woman's reduced price. When I rejoined with my travel companions outside the store, I asked a young woman in our group (who just happened to be cute) what she had paid for the same soft drink I had just purchased. It too was less than what I had paid but more than what the elderly woman had paid. Apparently, my subsidy had to cover the (cute) young woman as well. After that experience, I decided that I needed to get more assertive when it came to bartering prices.

Earlier in the week, in a small store on Cuzco's main plaza that sold canvas oil paintings done by local artists using mass production methods, I tried to make up for the soft drink indecent in Mexico. The paintings were in the style of Cuzco Baroque, which I loved, and I was determined to return home with one. They also sold carved gourds that were stained in a beautiful color. I wanted one of those too, but I wanted to pay a price that didn't make me feel foolish. So, after eating pizza on a restaurant's second-story balcony that seemed as though it would collapse onto the street at any moment, I convinced my travel companions that we needed to pay one last visit to the art store. After all, reinforcing my request, we would soon be leaving Cuzco and may not have another chance. My travel companions were seasoned barterers and I was still trying to get the hang of it, so I needed them along for moral support. I found a small oil painting that I wanted and inquired about the price. I don't recall what the salesperson said, but I was certain that it was unacceptable and told her so. I counter-offered with a price that was one-third of what she had requested. I stood firm and tried every angle to convince her that I would leave without purchasing it if she didn't come to my terms. I tried ignoring her, I tried emotional appeals, I tried the hard sell angle, and I tried to convince her that I had very little money. She responded with indifference. After a while, what seemed a half-hour or longer, she conceded. Not because that was a fair price, but because (I'm convinced) she wanted this obnoxious

American tourist out of her shop and was willing to take a loss on that painting (if necessary) to do so. I never did get the gourd.

Back at the market stalls in Puno, I saw a pile of hand-crocheted Christmas ornaments. They were cute! There were adorable little Andean people, colorful lizards, cactus studded with bright flowers, woolly llamas, rotund turtles and other characters stuffed with llama wool. I wanted to purchase at least one of each. I asked the woman the price and she politely said, "25 cents each." Her four young children cheerfully climbed and played on the same pile of textiles she was sitting on. Still smarting from the Cuzco art store incident, I asked her (in my most polite American-accented Spanish) if she would take 20 cents each. In my mind, I though I could save face (and not be a foolish tourist who pays full price) by asking for only a 20 percent discount from her offered price. The 2/3-price reduction I had asked for in Cuzco had gone too far. The woman shot back at me in an angry tone, "NO! It is hard to sit here all day and crochet those little ornaments with tiny crochet needles- my hands hurt from making them!" I withered.

In the moments that followed, I thought about this woman's work, her handcrafting skills, the children she had to support, what she had and what I had. She was not a beggar on the street pleading for a handout (I only found them in the major cities) but a woman who proudly worked her craft and wanted to be paid for it. I wasn't purchasing things from a faceless entity in a large department store, I was purchasing them from the hard-working woman who handmade them. At that moment, I realized the difference between large-scale commercial enterprise and local economics. Large-scale commercial enterprise sets the price for its commodity and if you are unwilling to pay the price, you will have to live without the product. It is that way with market commodities; even the very food people eat. The cold fact is that if you cannot afford to pay for commercially produced food from an American supermarket, you cannot have it even if it means that you will starve to death. The rationale is that public food assistance programs and charities, not commercial enterprises, should be the ones to help people in need. The local economics I was seeing in the villages of Peru and Mexico were based on human relationships and local contexts. The cashier I encountered in the Yucatán village store was not a bad businessman because he adjusted his prices for the local elderly woman (I will not concede on the price for the cute young woman, though); he was selling her something at a price he knew they both could afford. This way, he kept a loyal customer and she got what she wanted at a price she could pay. This kind of economics is humane and builds the community. It helps people who are in times of need. Small-scale, subsistence and urban agriculture are usually these kinds of local economic systems because they are built on sharing, negotiated pricing, local context and value that is based on a person's individual situation. I gave the woman at the market stall the full price for the Christmas ornaments, plus a small *propina* (tip). In fact, I recall her and my poor bartering savvy every Christmas when I hang the ornaments on my tree.

The next day in Puno was perhaps the highlight of my entire Andean trip. My travel companions and I secured the services of a tour guide who would take us to the village of Los Uros on Lake Titicaca. Los Uros consisted of a collection of two- or three-dozen floating islands on the lake. This floating village pre-dated the Inca period and was constructed as a way for the Uru people to escape capture or conquering by invaders. We found our way to the docks where a boat would carry us out to the Mother Island. While waiting, we were greeted by the ubiquitous street vendors. These particular vendors told us that the Uru people were shy recluses who did not like visitors. But, if we took them gifts, they would be more agreeable to our unwelcomed intrusion into their watery domain. With that, they produced pencils (for the school children), candy and lollipops that, they assured us, were things that the residents of Los Uros most wanted. So, after a round of brisk bartering, we purchased pencils for the school children. We would have purchased a handful of lollipops, but the price seemed too high and, with the other tourists boarding the boat, we decided to pass on the candy. Moments later we boarded the vessel for the village of floating islands.

After a twenty minute boat ride, we arrived at the Mother Island. Our guide talked to us along the way, introducing us to the customs of the Uru people. He told us we would be visiting a school, a newly completed museum, restaurant, gift shop and even a family island or two. These did not seem like people who were trying to avoid contact with the outside world, as the street vendors suggested.

We arrived on the Mother Island and were greeted by several friendly townspeople. They seemed to be expecting us. The place was really remarkable, if not captivating. The Uru created these islands by cutting the native reeds from the lake's marshes and piling them up on the water to create a floating mass that eventually became large enough to build and live on. Because the reeds slowly decomposed, the islands had to be continually replenished. The Uru people also used the reeds to construct their buildings (both walls and roofs), boats, sails for the boats, storage containers, baskets and almost anything else that could be fabricated from the tough, straw-like material.

After touring the school (and being serenaded by the schoolchildren), museum and restaurant (next to a bar that sold Cusqueña beer) we were given a ride to a family island by our guide. He paddled us across the water in a reed boat until we reached a small island that was only large enough for two huts (one for storage, which also was a small gift shop, and one for shelter, with mat-like beds), a place for cooking and an area for the children to play. The family who lived on this island harvested most of their food from the lake and its expansive wetlands. Fish and waterfowl were the main sources of protein. Some of the marsh plants were eaten too. My travel companions and I respectfully looked around the family's island, asking a few polite questions. The two children, a boy and a girl, were cheery and seemed thrilled to have visitors to chat with. They told us about their mommy and daddy, how they liked to fish and go to school. Each child produced a small piece of gray cardboard that had been cut from what appeared to be a discarded box and asked me if I wanted to buy a postcard. I took them from the children and looked at them. On one side, there were pictures drawn with crayons- one was a picture of an Uru woman frying fish in a pan over an open fire and the other was a picture of their little island home. My heart welled up with love for these two children. I asked them to tell me who was in the picture and they giggled and shouted- "That's my mommy!" They beamed with pride! I told them how much I loved the postcards, asked them what they wanted for them, paid (with a small *propina*) and thanked them for their beautiful work. The little girl and boy beamed with pride.

A friend who had gone to the family island with me did not have such a charming time. She poked her head inside one of the huts for a look but had to pay the owner a *propina* to come out. The family's hut was interesting, though. It had a solar panel on the roof that powered a small black-and-white television set, a radio and lights. These, they said, were given to them by the government. In fact, all of the energy for the village of Los Uros was generated by solar panels. Interestingly, it has been almost twenty years since I visited Los Uros and there still is not a single solar powered village in the United States.

On our return boat ride to Puno, our guide told us that he was born and raised in this area. He became a guide because he wanted to share his culture and heritage with others, but feared that their way of life was slowly being threatened by development and commercialism from outside. Our guide was concerned about the lake's water, which was once clean and clear but has become clouded by pollution from Puno. He told us how the local diet has been increasingly changed by processed foods imported from commercial markets. I remembered the candy sellers at the docks. At first, these dietary changes came to Puno, but are now impacting the Uru people. He noted how tourists continually bring candy to the islands of Los Uros as gifts, but this has had the unintended consequences of causing obesity and tooth decay where it once was rare. My travel companions and I exchanged nervous glances of relief. He didn't know if the children living in Los

Uros would continue their family's traditions or abandon them for a modern city.

In contrast to the Andean villages I visited in the Urubamba River valley, in Puno I found a serene, floating village that did not rely on agriculture for their food. Farming was unknown to the Uru people. Instead, they sustainably harvested from the lake environment around them. This practice of sustainable harvest allowed the village of Los Uros to thrive for more than six centuries, but the Uru children could soon find themselves dependent on a new and unsustainable commercial food market system. Once dependent on commercial food products, the knowledge of how to feed themselves sustainably from the environment will be lost and they will no longer care about the health of the lake that brought them into being.

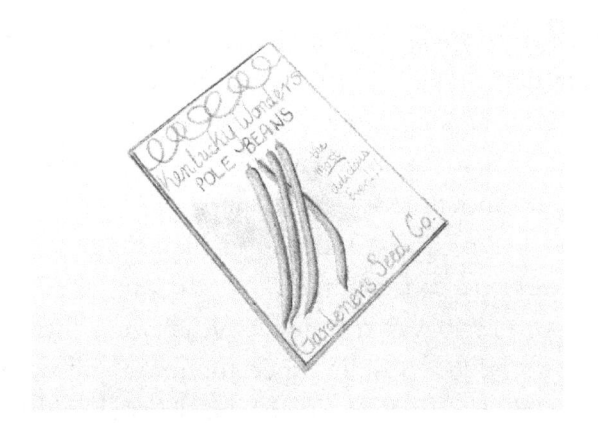

9. HOME AGAIN

I moved into my second home in 2006. This home was larger than my first, although the lot size was the same. I did only landscape maintenance until interior renovations were mostly completed. Landscape maintenance consisted of bushwhacking the weeds so that the home would not appear run-down or abandoned. I started my first vegetable garden at my second home in the fall of 2006. Recalling the failures of my vegetable garden at my first house, I was determined to learn from my mistakes. This re-invented garden was small, perhaps 75 square feet. I grew tomatoes, cabbages and beans in the sterile sand with moderate success. By mid-2007, I started to consider permanent landscaping for the property and to think about what could be done with it. I decided that, as an ecologist, I would take an approach that was environmentally friendly. I also needed landscape that was low maintenance. With these two restrictions, I decided that there would be no lawn.

The home was situated on a ¼ acre lot, typical for most urban residential lots in the area, with a large mango and small plumeria tree in the front yard, and a loquat and large oak tree in the backyard. The rest was dry white-gray sand and weeds. I'm certain the property had never seen grass, except for the weedy ones. I installed low-maintenance landscaping in the front yard, enough to make it presentable at first, and added to it over the next several years until it became the best looking front yard on my street. No grass, no irrigation and almost no maintenance. I was enormously pleased! Now, what to do about the backyard?

In the summer of 2007, I tried my first summer food garden, planting peanuts and sweet potatoes. I had only moderate success with these too, but it was my first time growing them and stellar success was not a reasonable expectation. As fall approached, I thought about my backyard and its future- what should I do with it? Besides the small vegetable garden, which had been placed in a fairly random location, there had really been no changes to it since I purchased the house. But, it was time to start thinking about what to do with all of that space.

At the start of the 2007 vegetable growing season, in September, I doubled the size of my small food garden. I had realized that my growing space was too small to contain all of the varieties of vegetables I lusted after in the seed catalogues. To me, seed catalogues were like travel brochures to exotic destinations. They were dripping with carefully enhanced re-touched photos of perfect models that lured and tempted me to purchase what they were selling. I have limits both to how much of this kind of temptation I can resist and how much I am willing to spend. Having more growing space definitely changed the balance that my conscience and good sense had become accustomed to. With more "luxury" garden space to fill, I was now venturing where angels feared to tread. My heart raced as I flipped the pages of the seed catalogue and indulged my fantasies.

As we all have known since childhood, but often forget in the heat of passion, fantasy is very different than reality. This season, I tried to grow Brussels sprouts and artichokes; both died before reaching bearing stage. Sadly, these were not quick deaths. They were slow, painful, excruciating deaths- the kind that scars you with guilt. Although I added purchased soil to amend the dry sand, the growing conditions in my backyard were seemingly too harsh to grow anything that needed more water than cactus. During the day, the hot sun baked the garden, wilting the tender vegetable plants even during the shortest days of the year. It seemed that only daily watering could alleviate the soil's dryness. Regardless, I was not going to be without my vegetable garden. I was going to solve these problems.

Although food gardening was a struggle, the weeds thrived effortlessly. If I did not mow them down frequently, they would have reached great heights and breadths. The weed patches apparently had no redeeming qualities- they were masses of only a few species, hardly anything that I would have thought of as being beneficial to anyone or anything. I decided to try something different- to plant a small area in wildflowers and wild grasses that were beneficial to wildlife, like butterflies and bees and birds. Thinking back to my college courses in ecology, it seemed that if I selected plants that preferred to grow in the kinds of conditions I had to work with, these new plants could offer enough competition to control, if not conquer, the nuisance species. With this thought in mind, I purchased several wildflower mixes and began to plant a small test area. I added in birdseed as well, which was mostly millet and sunflowers. I referred to this new, little patch of planted area as my "prairie garden" because a true prairie consists of a mix of wildflowers and grasses. That is exactly what I was creating. My goal was to make it a place for wildlife and that it would be mostly self-sustaining and low-maintenance.

In late 2008, the vegetable garden was expanded again and over the summer of 2009 I grew peanuts, sweet potatoes and two varieties of squash with moderate success. The little prairie garden became a magnet for birds and bugs. Most importantly, I found that ladybugs and other insects that control agricultural pests now had a safe haven to reproduce and thrive. Wildflowers bloomed in their season and families of butterflies took up permanent residence. Swarms of bees buzzed about searching for nectar. The millet and sunflowers grew tall and produced ripe bundles of seed; cardinals, blue jays, woodpeckers and migratory birds flew in and perched on the tall stems to eat from the dry fruiting heads. A box turtle appeared and night visitors too, like the screech owl and crickets. The small prairie patch was a success!

In October 2009, I began to think about planting the winter vegetable garden. I was once again frustrated with my limited food growing space. My garden beds would be completely filled by the must-have types of vegetables and there would be no room left for anything else. Yet, I had an ever-expanding list of vegetables I needed to grow. I say "needed" because my desire to grow a robust variety of vegetables was strong. I didn't want to buy them, I wanted to grow them. Not only did the homegrown vegetables taste better, but growing them gave me a genuine pride that I had earned honestly. Certainly, I thought, there was more space in the backyard- after all, I was on a quarter-acre lot. But, another part of me resisted; that part of me felt that the garden was already as big as it should be, for a reasonable person anyway. Reasonable meant the size of gardens I had seen other people grow in the city.

Somewhere inside of me, I had acquired the idea that a backyard food garden should be no bigger than what I had seen my neighbors grow (small). This feeling came from the same place that told me I should have a verdant, weed-free lawn, like all other urban residential homes should. That way, I would take my equal place in society by achieving the American standard for urban residential living. I thought back to my struggle with growing a lawn at my first house and how that effort was more or less fueled by the desire to fit in with the neighbors' expectations. I also knew how that lawn was one more straw sucking water from resources that were already stressed and that made me feel uneasy. At this house, I had no lawn in the front yard and it was actually more attractive than lawn…that was a success! My uneasiness had vanished with the turf grass. As I thought this through, I realized that I had choices, this was my property and I was the one who had control of what I did on my land. Alternatives *were* possible.

Feeling freer to think, I looked around my backyard. It seemed that the only place where I did not have a patch of weeds, which required regular mowing in the pleasant dry season and continual mowing during the miserably hot rainy season, was the vegetable garden. I joked to myself that the solution to the weed problem was to expand the vegetable garden across the entire back yard! Of course, that was absurd...but what a fun thought it was nonetheless.

But, well, maybe not so absurd after all...

I recalled my Aunt Elizabeth. Her entire backyard *was* a vegetable garden, or at least the places where she didn't grow flowers; they were relegated to odd corners and borders. Elizabeth grew all or most of the vegetables that she and her husband needed from her garden. The best part was that the garden was conveniently located outside the kitchen door- that was a real kitchen garden! When leaving her house after a visit, our arms were loaded up with fresh vegetables, a box of juicy concord grapes, flowers growing in old tin cans and canned goods from her cellar. I would love to have those things again!

I knew a woman, Anne, who was from rural Michigan. Her and I spoke once about vegetable gardening and I recalled that conversation as I considered my own backyard vegetable garden. She was young-ish, in her late 30s, and was married with children. Anne had a large food garden in her expansive yard. The half-acre garden grew more than 60 types of fruits, vegetables and herbs! From that garden, she grew about half (she was not quite sure exactly how much) of the food for her family. "My parents and grandparents all grew their own food," she told me, "I lived on my grandparent's farm for a year when I was a child and I loved it. They had a greenhouse on the side of their house to extend the growing season. Growing food is an essential part of our family life." Recalling this conversation encouraged me.

So maybe the thought of having a backyard that was mostly food garden wasn't so absurd, but it certainly was for me living in metropolitan south Florida, the subtropical paradise carpeted with emerald lawns, gated communities and golf courses, only a few miles away from the opulent seaside mansions of Palm Beach. It seemed to be a rather strange idea- to recreate a little piece of Iowa here in West Palm Beach...it was abandoning all of the unspoken rules. Then the scientist in me got involved and fantasy transformed itself into intrigue and inquiry. By late November 2009, I made the decision to expand the food and prairie gardens to fill all of the available backyard space. The weeds were now on a run for their lives!

As I began to get my backyard garden together, I made a decision to return to college. I wanted to teach college someday and a doctorate degree was required for me to teach at the university level. With the home renovations mostly completed, there was time to dedicate to that new goal. However, I would only go back to college under one condition- it must be an enjoyable experience. I had accomplished enough in my career and I didn't need to do this. Unlike my earlier experiences with education, this time it would be fun or not at all.

The first night of class that launched me on my journey towards a Ph.D. was on January 12th, 2009. I walked through the corridors of the Physical Sciences Building on the campus of Florida Atlantic University for the first time in 12 years. I had been among the first students to attend classes in this building after it was constructed. Back then, we worked around stacks of unpacked boxes, wrote on whiteboards that had been propped against walls and sat in computer labs that were still being set up. Now, walking through these halls more than a decade later, I could see how the once-new building had aged. Not well, in some respects. The elevators were creaky and slow, and there were grimy stains on the walls from the brush of thousands of student's hands as they passed through the corridors. The bathrooms appeared old. The floor tiles were worn. My memory echoed with visions of the classes I had taken long ago as I approached the classroom that had been assigned for my course in Environmental Restoration. It turned out to be the same classroom where I had attended my first course in this building! Looking at that classroom and examining the building as I made my way in, I remembered the excitement everyone had about the new structure. It was innovative, state-of-the art and modern- a picture of the future of university buildings. The building was designed to provide for students', professors' and staffs' needs in ways that older designs could not. No one feels that way about the building any longer- its flaws are clearly visible and the blinders of first love are not worn by the generation of students now walking its halls. What this outdated building could teach us now is what not to do when the next one is built.

I sat in one of the few available seats at the long table closest to the front. At 48 years old, I needed to be right up front to see the whiteboard and to keep my attention on the instructor. Another student arrived after I did, an older non-traditional student like myself, and took the seat to my right. Class started almost immediately so there was little time for introductions or pleasantries. But, during breaks and during the remaining semester, we became classmates and eventually, he became a good friend both in and out of school. Dean, like myself, was returning to college after many years. But, I had applied to the geosciences program at Florida International University in Miami (which was approximately 1.5 hours drive from my house) and was not intending to attend Florida Atlantic University (which was approximately 25 minutes drive from my house) because there was no such program at FAU. I was taking several college credits at FAU to be transferred to FIU. This way, I could get an early start on my degree and take fewer courses so far away from where I lived.

Three weeks into the semester, Dean informed me that the Geosciences Department at FAU was preparing to start their Ph.D. program in the coming fall. He also encouraged me to switch schools, which would be easy since I had not yet been formally accepted into the FIU program. I spent a month weighing the pros and cons (or, at least pretended to be weighing them because the choice was obvious). I submitted an application for the doctorate program at FAU and was promptly accepted into the fall 2009 class. I was now on my way to do something I had never dreamed I would do- achieve a doctorate degree.

By late November 2009, I was completing my first year of classes for my doctoral program. I would not begin my dissertation research for another year or two, but I still felt like I wanted to do some small study in the interim- something independent from school. I also knew that I wanted to do something more in my own sphere of influence- something in my own backyard that I could study, be immersed in and fully involve my hands, mind and expertise. As I turned my attention to the vegetable garden and its impending expansion, I started to see it as a possible research project. For the fun of it, I sat back, looking at the backyard space and thought broad and bold thoughts of fantasy. Well, if I did plant most of my backyard space in vegetables, I might as well make it a research project so that some good, beyond tasty produce, could come from it.

All research begins with questions and I first needed to have questions for the research to address. At first, the questions were broad but after trial and error, they became more specific. The garden would be a wonderful alternative to lawn. But, given the abundance of relatively inexpensive produce at the grocery store and food markets, was it really worthwhile to grow it yourself? In the past, so many people told me that it was too much work and too much of a bother. I knew those people were convinced it wasn't worth the effort.

I also started to think about the benefits that a home food garden could give to a household and to a community. How much food can someone grow in a home food garden? How much food can I grow in my backyard? Can I grow enough fruits and vegetables to meet the needs of one person? Two people? A family? I knew my aunt Elizabeth had grown enough vegetables for her household from her backyard garden. Why couldn't I do the same? How much would it cost to grow your own food? Clearly, if growing your own food cost more than buying it, there was no amount of environmental or scientific rationale that could convince most people to grow for themselves. I knew I could measure how much I was growing and I could estimate its value by going to the grocery stores and pricing what I was harvesting (and where it was coming from). Assuming a food garden actually pays for itself, how could a home food garden contribute to the household's finances and how much could the collective value of many backyard food gardens contribute to the community's economy? By collecting the right kinds of data, I could put real numbers on some of these unknown values. I started to feel really, really excited about this idea.

Drawing from my experience as a scientist, I thought about the garden as a part of the urban environment. As far back as my grade-school classes, I was shown figures of different types of cycles. For example, there was the water cycle, which showed how a molecule of water moved from clouds to the soil, lakes, streams, plants, then back to the atmosphere again. I could envision cycles of other things too, such as nutrients and energy and carbon dioxide. If I collected the right kinds of data, I could measure some of the parts of those cycles too. I started to think beyond the cycles and to the urban ecology, about the organisms that lived in the city. These organisms included butterflies, birds, wildlife and insects. I started to see the vegetable garden as a habitat that supported different species (including humans). In one way or another, I could measure some of that too.

Besides the financial and environmental issues, I saw how agriculture was linked to people in other ways too. As I started to connect the dots between agriculture and the important issues of human health, environmental health and sustainability, it was clear that I had stumbled onto something that was desperately missing in the area of agricultural sciences. Although my backyard food garden was small, it too was agriculture and was connected to these important issues in unique ways. I searched through the scientific literature and popular book titles and could not find a single study that did what I was proposing to do- measure the financial, environmental and ecological benefits of an urban backyard food garden. There were, however, thousands of science journal articles and books that delved into the minutia of commercial agriculture…university agriculture departments, their students and agricultural extension agents are well funded for that type of research. There were many persuasive public figures that lectured on the subject of local food growing and urban agriculture, and there were a number of well-written books on the concepts too. But, I was still unable to find studies with hard numbers to prove what these public figures and conceptual books touted. There were already some people who believed in the benefits of urban agriculture. But, why should policy makers and community leaders pay attention if urban agriculture was a good idea but nobody could say how good it was?

Although my first impression of this backyard food growing study bordered on fantasy, I began to think it through more deeply and it became more serious. After working for more than a decade with a government agency that focused on natural resource conservation and management, I was very much aware that policy makers and community leaders are bombarded with great ideas every day of the week. Their challenge is to separate out the most critical ones to act on. Ideas that are backed by sound science and can prove their benefits are those most likely to get attention. Dire problems also get attention. If successful, this study would give supporting data to address both a sound idea and a dire problem.

A sense of urgency began to grow inside of me. Almost daily, there were news stories and published science articles warning about the unsustainable use of our natural resources, the threats from pollution, the coming impacts from global warming, the concerns about how to feed an exploding world population, food safety and food security within our communities. There were heated policy discussions at the highest levels of government about managing carbon dioxide emissions, non-renewable energy consumption and hunger in our communities, but few of these discussions included how agricultural systems are related to these issues and the potential role of urban agriculture in alleviating these problems. Although I had a single urban backyard food garden, my small study with big ambitions had the potential to contribute to these conversations in important and significant ways. Especially if my one backyard food garden would be multiplied by tens of millions, as had been done during the Victory Garden campaign of World War II.

By the time all of this had tumbled through my mind, I was convinced it was a study that *had* to be done and I wanted to do. I could be finished with it by the time I was ready to begin my dissertation research. Great! The timing was just right! I sat down and made a plan for the study. I made a decision about what kind of data I needed to collect and how it should be collected to satisfy scientific rigor. Now, it was time to begin planning the garden!

I got out my seed catalogues and began to browse them in earnest. After I had selected the basics, I had additional space that could be planted with things I have always wanted to try, but never could! This was thrilling. The basics included green string beans, green cabbage, carrots, onions, potatoes and tomatoes. The luxury vegetables included the stunningly beautiful royal burgundy string beans, which had a color and texture of a fine purple-blue velvet that quickly changed to bright green when cooked. There was the Asian green bok choi (with the even more exotic name Shanghai Psai Tsai), deeply-colored black beans for Cuban-themed dinners, succulent Napa cabbage with a mild nutty flavor right from heaven, sweet golden beets and flavor-filled Roma tomatoes for sauces and home-made ketchup. There were the herbs, too, which I never had enough space to grow before- cilantro, rosemary, basil, tarragon, parsley, thyme, mint, dill and lemon grass. By late 2009, I had finished the large-scale expansion of the beds, filled them with vegetables and officially began my research. I watched like a mother hen over her chicks. Perhaps this was all one great fantasy, but I had taken my first steps down a path that would become very long and curvy, and more rewarding than anything else I could possibly have imagined.

At the start of the study, I had not committed to collecting research data for any longer than this one season. In fact, I was not even sure when the season would end. I would just have to play it by ear. On my 49th birthday, December 12th, 2009, I began to keep a daily garden log to track all of the problems I ran into, things I had learned, ideas that I had thought about and all of the research data I was collecting. As the study progressed over the 2009-2010 season, I refined my research questions and learned that some data were too difficult to collect, so I let those parts of the study go.

When I was in my younger 20s, I worked for a local fruit company that purchased, packed and shipped citrus and other tropical fruits to customers around the United States. During the 5 years I worked at the fruit company, I became involved in purchasing fruit for the store, sometimes driving to fields to buy a truckload of melons or to a wholesale broker for boxes of vegetables for retail sale. I became aware of the many stages involved in the production and transportation of food as it traveled from farm field to point of sale. I became interested in how much energy and carbon dioxide emissions to the atmosphere were associated with the conventional commercial agricultural system, as compared to local and backyard food growing. Just how much does our dependency on the industrial agricultural system contribute to global warming concerns? Although I could not measure precise numbers, I could come up with some fairly good quantities for comparison.

A second tweak to my research project came from my determination to find high-quality fruit and vegetable waste for composting. In keeping with the desire to use "organic" methods, I wanted to use no synthetic, chemical or mined fertilizer in my garden beds. Although I would use purchased organic fertilizers, these are relatively expensive and a high-quality compost was needed in large quantities. Unfortunately, my household did not produce enough compostable material to feed even one fraction of my many garden beds, but one convenient source would be from my cafeteria at work. At that time, I worked for a government agency that had a small cafeteria, the operation of which was outsourced to a for-profit company. They only served breakfast and lunch on weekdays, usually Monday through Friday, to those workers who chose to dine on site. It was never a lucrative operation, a situation that had significantly worsened because of the multi-year economic recession that the United States was going through at that time. As such, the cafeteria staff always seemed overworked and stressed. I had to be careful in my request for their vegetable and fruit scraps- if it was going to cause them any costs, additional work or interfere with operations in any way, I was guaranteed a decisive "NO."

In late December 2009, I approached the cafeteria manager with my inquiry; I was quite surprised when she, almost without thinking, heartily agreed to do so. She explained that her company had a commitment to environmentally friendly practices, but that was not the whole reason. Through an entirely fortuitous circumstance, earlier in the week she had received orders from the regional manager to begin separating out and measuring all of their vegetable and fruit waste from the garbage stream. Corporate headquarters wanted the individual food service units to be aware of how efficiently they were using the produce they were purchasing, which was among their larger operating costs. Through careful discussion, I was able to take my need and turn it into something that was able to make the manager's job easier- I offered to weigh and measure the volume for her if she would set it aside in a bucket each morning. I would pick up the bucket over lunchtime, weigh and measure at home that evening, then provide her with the numbers she was looking for. It was a win-win situation!

The new garden plantings were beginning to grow wonderfully by early January 2010. Then, something that had not occurred in almost two decades descended on the tender tropical vegetation in West Palm Beach- frost. Not just one night, but several. Each night, I collected every sheet, pillowcase, blanket, rag, bucket, barrel, bin and box I could find in the house and shed. I covered, blanketed, wrapped, protected, clothed and sheltered everything that was exposed. It was only marginally helpful; the cold was too sharp and penetrating. The January frosts damaged or killed a substantial part of the garden, which took a week to be fully known. Waiting until it seemed that the worst of the cold weather had passed, I found myself having to replant a substantial part of the garden only weeks after I had begun to collect study data.

The frost also nipped the growing tips of the old mango tree in my front yard. I estimated the tree to be at least 50 years old at that time. It was an old commercial variety of which entire groves had been planted on the coastal sand ridges of Palm Beach County. Remnants of these groves can still be found today in front yards and along streets in neighborhoods in the area. These Florida mangoes were renowned for their flavor and size, but for unknown reasons, are no longer being planted or grown commercially. Curiously, the mangoes in our West Palm Beach grocery stores come from Mexico and Haiti during the same time when our local mangoes are ripe. My robust and energetic 70-year old brother-in-law had come down to visit over Christmas, as he did most years, and I recruited him to help me trim my mango tree back. The tree produced some fruit, but I was not particularly enamored with the quality. I did know that severe pruning of old mango trees could rejuvenate them and improve fruit quality. This was not the reason for the pruning; nor was the fact that frost had most likely damaged the new growth and there would be little harvest anyway. The previous year, the tree's wide and spreading branches, which overhung the neighbor's driveway, bore clusters of fruits weighing up to two pounds each that precariously dangled some twenty feet above the neighbor's new vehicle parked below. Lying in bed at night, the resonating THUD of falling fruits as they crashed to the ground was enough to wake you from a light sleep. Something had to be done to prevent inevitable disaster.

As the growing season progressed into late March, the height of the dry season, it became a challenge to keep the vegetables alive. The sun's strong intensity and the prolonged periods of dry, sunny weather made the garden's toughest plants shrivel. By mid-April, it was time to surrender gracefully and withdraw with dignity. Even if I could make it to the beginning of the rainy season, which normally happened in mid-May, the daytime and nighttime heat would prohibit cultivation of most vegetables I was familiar with. I pronounced the end of the study's 2009-2010 growing season in May, with cleanup in early June, and analyzed my data.

By the end of the study's 2009-2010 growing season, I had harvested 66 varieties of vegetables and herbs weighing a total of 167 pounds! But what was more interesting to me was the value of what I produced. If I had purchased these fruits, vegetables and herbs from the supermarket, they would have cost me about $475 if they had been grown using conventional (industrial) agricultural practices. But, I was using organic methods and those prices were much higher-closer to $775. There were many other results from this study that were exciting too, such as how much compost I was able to make from the cafeteria waste that was diverted from the landfill, how much water I had used, how far the vegetables in the grocery stores had traveled and how much energy I had saved by growing my own food instead of buying produce that had been transported here from afar. When I looked at these results, I knew that I had to continue the study at least one more year. Without the killing frost, I certainly could produce more, especially since I was learning how to grow better.

In spite of the problems, this had been a good growing season and this study had yielded good data! I felt a thrill that other research scientists understand- that point where you spend a lot of time collecting data and information, and the big day comes when you finally get to see the results of all of your hard work. What I found was meaningful, if only to me, and I knew that it was important enough to continue. The data from these 171 growing days may be compared to other regions with similar growing season durations, even in temperate climates. Although you can grow food in south Florida all year, you can only grow the "winter" vegetables for about five months, those that are grown "up north" in temperate regions in the spring, summer and fall. These are the types of vegetables and herbs I was producing. The actual growing season duration for winter vegetables in South Florida is comparable to that of many temperate zone regions, such as Chicago and New York City.

Around this time, I had been attending a series of research presentations as part of my doctoral program. At one of these presentations, a professor of climate studies presented his study of the regional weather phenomena known as the "Summer Drought," which is somewhat recognizable in rainfall patterns from south Florida, but is a significant weather pattern in the Caribbean islands of Cuba, Jamaica and the Cayman Islands. The summer drought is an annual period of low or no rainfall that occurs during July and August. The rainy, or monsoon, season in south Florida is from May through October. The summer drought in south Florida is often expressed as a two or three week period around mid-July when little rainfall occurs. This is both noticeable and unusual for occurring during the middle of the rainy season. The Summer Drought in Jamaica and the Cayman Islands is so prolonged, that it interrupts food crop production. It appears that one of the main crops that were affected was cabbage. This surprised me, since that is a vegetable whose best growth is usually associated with cool weather. Or so I understood from my seed catalogues and the vegetable-growing experts from temperate climate zones. How could they grow cabbage in the summer in the tropics? Either they are growing a variety I am unfamiliar with or they are growing it without regard for what the seed catalogues and temperate climate vegetable growing experts say. My interest was prodded and I found that I needed to think beyond the confines of the gardening knowledge I grew up with. I had to adapt to the regional climate I was growing in and adopt fruit and vegetable types that do best here. Up until now, I had been trying to grow my familiar Iowa vegetables in a climate they did not particularly like. I was fighting nature.

In April 2010, I went to a plant sale at Fairchild Tropical Botanic Garden in Miami with a group of adult students from my Florida Landscape and Garden class. As we were leaving, I passed a vendor who was selling tropical vegetable varieties that were commonly grown in the Caribbean. These vegetables had unfamiliar and exotic names such as cassava (yuca), malanga (taro), boniato (a yam), malabar (vine spinach), roselle (red hibiscus), calalu (an amaranth), tepary beans (a bean native to the Southwestern United States and Mexico, which was important to the indigenous people), winged beans and gandules (pigeon peas). These were varieties of tropical vegetables that could be grown here in the summer! I felt like I had struck gold. The next step to my research was in these trays. I purchased several of each variety and took them home to plant in my garden.

These two recent experiences, the presentation on Caribbean agriculture and finding a local source for tropical vegetables, made me rethink my way of food gardening. I realized three very important things...first, I was growing a garden that was centered around European traditions that were carried to the United States with immigrants and these may not work as well as indigenous food growing methods. Second, I had not adapted my food garden and diet to the climate I was living in. Third, I had placed limitations on my gardening practices based on what experts in another region told me were the right ways of doing things. These limitations had restricted my learning and productivity. In other words, seed catalogues, gardening guides and most of what I had learned about growing vegetables had come from another region and did not work here. It wasn't that the growing season in south Florida was opposite that of the temperate north (plant in the winter, rest in the summer), it was that our climate was turned "inside out" as compared to the temperate north. Temperate climates started cool, got hot, then turned cool. Gardening advice was based on that temperature regime and plants from temperate regions prefer that climatic pattern. Here, it was hot, then mild, then hot. As I sought out information and materials for vegetable gardening in this subtropical climate, I realized that there was very little, if any. Most of it was scattered, locked up in the minds of local growers and not broadly accessible. It was too small of a region for anyone to study seriously and to publish materials for those living in this area. If I was going to be successful, I had to forge new ground and talk with people who had been growing food here. I had to rethink and relearn almost everything I knew about gardening. There were no other options.

Most of the tropical vegetable seedlings that I purchased from the vendor at Fairchild Tropical Botanic Garden died within a month after planting them and I did not know why. I began to search for local vegetable gardening information and for other kinds of tropical vegetables to grow. I found a few of these listed in seed catalogues, but doubted that they were varieties that were appropriate for my local growing conditions. I knew that I had to keep an open mind and an open ear, and if I waited long enough, I would find what I was looking for. Fortunately, I did.

10. GARDEN CITY

When talking about urban agriculture, I have been referring to the entire range of food growing that occurs within developed areas. This includes home vegetable gardens, patio gardens, rooftop gardens, wall gardens, fruit trees along city streets, community gardens, urban farms, aquaponics, hydroponics and any other ways that people use to grow food. Some of these are carried out by individuals or a family on their own property. However, some kinds of urban agriculture involve the participation of many people who are usually unrelated, but share a common interest in growing food. Examples of this kind of urban agriculture are communal gardens and community gardens. Urban food gardens that contribute to a community's economic and social development are referred to as "civic agriculture."[39]

Civic agriculture can be multi-dimensional, playing roles in the community that are unique and sometimes profoundly important. Traveling across the United States and visiting many expressions of civic agriculture, I have been dumbfounded by the diversity of purpose and the depth of caring these gardens demonstrated. Given the minuscule support that civic agriculture receives from government funding and the enormous community benefit provided by it, civic agriculture is perhaps the least appreciated and most productive societal activity.

Civic agriculture, in one form or another, has been around for a very long time. In fact, when comparing industrial agriculture to civic agriculture, industrial agriculture is in its infancy. Besides growing food for oneself, people in cities have always gathered to grow food on publicly accessible spaces, whether the land was privately or publicly owned. Communal gardens, which are nothing more than a piece of land which is used by a group of local residents for food growing, have been around for thousands of years- probably as long as there have been cities. In most places, local residents use land with the permission of the landowner. However, some communal gardens are on property that is being used without the landowner's knowledge or permission. This too, is a very old practice. I know a woman in the Midwest who lives next to a farm that has expansive cornfields. Among the young corn plants, she and some of her neighbors sow their own vegetable seeds in the spring and harvest before the corn crop is picked in late autumn. Despite having a long tradition, using someone else's land without permission is illegal, but the consequences are usually benign. Over the past several decades, activists have used illegal food gardens to improve neighborhood aesthetics, make political statements or to call attention to social issues; these forms of illegal gardens are called "guerrilla gardens."

I drove past a guerrilla garden in south Florida one day. It was located on a moderately traveled street and was rather unimposing; in fact, if you didn't know what you were looking for, you would miss it. When I said that the garden was located on a street, I literally meant "on." The guerrilla garden was planted on top of a cross street that was no longer being used by traffic; the city had erected removable barriers on the crushed-rock surfaced road to route traffic onto main thoroughfares and to reduce the costs of maintenance. Over a relatively short span of time, a few local residents hauled in truckloads of compost and mulch, and planted shade trees, fruit trees, shrubs and vegetables. They put this underused piece of land to better use. Guerrilla gardens have also been planted along sidewalks, on empty city lots and in obscure urban locations.

The viability of guerrilla gardens is questionable, though. Usually, the soil is untested and may be contaminated by urban pollution. Should city officials or the landowner decide to alter the site, the garden will have to be removed at the expense of someone other than the gardeners. But, even with the problems, these gardens make a strong statement about the lack of food growing space in cities, are an expression of frustration with limited food choice and demonstrate how food can be grown unnoticed in urbanized areas.

Community gardens, as we know them today, are like communal gardens but the landowner has legally granted access to the property and the community's governing authorities are supportive of the gardening activities. Unlike guerrilla gardens, some type of an organized leadership runs community gardens. Community gardens in the United States can be traced back to the 18th century, but most came about during the 20th century and in the past decades have taken on a variety of roles and causes. In the United States, community gardens are most numerous in the northeast and the western states. Other countries with notable community gardens include Brazil, Canada, Cuba, England, Germany, Guatemala, India, Italy, Japan, Malaysia, Mali, Mexico, New Zealand, Peru, South Africa, Spain, and Taiwan. In fact, it would be difficult to find a country without one. One country that seems to be racing forward with establishing community gardens, likely because of government support, is Australia.

Quambatook, a town of little more than 250 people in the southeastern Australian state of Victoria, is known as "The land of wheat and wool, home of the tractor pull" (the town's motto) and would be one of the last places one would expect to have or even need a community garden. The climate is warm and semi-arid, with only about 12 inches of rainfall a year. Sheep and wheat farmers inhabit the area surrounding the town, whose residents are typically older. Although the town is surrounded by agriculture, there is a coalition of residents who are looking for a permanent space for a community garden. More recently this coalition turned its attention to a local disused recreational park where there were nine grass tennis courts. The community garden's leaders brought forth a proposal to keep two or three of the tennis courts and turn the remaining ones into food gardens. In exchange for access to the unused courts, the community garden would help promote the use of the recreational park and remaining tennis courts- a win-win situation for the community. "The tennis courts are already fenced off and there is great access," says Jolene, who is heading up the effort. "It is central to most people in town, has water, a structure which could quite easily be utilized as a possible hothouse, garden sheds, clubrooms, etc." She is excited that up to now, there has been wonderful support from various companies and small businesses that have donated seeds, fertilizers, fruit trees, hardware and the list goes on! "Obviously, they can see the benefits in such a project too," she says. "As for local support, there are a lot of people in town and in the surrounding district who are very keen on the project and can't wait to see it up and running." Jolene hopes that everyone in town will participate in the project and offer their skills, such as helping with setup, construction, offering advice, educating people, donating time and/or goods, anything they have to offer. "After all, this garden is for each and every one of them." Jolene says that what she hopes to see from the project is the empowerment of individuals, positivity and development of a sense of community. She hopes that the garden can be a place to develop friendships, learn, rest, socialize and to provide opportunities to build physical health and mental well-being. The list is long. This garden is already becoming a milestone in this town's history and, in the future, people here will use it as the reference point that divides the era before and after the garden.

Across the Australian continent, about 260 miles north of Perth, is the City of Greater Geraldton. It has a population of about 35,000 people and a mild Mediterranean climate that is great for growing many types of food plants. Their community garden is relatively new, having been formed in 2013, and it is in a suburban park. Tammy, one of the garden's leaders, told me, "The garden was founded through a grant from the Australian federal government, which has a program to support the startup of community gardens." Under guidelines established by the grant, volunteers must run the garden and the money could only be used for infrastructure. They grow in wicking beds, which are lined garden beds that have a water reservoir on the bottom that, when filled, keeps the garden soil moist. These garden beds are very water-efficient. "The garden assimilates food scraps from the community to create worm casting and compost. There are no assigned beds; whoever volunteers at the garden gets to take a share of what is produced." Tammy points out, "For us, it's not about taking home the produce, it's about bringing a community together."

In the far north of Queensland, Australia, another recent (2013) community garden has taken shape on what was formerly a disused basketball court at a community center! Ravenshoe is a town of nearly 2000 people and residents have to drive one hour to get to the nearest major shopping outlets. Julie, one of the garden's leaders, explained, "We grow for ourselves; those that participate get a share of the weekly harvest and any surplus is usually sold at a local shop. Food is given to the needy through the local community center." Julie is excited about how the garden has come together under improbable circumstances and strictly by community interest. "We are hoping to encourage people to have their own food gardens and hope to one day have street 'pods' where some streets have smaller food gardens under the guidance of our main garden." They grow according to organic methods, compost, have a worm farm, own their own greenhouse and have even had a series of garden-to-plate cooking classes!

Although civic agriculture is about food production and community involvement, it has had other unintended benefits. It would be hard to understate the important role that civic agriculture has played in keeping local food traditions alive. The need to grow one's own food and to can, freeze or store produce during the normal harvest season vanished with the rise of industrial agriculture and would have been entirely lost by the successive generations, if not for political events on another continent thousands of miles away.

During World War II, governments in the United States and Great Britain encouraged civilians to plant food gardens as a way to help conserve valuable resources that were needed for the war effort, such as energy. Public support for these "Victory Gardens" was tremendous. In the United States, major cities such as Boston, New York and Chicago established Victory Gardens on public lands and the number of private vegetable gardens during that time reached tens of millions.[40] These wartime food gardens supplied an estimated 40 percent of the United States' fresh vegetables in 1944,[41] producing roughly the same amount of vegetables as the commercial food system at that time. In England, Victory Gardens were estimated to have covered approximately 300,000 acres and met half of that country's fruit and vegetable needs during and after World War II.[42] The role that home and community food gardens played in conserving natural resources during that time cannot be understated. Governments at that time realized that large-scale agriculture and long-distance food shipping consumed non-renewable resources, such as energy, metals for manufacturing farm equipment, mined materials for transportation infrastructure and natural resources. It was also recognized that high numbers of local small food growers led to a more sustainable and stable national food system.

Unfortunately, Victory Gardens were abandoned soon after the war. The decline of urban food gardens after WWII occurred because of the robust economy in the 1950s and the advent of industrial agriculture that was able to supply food through a single source (a broker) rather than from multiple individual farms.[5,43] The decline also occurred because the government ended support for the food garden campaign. Since the war was over, Victory Gardens were considered to be no longer necessary.

It was not until the mid-1970s that civic agriculture would begin to take hold again, supported by followers of the back-to-nature movement and maturing hippies of the 1960s. The first significant community garden program in North America was started in Montreal, Canada, which grew to include more than 76 garden sites with 6,400 plot allotments and 10,000 participants.[43] In 1989, 405 community gardens in Newark produced $450,000 worth of produce.[44] Seattle, Washington initiated a community garden program in the mid-1970s and by 2009 it had more than 70 organic gardens that produced between 7 to 10 tons of produce annually. Urban food gardens moved from public spaces and into schools when, in 1995, California began its school food garden program. By 2009, that state had over 3,000 school food gardens. These efforts were complimented by the on-going expansion of urban agriculture in other major cities in the United States, such as New York, Milwaukee and Chicago. The City of Detroit established the Garden Resource collaborative in 2003 to provide technical information, marketing resources and seeds to urban food gardeners. By 2008, that one program supported 169 community gardens, 40 school gardens and 359 family gardens with an estimated combined production of over 163 tons of produce.[43]

Beyond the big cities, interest in community food gardens reached even small cities like Dubuque, Iowa. I remember my sister getting her own plot at a community garden on the edge of town in the mid-1970s. A generous landowner donated the space to anyone who wanted to plant his or her own food crops. There, along with other city residents, she grew tomatoes, peppers and lettuces. Some adorned their plots with handmade signs, marking the locations of their beloved plants. Although the plots were small and weeds numerous, these growers were excited about returning to the food gardens they once knew as children. By the 1980s, these ambitious garden plots were buried beneath strip malls as urban sprawl pushed well beyond Dubuque's city borders and absorbed the prime farmland that fringed the city. When the community food growing space closed, these residents returned to supermarkets and the produce supplied by the industrial agricultural system. Today, driving past the site where tomatoes once grew for appreciative families, you would never know that community food gardens had ever been there. It was not the loss of interest that killed the community garden in my hometown of Dubuque, it was urban sprawl.

The number of community gardens in the United States has exploded since 2005. When I began studying local residents' attitudes and perspectives about urban agriculture in 2012, I knew of only a few community gardens in Palm Beach County. By 2014, there were at least 14. They are popping up across the world in numbers that nobody could have foretold a decade ago. One reason why community gardens are in such demand is because they offer city residents, who often have little gardening space of their own, a place to grow food and socialize with others. They are also rich storehouses of local food growing knowledge, assistance and experimentation.

At one community garden in a south Florida master-planned community, which is situated on land that has been generously offered for use by a Christian church, I talked with Emily about why she was there. Her graceful gestures and refined manner of speech indicated to me that she was highly educated. She and her husband had been married for 44 years. They lived in a single family home that was situated alongside a golf course in an affluent community where famous celebrities and old-money families spend their winter months. "In New Jersey, we had a huge garden for years," she told me, "but, there are landscape restrictions where we live now and even if I could grow a vegetable garden, I would be afraid to eat food that had been exposed to the sprays they use to maintain the golf course." Emily told me that she is just getting started at a community garden and is learning about different soils and fertilizers. "I would love to see many, many more community gardens," she says. "I love the community aspect, it's healthy; the people from all ethnic groups and the children are involved too, it's wonderful!" Emily's excitement for food gardening was particularly pleasing to see- neither her parents nor her grandparents knew how to grow food. At 65 years old, she was experiencing something new.

Emily was not the first person I met at a community garden that had broken from their family's non-food growing heritage. Two friends, Jackie and Karen, have immersed themselves in their local community garden. Jackie is 48 years old and from New Jersey. Karen is 54 and is from Boston. Both have vivacious and outgoing personalities that are fun to be around. Their stories are surprisingly similar. Both have grandparents who immigrated to the United States and settled in big cities. Both had parents and grandparents who did not grow food for themselves, so neither woman grew up with a vegetable garden. Both women were born and raised in major metropolitan areas and now live in residences where there is no land for gardening. These women each told me, "I grew up during the 1960s and was profoundly influenced by the hippie movement." In fact, the hippie movement inspired all of their siblings to start growing their own food too. Out of a desire to have vegetable gardens, Jackie and Karen joined their local community garden because, as Jackie says, "Gardening makes the world a better place and is pure enjoyment!" What could be more special and entertaining than two gregarious and fun women at a community garden? Well, three! I found these three interesting women, who were sisters, in Kentucky.

While traveling between Florida and the Midwest in 2014, Eddie and I spent a couple of days in Louisville, Kentucky. Louisville is an interesting place. It is situated along the crossroads between the Deep South, the Midwest and Appalachia. True to its Southern influences, it is personable and friendly. One never feels rushed. But, it is also connected to the agricultural heritage of the Midwestern heartland. Food, and food growing, is very important to its residents. Down-home, no-nonsense, make-do-with-what-you-have attitudes have drifted in from the Appalachian Mountains to the east. My friend Barbara, who lives and works in Louisville, participates in a community garden. This garden has the distinction of being the oldest in Louisville- it was founded in 1999. The annual cost per plot is a meager $10. People who have plots in the community garden respect each other and watch out for each other. A monthly potluck brings members together to socialize and to share gardening stories. Nobody grows the same things or in the same way as another; one bed is all flowers, another all squash and another is experimenting with new growing methods.

On the day of our visit to the garden, I approached a woman who was sitting in her vegetable bed tugging at weeds and fluffing sagging plants. After initial pleasantries, I asked her what got her involved with this community garden. She introduced herself as Lisa, in that kind way that people here usually do. "Well, this is my second year. I got a bed here after a neighbor of mine gave me an eggplant that she grew here- it was the best eggplant I had ever had. It was so good that I decided to get a plot here *and* at my church's community garden too." Looking through her bed, she had robust plantings of potatoes, eggplant, garlic and Brussels sprouts. Her plants looked twice the size of those I could grow in my backyard in West Palm Beach. Lisa told us that her parents grew food, but had never taught her how. This garden had many people who were glad to teach her. During a lull in our conversation, she stopped and asked, "Do you know anything about Brussels sprouts?"

After an encouraging chat about Brussels sprouts, we left Lisa to her weeding and spied an elderly lady doting over her vegetables in another bed on the other side of the garden. Barbara smiled and said that we must meet her- she is one (the eldest) of three sisters who have plots in this garden and they are such a joy to be around. We migrated towards the elder sister. She eyed us cautiously as we approached, probably to see whom she knew and whom she didn't know, then broke out in an energetic smile. I looked down into her plot as we approached; it was immaculate. She seemed thrilled to have a spontaneous audience and I could not wait to hear what she had to say.

Beaming with pride, the elder sister began talking about her garden. Her words were carried along on the chords of a lilting Appalachian Mountain accent that was charming and earthy. Pointing at the plants in the bed, she started, "Daddy was raised on a farm. He always told us to plant the week *after* the Derby (Kentucky Derby); but this year, I had to plant *two weeks* after the Derby because of the rain." This last point was said in a way that made you feel that the one-week delay might threaten the entire vegetable crop. The elder sister's plot was virtually weed-free, clearly the most weedless garden bed in the entire community garden. "I love working with my hands," she explained, "I'm 70-years-old; I weed and plant and even till the soil with my bare hands. I love the feel of the soil." She told us that she would work in the garden from sunrise to sundown, if the weather would let her, and she would still work in her garden even if she couldn't walk and had to crawl on her hands on knees. This was a woman that loved her vegetable garden.

The elder sister was a long-time resident of the neighborhood where the community garden resided and intended on staying there until she died. The place where the community garden sat once was the site of an elementary school, the school where the elder sister used to teach classes. Wrapping up the talk about her own vegetable plot, the elder sister took us on a tour of the rest of the community garden. We passed one plot that had not been planted and had a few sad weeds. This reminded me of other plots I had seen before- not in a community garden but in a cemetery, after the casket had been buried and, as though in mourning, the bare earth sat waiting for grass to grow back over it again. The elder sister pointed to that plot and explained that it belonged to Clara, who had died the past winter. The plot sat there empty and unattended. Our tour continued past a garden plot that had a plastic pink flamingo foraging among the onion and garlic plants. To the left of the grazing flamingo, the elder sister pointed to a group of plots, "This is where I taught kindergarten, our classroom was right there." The woman's face briefly slipped into a stare of reminiscence, then returned to us. "One thing about children," the sister said, "you can't doubt them, you have to encourage them." We continued, then stopping in place, she pointed to a particularly ubiquitous weed and asked if we knew what that was. In fact, I did know that weed and this was the only time during our conversation when I felt that I could contribute something meaningful to her.

From nowhere, the second of the three sisters appeared. Her vegetable bed was next to the elder sister's and was somewhat less perfected. The second sister joined us on our tour. Wanting to stir family rivalry, I asked the two sisters where their third sister's garden plot was. The entourage flowed around raised beds and stopped in front of a particularly bountiful vegetable plot. I asked, "Which sister has the best plot?" The two sisters replied instantly, "She does, but we all plant how Daddy said to plant and grow."

Driving away from the community garden, I asked Barbara if she could go through alleys and back streets. I wanted to look into backyards to see how many people had their own vegetable gardens. One house had pole beans growing up a chain link fence along their property line. A neighbor had grapes on their fence. Another backyard held a large vegetable garden with robust and healthy plantings. I counted. About one out of ten homes had a full vegetable garden, a garden that was much larger than the plots back at the community garden. Arriving at Barbara's house, we saw her neighbor's vegetable garden in the front yard next to the sidewalk. Herbs, kale and other vegetables greeted passersby. This was a city that loved its urban gardens.

Many communities have an aversion to growing food in front yards, referring to these kinds of gardens as magnets for weeds. Grass and flowerbeds are acceptable, but not cabbage or collard green plants. It is not that grass and flowers are profoundly more valuable than food plants (they are not) nor is it because cabbage and collard green plantings are more likely to be unkept (they are not), it is the fear of untidiness that has been channeled against food plants. These communities blame the weeds.

Weeds. I began my garden study thinking about weeds. I was

certain that they would cause me many hours of frustration, sprouting up in every corner of the garden and forcing their way into my neat rows of vegetables. As much as my garden project caused me to rethink my food growing, it also caused me to rethink weeds. Of course, the messages that I had been given by the gardening media (books, magazines, guides, etc.) taught me that my food plants were vulnerable, innocent and child-like, needing the same nurturing care as human babies. Weeds were the bullies on the block that needed to be met with fierce resistance; they were, after all, out to steal space, nutrition and water from the poor vegetables. Weeds were to be dealt with swiftly and strongly, hit hard and hit early.

Then, there were the things I learned in college. There really wasn't a thing as a weed in botanical science. There were some species that were considered to be "weedy" in the way they establish themselves, but many of these were not native and they tended to grow very well in places you didn't want them to. In their homelands, they were usually not weeds at all. There were other types of plants that were considered to be "invasive," but these were species that tended to move into an area that was either disturbed or the conditions were just right for them to proliferate. These were not quite weeds either. One great definition of a weed is that it is a plant that grows in a place you don't want it to. My neighbor adores her flowers, but one of them likes to seed itself in my yard, just across the chain-link fence. The flower is beloved to her but a weed to me (to avoid unnecessary emotional pain, I tear them out when she is not at home and quickly push them into the compost bin). I encountered another great definition for a weed, which is credited to Ralph Waldo Emerson; this definition says that a weed is a plant whose virtues have not yet been discovered. Like the first definition, the second one leaves the door open for interpretation and personal perspective. The idea of a "weed" is not an ecological concept, but a human invention, devised from the dislike of plants growing in places that we have deemed unacceptable. It is this same dislike that teaches us that tidy lawns of a single grass species are considered to be more desirable than a diverse collection of food-producing plants.

Western culture's preoccupation with order knows few bounds. It has given us the concept of a weed, a concept that has spread weed-like throughout our social consciousness. This has had unfortunate negative consequences. It has caused us to abandon nutritious food plants because they arrive as uninvited additions to our gardens; these plants we classify as ruderal and vulgar. They grow among our genetically weak cultivated vegetables, begging for a place on our plates but our response is to pull them out and toss them onto the trash pile. These weeds have an important message for us: wake up and realize that they are better plants to grow than the needy imports that require babying, soil amendments and irrigation just to survive.

With the apparent race to breed and genetically engineer as many new hybrids as possible, agriculturalists ignore the menu of wild food plants that long ago learned how to tolerate local conditions and resist local pests. Some examples from North America include ferns (the fiddleheads of some species) and violets (*Viola* spp. young leaves and flowers), and the wetland plants pickerelweed (*Pontederia cordata* leaf stalks and seeds) and cattail (*Typha* spp. roots and shoots). Native American tribes did not have to order vegetable seeds from catalogues or purchase seedlings at garden centers. Nor did they have to purchase chemical fertilizers or manipulate plant genomes- the world around them provided an abundance of food plants that, unfortunately, have been lost to modern gardeners. These ancient food plants are the true heirloom vegetables and herbs. Many of them are considered to be weeds.

Even some introduced wild food plants have become naturalized and are common in our own backyards. One particularly prolific "weed" in my garden is purslane (*Portulaca oleracea*)- this was the weed that the elder sister at the Louisville community garden asked me about. After trying it in salads, soups and stir-fry dishes, I was amazed at its quality and flavor. A Russian visitor to my backyard garden lit up with joy when he found it among my vegetables- it reminded him of his homeland and was a plant that his family once treasured in their gardens. It is known as a tasty and cultivated potherb throughout the Caribbean and parts of Europe, but is virtually unknown (if not denigrated) in the United States. After discovering its qualities, I no longer have a problem with purslane as a weed. In fact, there never seems to be enough of it. It is surprising how rare the weeds become when they become food!

Another food plant that has been terribly wasted is millet. Millet is indigenous to several parts of the world and many types thrive in warm and semi-arid regions. Because it grows well in hot weather, tolerates drought, is highly productive and has a relatively short life span, millet makes an ideal crop plant for agricultural production in drier regions. Millet is an ancient food plant and has been cultivated by humans for some 10,000 years, but today nearly all (97 percent) of the world's millet production occurs in developing countries.[45] In the United States, we believe it has so little value that we set it out for birdseed.

Challenged by the weeds in my own backyard, I set out to learn more about them. Over the course of my food growing study, I made a list of the pesky weeds that inhabited my yard- those that came up in cracks between patio stones and those that flourished in great abundances, reaching waist high if I would let them. There were also the subtle ones that peered out from beneath hedges and those that climbed fences and clamored over hedges. What I found was that about half of my worst weeds were edible…not just edible, but common food plants in other cultures!

Besides their potential as food plants, my weeds also were important ecologically. Weeds excel at extracting precious nutrients from soils and concentrating them in their tissues. If you harvest them before they set seed and use them as mulch or place them in your compost bin, you can recapture those nutrients. After researching the plants that beneficial insects use as food or for reproduction, I found that 11 of my backyard weeds were larval or nectar plants to 29 species of local butterflies! Many flowering weeds attract bees and other pollinators- the pollinators that my food plants depend upon for producing fruit. These weeds were drawing the beneficial insects to my garden without any effort on my behalf. That fact alone was deserving of my respect. With these revelations, I stopped treating my weeds with chemical sprays and started eating and harvesting them. I no longer have a weed problem.

11. LETTING GO

One and a half years into my doctorate program, I found that I wasn't enjoying it as much as I should. I would be well into my 50s before I finished my degree and going back to school was purely voluntary. If this wasn't going to be a pleasant experience, then I would not do it. One reason why I was not satisfied with my program was my field of study. I had always thought that I would end up in a biology department; after all it was the focus of my other college degrees. I should stay with it, I thought. But, I found that biology departments had changed a lot since I started college in my teens. Back then, biological science departments were focused on the traditional areas of plants, animals and ecology. However, a revolution had occurred in the interim period- the advent of bioengineering and biotechnology. My university had also moved toward advanced degrees in medicine. These new programs competed with the traditional biological sciences for funding and positions. As a result, when biological science professors retired, their positions were not replaced. When I began looking at the traditional biological sciences doctoral program, there simply were not enough professors left to complete a program.

While searching school programs for alternatives to a biological science major, I discovered environmental studies and geoscience departments. Both of these were integrative subjects, meaning that a range of fields could be involved in your research and studies. I began my doctorate degree in the geosciences with a focus on biogeography, the study of why and how species are distributed through time and space. It was also an extension of what I had been doing as a career since 1991, the year that I went to work with Duke University in the Florida Everglades. When I went back to school to get a Ph.D., I was near the pinnacle of my career as an environmental scientist and my doctoral research proposal seemed to be more of the same. I was bored. Looking around the geoscience department at the university, I saw many of the wonderful things that were being researched by other students and professors. Geology, hydrology, human geography, economic geography...I was amazed at the diversity of topics being studied and, like a kid suddenly placed unsupervised in a candy store, was thrilled with the idea that there was so much to choose from. I missed being thrilled about my field of study.

One evening in class, we had a guest lecturer. She was a professor from our department who I was only vaguely familiar with. My lack of knowledge about the professors in the department was understandable- I was working a full-time job during regular business hours and needed to arrive on campus as close to the beginning of class as possible and leave immediately after class to return to my job. There was just no spare time available to get to know other students or professors in the department. Although I found the class material interesting, the guest lecturer this evening was particularly fascinating, if not electric. Dr. Fadiman was young, energetic and affectionately kind. This stood in stark contrast to so many of the professors I had studied under in the biological sciences- they were stoic, carried very high opinions of themselves and believed that their particular research was among the most important on earth, something that students standing in their presence were expected to recognize as well. When Dr. Fadiman came to the front of the class to begin, she immediately held everyone transfixed by her effervescence and genuine interest in what each student had to say. She was not a lecturer, she was a listener. It was as though a great net had been cast out over the room and everyone was gathered into the conversation. She fired quirky questions out to the audience, animating with wide gestures and theatrical facial expressions, and students were immediately caught up in the energy. She was masterfully in control while allowing a loose, but intelligent, discourse to unfold. I thought to myself, "Wow, it would be so great to study under her!" Clearly some of my fascination was grounded in her ability to liberally broadcast her feelings for all to see and to draw out other people's thoughts in a supportive way. How very different from the stoic German immigrant, Upper Midwest, emotionally conservative upbringing I have had! I come from a people who never speak of their own feelings and are terrified of hugs. What I experienced in the classroom that night was the kind of excitement I longed to have in my program.

As the time to commit to my dissertation topic approached, I felt more trapped and more certain that I would be happier doing something else...something that resembled work less and fun more. The day came when this reality stared me straight in the eye and I needed to talk to someone high up in the department about it. Having had a course taught by the department chair, I knew him to be a practical, down-to-earth and no-nonsense kind of man. He was someone, actually the best person, I could talk openly with. I scheduled an appointment with him in early January, 2011.

The meeting day came and I began the discussion with a bit of background, which then led up to the point where I told him that I wasn't feeling like my program was exciting me. In fact, it felt the opposite, I said, and I wanted my experience to be fun and not draining. He was very understanding. He was also very supportive. It may have helped that he was near to my age and could sympathize with the feelings of a non-traditional middle-aged student. After patiently listening, the question he posed to me was "Do you have another topic that you want to study?" I immediately felt liberated. "Well, for the past year I have been researching food production in my backyard and..."

I launched into a summary of what I had been doing in my backyard and how important this kind of information was, particularly to issues of sustainability. He listened carefully and told me that he could see that it was a topic that I was passionate about, much more so than the current ideas for my dissertation. When I got done talking about my ideas, he asked me a simple question- why should anyone care about the research I was doing in my backyard? What he was getting at was that I could collect all of this information from my garden and come to some interesting conclusions, but why would the average person care? All of this research sounded good, but how could it stimulate interest in the average person and inspire them to make a change? This was something I had not yet thought through. I knew from my years of working in environmental research that scientists were particularly good at doing studies and publishing them in journals that are read by very few other scientists. Nearly all of that information stays in the world of academia, on library bookshelves and in electronic databases. Much of the non-academic world is completely unaware of it and does not benefit from it. What he was asking me was how my studies could bridge the gap between academia and ordinary people. If that didn't happen, then my research would never benefit society.

Nearing the end of our conversation, he made it clear that he was fully supportive of my change in direction, suggested a different advisor (more in line with my new topic) and outlined how this change would occur. It was official- I was going to be an urban agriculturalist! Walking out of his office after this one-hour meeting, nothing of my old program remained. A new career had been born and I was walking on clouds.

The department chair suggested Dr. Fadiman as my new advisor and set the wheels in motion to make that happen. My dissertation research shifted from quantitative ecological research to qualitative surveys of people's attitudes and perspectives about backyard food gardening. This was a very big change from the way I had been doing research! Up until now, I would design a study, collect measurements, go back to the office, crunch the numbers, summarize results and write a technical document. For each of these steps, I preferred to work alone. My new advisor pushed me toward wildly unfamiliar territory...directions that were contrary to my stoic German immigrant, Upper Midwest, emotionally conservative background. My dissertation research would focus on recording the experiences, feelings and thoughts of my study participants. I needed to interact with them in personable ways and express my own feelings on topics. There was no college course that could prepare me for this!

Most importantly, I needed to find out how people felt about urban agriculture and growing food in their own backyards. Some communities had strict rules about how homeowners were required to maintain their properties. In some neighborhoods, a grass lawn was mandatory and it must be kept green and regularly cut so that it did not grow taller than a set height. There were also restrictions about planting any landscape plants or flowers. With so many people living in restricted communities with the apparent fear that a food garden might destroy the neighborhood aesthetics, it may be that these rules only reflected the values of the local residents. If this were the case, then there would be few people who would actually want urban agriculture in their neighborhoods.

I became interested in knowing about the people who were growing their own food- who were they and why did they grow food? Why was it important for them? For most people, this was an emotional rather than an intellectual response. Discussing other people's feelings and experiences made me more comfortable about discussing mine. I also wanted to know about the people who did not grow food, why they didn't and what would make them start. It seemed to me that even though there were very good reasons why people should be growing food in cities, the sober fact is that if residents' don't want agriculture in their neighborhoods, it won't happen. In essence, the results from my backyard food growing study were meaningless if people just didn't care and hopes for reaping the benefits of urban agriculture could never be realized.

As my college program progressed, my backyard food garden study began to flourish. I was encouraged by the results from the first year and, in September 2010, began the second growing season. The actual size of the food garden "footprint" (its total area) was approximately 1500 square feet, which included pathways, a composting area, a potting area, a place to store mulch, fruit-bearing trees and vegetable beds. The 1500 square feet was approximately half of my backyard and could fit into residential lots that were half the size of mine. Although the size of the total footprint did not change much through the years, the area of planted vegetable beds did change each growing season.

Each day, I meticulously recorded data and any other information that I thought was important. I knew that only good data could give good results but, like all other farmers, I was at the mercy of the weather. There had been frosts during the last growing season and I needed to collect data during a season when there had been none. With a rare frost event out of the way, I expected the second year to have a more normal weather pattern and looked forward to ending the study in August 2011.

I tried to stretch the growing season to see if I could get more production out of the garden. Beginning Labor Day 2010, I began planting. The first vegetables I planted were those that tolerated summer heat "up north"; these were beans, beets, bok choi, carrots, sweet corn, cucumbers, okra, pumpkins, tomatoes and herbs. Within a month, nearly all of these early plantings had died. Pests ate those that remained. It was well into October when my plantings began to survive. Like people in temperate climates who plant too early in the spring and lose their seedlings to cold weather, sometimes it just isn't worth the effort to fight the natural timing of seasons.

By December, the garden was looking wonderful and was planted to capacity. Then, in mid-December, an unusually strong cold front passed through, unusual for that time of year. In south Florida, it is normal to have one or two cool nights after a cold front passes through. In the daytime, though, temperatures quickly warm into the 70s (degrees Fahrenheit). This cold front, and those that followed behind it in quick succession, pushed through with such force and persistence that it warmed up little during the day and nighttime temperatures plunged into the 30s and 40s. This weather pattern was enough to damage or slow the growth of most food plants.

In late December, 2010, frost struck. Then again in January, 2011. Temperatures in Palm Beach County's agricultural areas plummeted into the upper 20s. Vegetable and fruit crops from central Florida to south Miami were devastated. Each cold night, every vegetable in my garden was covered, wrapped, clothed and sheltered to protect it from the damaging cold. Once again, most of the warmth-loving vegetables were lost. This season, there was the double punch of frost coupled with unusually cold weather that lasted well into March. Sweet potato vines turned brown, withered and died back to the ground. Some of the more exposed plants collapsed into twisted masses of brownish green. I lost most, but not all, of my okra, beans, pumpkins, squash, mustard greens, bok choi, peanuts, yams and potatoes. Plants that were too damaged had to be pulled from the garden beds while the survivors were coaxed back into production. With the frost came the certainty that my garden would produce much less this year than it normally would have. With so many commercial agricultural crops destroyed, it also meant higher vegetable prices were soon expected in the grocery stores.

I could not have imaged that the coastal area of Palm Beach County would experience two back-to-back seasons of frost. This wildly unusual weather pattern must have meant that the worst had been dealt to us and I could look forward to relatively normal weather for the rest of the growing season. I could not have been more wrong.

The rainy season had ended early- it fizzled out in September 2010 and October turned out to be quite dry. Usually, south Florida's rainy season continues into late October, but it didn't this year. November was unusually dry as well, as was December. The dry spell didn't end and by early 2011, this region was classified by the U.S. National Drought Mitigation Center as being in the Extreme Drought range. Water managers imposed mandatory water restrictions and I had to adjust my watering schedule to accommodate the guidelines. The rains did not return until April, when it became too hot to grow most winter vegetables. In the end, the period from October 1, 2010 through the end of March 2011 (the period when most vegetables are grown in south Florida) was the driest period on record for those months. Rainfall for that period was down a remarkable 15 inches from normal.[46] Once again, I thought that this wildly unusual weather pattern must certainly have meant that the worst had been dealt to us and I could look forward to relatively normal weather over the rest this growing season. Again, I could not have been more wrong.

Following on the heels of killing frost and extreme drought was one of the hottest summers I could recall in my more than 30 years in Florida. Day after day, temperatures soared into the mid-90s. Nearby weather stations regularly reported temperatures between 95 and 101. April and July were record hot months with temperatures 6.4 and 3.2 degrees above average, respectively. August temperatures were the 5th warmest on record. By the end of the year, the heat wave's full extent had been recorded- 2011 was the warmest year on record for West Palm Beach. There were 119 days of temperatures at or above 90 degrees (the average was 56 days) and West Palm Beach recorded a streak of 46 consecutive days of temperatures of 90 degrees or higher (July 8 through August 23).

Let's see...that's killing frosts, extreme drought and record heat. Hmm...what else could be missing? A hurricane, perhaps? Why not! In late August, Hurricane Irene passed east of the Florida coastline packing sustained winds of 120 miles per hour, producing strong winds, locally heavy rainfall and flooding. At least it broke the drought and heat.

With the water use restrictions and extreme drought conditions, I decided it was time to install rain barrels to capture runoff from my roof to use for watering the garden. I knew a woman that sold them; they were recycled food-grade containers refitted with brass fixtures and screens to filter out debris coming off of the roof. I installed a single rain barrel, with a 50-gallon capacity, in June 2011. With the first refilling rains, I was elated. But, I soon found out that the garden's thirst was well beyond that of a single rain barrel's capacity. I installed a second rain barrel the following month. In keeping with my research goals and data collection fanaticism, I tracked how much rainwater and how much well water I was applying to my garden.

To say that this past season, the first of my study that lasted throughout the entire year, was fraught with difficulty would be to grossly understate the obvious. The ever-present pests, diseases and weeds, coupled with killing frosts, record setting drought, intense heat and a hurricane would have been enough to cause the most dedicated gardener to give up. This season, I tried to grow food under the worst possible conditions; there were many areas of the garden that produced very little or nothing at all. Add to that the prospect of trying to coax edible food from sterile dry sandy soil, I could not imagine that my study results could show anything except that this whole effort was a waste of time- go buy your food from the grocery store and be done with it, it simply is not worth it to grow your own food. In late August, at the end of the growing season, I began to look at the numbers. What I found was shocking.

During the second year of my garden study, I began to record how much fruit I was growing, now that my mango tree was producing after being pruned and other fruit trees had become established. This season, I harvested more than 550 pounds of fruits and vegetables from my food garden. Of this, 323 pounds were vegetables! I had produced almost double the amount of vegetables during this season than I had the previous season! I had also expanded my selections, harvesting 89 types of vegetables and herbs, and 5 types of fruits.

It was undeniable...I had to do another full year of data collection.

If I had produced so much under what were clearly the worst possible conditions, I had to know how much I could grow during a normal year. With this, the garden was again planted and the third growing season (2011-2012) was soon underway. That season, the weather was more normal for the climate. Although I wanted to stop the study at the end of the third year, I eventually decided to continue it for at least two more. I thought that the five-year mark would be a good place to stop and see what I had accomplished. After analyzing the data, the results were groundbreaking!

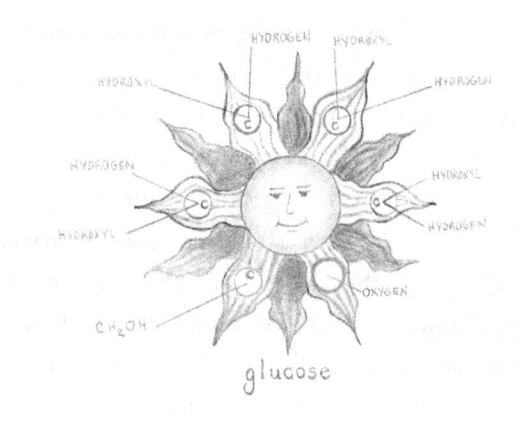

12. THE CIRCLE OF LIFE

I have been an ecologist for over two decades. Unfortunately, every college course I have had on the subject focused on rural ecology, as though it was the only place on Earth where ecological things happened, such as birds nesting, rain falling, wildlife looking for food and wildflowers tempting bees. This is not true. Fortunately, the concept of urban ecology is beginning to take hold in universities, and students and researchers are studying cities using the same methods used by rural ecologists for generations. One fundamental concept in the study of ecology, rural or urban, is the idea of cycling, or as it is better put- recycling.

Cycling is when a certain thing is passed around through various channels, sometimes taking on different forms along the way. When this happens in nature, it is called cycling. When this happens to plastic or other materials and is assisted by humans, we call it recycling. The goal of recycling is to mimic the natural process of cycling- to reuse the same materials over and over again. Things in nature that cycle include water, nutrients, energy, carbon dioxide and pollutants. Most of us have seen a stick-like drawing of the water cycle, where a drop of water falls from a cloud onto the land, where it eventually finds its way into a creek, then a river, then to the ocean where it evaporates back into the sky and forms clouds. Sometimes that raindrop ends up in a wetland or lake, where it will evaporate into the sky to form clouds. There are other paths the water drop can travel too. Rain can fall to the earth and be absorbed into the soil, where it forms something called groundwater- a great reservoir of water underground that is stored within soil or rocks (aquifers), hidden from view. This is the water that our wells draw from and is a main source of drinking water for many city residents and some agricultural operations around the world. Sometimes the roots of plants absorb water from the soil. This water is carried up though the stems and into the leaves, where it can be released into the atmosphere, forming water vapor- the stuff clouds are made of. Understanding how things move through cycles within the environment is helpful; it is also a fundamental concept in the study of sustainability.

In nature, nutrients also travel through cycles. In the Everglades, where there is very, very little of the nutrient phosphorus, plants and other organisms rapidly absorb it whenever some of it becomes available. The lush growth in Everglades marshes is possible because of highly efficient cycling of the scant nutrients that are found there. The same is true for deserts and tropical rainforests. Most soils in rainforests are surprisingly low in nutrients. But, there are great quantities of them stored in the living plants. Once a plant dies in the rainforest and falls to the ground, it decays rapidly and the thick network of shallow tree roots rapidly take up nutrients that are released from the rotting plant material. So, natural ecosystems like the Everglades, Brazil's tropical rainforests and the enormous stands of redwood trees along the Pacific Coast do not rely on continual supplies of added nutrients for survival, instead they thrive on the efficient recapture and reuse of nutrients that are already there. Each organism gets to use the nutrient for a time, then it is passed on to others to use. In this way, many can live through the sharing of little. If the process of cycling is interrupted, so is the flow of nutrients and energy. Eventually the resources upon which life depends are exhausted and the ecosystem goes extinct. The cycling of materials is the way things work in nature and is the basis for the earth's circle of life.

Cities do not have all of the things their residents need to live, such as building materials, clean water, clean air, energy and food. Cities also create polluted air and polluted water, and these need to be cleaned before they can be used again. Fortunately, natural ecosystems have the ability to clean polluted water and air, recharge the groundwater that municipal wells tap into for drinking water and do other important things that, taken together, are referred to as environmental services. A city's "ecological footprint" can be thought of as the amount of natural resources (such as building materials, clean water and energy) and environmental services needed by the city's population.[21] Importing natural resources to sustain a city has three important consequences. The first is that the movement of resources into and out of the city requires energy and sometimes lots of it. For the most part, this energy comes from non-renewable fossil fuels and releases carbon dioxide into the atmosphere. The second is that obtaining natural resources for the city usually causes environmental damage somewhere else and urban residents are largely unaware of this damage. Without this awareness, there is no feeling of responsibility for the damage and little incentive to do anything about it. The third consequence is that waste is often transferred outside the city for disposal. This scenario is a lot like that faced by Farmer B who has more cattle on his land than it can naturally support.

For most of us, nearly everything we have ever thrown into the trash (not a recycle bin) and set out for pickup by the garbage truck has been deposited in a landfill. This includes things like a broken child's toy, bags, shaving razors, vegetable trimmings left over from food preparation and even the discarded leftovers themselves. These items may have vanished from our consciousness, but they still exist in some form under the piles of things that others have discarded. Things that are buried within the landfill are examples of waste products that are exported from the city.

Another waste that is exported from cities is polluted stormwater runoff. Oily residues from roads and bits of plastic and lawn care chemicals and other pollution wash into sewers during a rainstorm and end up in rivers or lakes far from where it came from. Carbon dioxide emissions and mercury vapor from coal-burning power plants are other types of waste that cities export since these are usually carried far from the place where they were generated or where the electricity they created was used. Some things that are thought of as waste actually have value and reusing them again (recycling) reduces imports into cities and decreases the amount of waste that is exported. Unfortunately, some waste products like mercury vapor emissions cannot be recycled. Instead, less of them must be created.

Sustainability initiatives try to reduce waste in two ways. First, practices that generate waste are changed so that they create less waste. For example, in order to reduce the amount of petroleum that is used, people purchase vehicles that are more fuel efficient, so they use less gas and generate less pollution from the tailpipe. A second option is to recycle wastes for other purposes. Recycling seeks to reuse materials over and over again, like natural ecosystems do. The best scenario is to have practices that create no waste at all. By combining efficiency and recycling, some practices can become "zero waste."

One example of how urban agriculture can play a role in reducing the amount of waste that cities export is in the reuse of compostable materials that are normally sent to landfills. The United States Environmental Protection Agency estimated that in 2012, Americans generated 251 million tons of trash, which is about 0.8 tons per citizen![47] Of this, approximately 28 percent is compostable materials such as yard clippings and food waste. Although most people would prefer to have the workers at the landfill separate and compost this material, the reality is that it is best to keep it from going there in the first place.

During my food growing study, I wanted to know how much

The Circle of Life

compost my backyard garden needed to grow my food. Over a two and a half year period, I picked up compostable waste from a small cafeteria. The cafeteria was only open for breakfast and lunch on weekdays, but generated a surprising amount of fruit and vegetable scraps. Over the period of a year, I picked up over 2000 pounds of waste and made it into a high quality compost for my garden. Because I collected this waste during the Great Recession, even higher amounts from this small cafeteria would have been expected under better economic times. Not only did my food garden need this much compost, it could have used three to four times that amount!

While picking up the compostable material from the cafeteria, it seemed to me that I was taking in more waste than I was setting out for pickup by the garbage truck. I was bringing in heavy tubs of food waste and setting out light bags of non-recyclable and non-compostable materials in my garbage can. To find out how much garbage I was setting out for pickup, I measured each filled trash bag over the period of seven weeks. When I compared how much compostable waste I was receiving and compared it to how much garbage I was sending to the landfill, it turned out that I was actually taking in 7.5 times more waste than my household was setting out for the garbage truck! Imagine how much less waste would be sent to landfills if many restaurants and food growers did the same.

These findings are important. First, they indicate how many thousands of tons of organic waste are discarded by tens of thousands of restaurants in this country each year. These restaurants and cafes can be reliable and rich sources of compostable materials. Second, this organic waste can easily be made into high-quality compost- a resource that is in short supply to local food gardens and agricultural operations. This compost is an inexpensive fertilizer that reduces the amount of waste taken to landfills. This is especially important because organic materials, when put into landfills, can contribute to the formation of methane. Methane is a greenhouse gas that is twenty times more potent than carbon dioxide.[48] Third, it is a terrible waste of plant nutrients. For every pound of plant nutrients that are recycled through composting, that is one pound that does not have to be manufactured or mined.

There are some communities that have recognized the value of these compostable materials and have implemented programs to recapture and convert them to compost. Orange County, North Carolina has such a program. The program collects waste from thirty-two food businesses and three schools, and has recently proposed an expansion.[49] Without the composting program, these waste materials would have to be trucked 90 miles to landfills. In 2012, New York City began to test organic waste curbside collection from select schools, residences and institutions.[50] New York estimated that approximately one-third of all waste generated by residents was compostable organic material and the pilot program, which ends in July 2015, is studying how best to capture some of that waste. In 2014, the state of Massachusetts enacted a ban on the disposal of organics materials by businesses that generate large amounts of organic waste (e.g., restaurants, grocery stores, institutions).[51] These businesses must sign up for separate collection services. Organic waste materials, which make up some 25% of the total waste generated in the state, will be sent to composting facilities. Other similar programs are either in place, under study or in development in many other cities across the United States. In Germany, a successful pilot study was conducted in 2011 to determine the feasibility and receptivity of home organic waste collection using compostable bags that were supplied by the municipal waste management company. This Germany pilot study, which included 21,000 households in Berlin, was conducted with the assistance of an internationally known chemical company. The company leveraged its laboratory expertise to create the biodegradable bags and demonstrated how major chemical companies can play a role in solving some of our environmental problems. Just imagine the environmental benefits that could be reaped if thousands of people were to recapture the compostable materials in our waste and use it to grow food! This is something that networks of individuals and food service businesses can do without

The Circle of Life

any effort on behalf of the landfill or government.

Just as water and nutrients cycle through the environment, so does carbon, but its cycling is a little more complicated and far more fascinating. This is a relevant subject to present here, because nearly everyone today has heard about carbon dioxide emissions to the atmosphere and its link to global warming.

Carbon is a natural and abundant element found everywhere on Earth. Carbon comes in many forms and flavors, some of which are invisible gases in our atmosphere. The one that scientists get most concerned about is carbon dioxide. People, and other animals, give off carbon dioxide when they exhale and plants take it up while they carryout the near miraculous chemical reaction called photosynthesis. Photosynthesis is a process that occurs in the greenish parts of the leaves and stems of plants by which carbon dioxide (taken into the plant through the leaves) is combined with water (taken into the plant through the roots) to produce sugar. This sugar is usually glucose. Within the sugar molecule is a bit of energy captured from sunlight. Glucose is an important source of energy for humans and other organisms; it is what doctors measure when they test your blood sugar levels. The "waste" product of photosynthesis is oxygen, the same molecule we breathe in. So, the very life of humans and other animals is tied to the wealth of oxygen that plants give off when they are busy making sugars.

As plants are creating large amounts of sugar, they store it in various ways. Fruit usually contains a lot of sugar to tempt animals to eat it; this is how some plants get animals to spread their seeds around. Sometimes the sugar is turned into other things, such as starch. Potatoes, yams (Americans call these sweet potatoes), cassava (which Cubans will know as their beloved yuca) and other similar vegetables are built from starch that was created from the sugars produced during photosynthesis. Plants also link sugar molecules together in long chains. One type of these very long sugar chains is called cellulose. Cellulose is one of the basic building materials of plants and is used to create roots, stems and leaves. It is also a main ingredient in paper and the cellulose sponge on your kitchen sink. Cellulose has a tendency to absorb a lot of water.

When plants die, the dead material falls to the ground and begins to rot. Besides nutrients and water, most of this dead plant material is made up of cellulose. Bacteria and fungi break up the cellulose chains into the individual sugar molecules they were originally made of. Then, the sugar molecules are broken apart to release the stored energy- energy that originally came from sunlight. As the stored energy is released, so are carbon dioxide and water, which evaporate into the atmosphere. Bacteria and fungi, like humans, need oxygen in order to use the energy locked up in the sugar molecules. The process of burning the energy stored in the sugar molecule is essentially the reverse of photosynthesis and through it, all life on earth runs on the captured energy of sunlight.

In wetlands, such as the Everglades, dead plant material falls into the water and sinks to the bottom. As dead plant material piles up on top of other dead plant material underwater, oxygen is cut off and decomposition stops. Each season, layer after layer of dead organic matter piles up until older layers become buried. This old plant material then becomes part of the soil. Soils that are made of this partly decomposed plant material are called peat. It is the almost continual flooding of peat soils that allows them to form and prevents them from decaying. When peat soils are drained, decomposition resumes and the soil is reduced to a greasy, dark material called muck, which sometimes resembles a soft coal.

Coal is a form of fossilized carbon. If plant material or peat soil becomes buried because of some catastrophic event, such as a vast flood or fallout from a volcanic eruption, it will eventually be transformed into a compacted, stone-like material. This is how coal is formed and why it is used for generating energy. Coal, and other deposits that were formed from dead organisms, are referred to as fossil fuels. These fuels contain vast quantities of the sun's energy that was trapped and stored during photosynthesis. During the process of burning fossil fuels for energy, the same molecules of carbon dioxide that were removed from the air millions of years ago are added to the carbon dioxide that is in the atmosphere today. This buildup of atmospheric carbon dioxide is believed by many scientists to be changing the world we live in.

This brings us back to the topic of cycling. Ecosystems are fine-tuned engines that run on the cycling of a limited quantity of the same materials, such as water and nutrients. When more water or nutrients are artificially added to an ecosystem, it will inevitably change how things work and what things can live there. The alarm over rising carbon dioxide levels in the atmosphere is based on this same principle. The best available data indicates that the world's climate has been gradually warming over the past century. The consensus among climatologists is that this is at least partly due to increasing carbon dioxide (and other greenhouse gases) levels in the atmosphere, although there are scientists in other disciplines that are unsure that one is causing the other. Although it is healthy and constructive to debate the science and conclusions, unfortunately, artificially enriching the earth's atmosphere with carbon dioxide is an irreversible experiment that may have catastrophic consequences.

Hardly a day goes by before a new study or news article is published about the concerns with carbon dioxide emissions to the atmosphere, climate change and the potential impacts of global warming. Although the earth's climate has been changing since it first formed, the changes in atmospheric temperatures over the past century have been alarming, as well as the approximately 1 foot of sea level rise during this same period. Some of the predicted effects of continued global warming include inundation of coastal areas (including some of the world's most notable cities), increasing frequency of extreme weather events (and the human toll from them), the expansion of deserts and a loss of productive agricultural land. Although natural habitats are already threatened by the expansion of human settlements and agriculture, global warming is also changing them. With a looming crisis born from exploding human populations that depend on rural agriculture, the loss of prime agricultural land to urban sprawl and the loss of farmland to the effects of global warming, the future of food supplies looks grim. There simply is no other option but to focus food production within cities. Doing so may actually make a difference in the global warming equation.

Of the carbon dioxide that is emitted to the atmosphere each year, about one-third of it comes from transportation- the burning of diesel fuel and gasoline to transport goods and people.[48] A significant part of the goods that are shipped long distances is food. Because food is one of the biggest imports into cities, food transport is a substantial contributor to carbon dioxide emissions. When considering the amount of energy that was used to grow food using industrial agricultural practices, then pack and transport the food to urban supermarkets, it adds up. This is especially true when you consider the amount of food that is consumed over the course of a year or during a person's lifetime. Because of this, our individual food choices can make a big difference with respect to energy conservation and carbon dioxide emission reductions.

One of the last courses I took in college was focused on the relationships between plants and people. I was required to do a class project and present the results to the class at the end of the semester. For my project, I went into grocery store produce departments and clandestinely watched shopper's behavior with respect to how they selected the fruits and vegetables they purchased. I looked for how they read the signs, which contained prices and place of origin. I was focused on how much effort they put into selecting their food. When I looked at the results, I did not find any evidence to suggest that shoppers preferred local produce over other choices. This was not so surprising to me, but the real interesting part of this small study was where the most commonly-purchased vegetables (cabbage, carrots, celery, head lettuce, green bell peppers and tomatoes) had come from. All of these vegetables were being grown and harvested in Florida at this time of year, with a substantial acreage of these crops in Palm Beach County.[52] Naturally, one should expect that these vegetables would have been available in our grocery stores. I should know because I was growing and harvesting these vegetables from my own backyard garden. At my neighborhood supermarkets, which sold conventionally grown produce, only half of these six types of vegetables offered for sale were grown in Florida. A quick estimate of the total miles that these six vegetables had traveled was 6,600 miles. At the organic supermarket, things were much more disappointing. Only one out of six of these vegetable varieties were grown in Florida. I calculated the total distance traveled by these six vegetables to be an incredible 14,500 miles! I challenge you to do the same at your grocery store.

One researcher found that the average distance traveled by supermarket offerings was 1,300 miles.[53] During my food growing study, I tracked where the fruit and vegetables I was harvesting from my garden would have come from if I had purchased them at the grocery store. I found comparable results. Using the average distance that produce at my local supermarket had traveled, I estimated the amount of energy my backyard food garden had saved. I do not realize this energy savings; rather it is energy that did not have to be used to transport my food from a distant commercial agricultural field. I estimated that by growing food in my backyard, each year I saved up to 6 barrels of crude oil from being consumed. This was equivalent to approximately 10,200 kilowatt hours of electricity-roughly enough to run the average residential household in the United States for a year.[54] This is also equivalent to enough gasoline to take my car off of the road for 3 to 4 months each year.

How much energy could be saved if 10 percent of a city of 10,000 grew food as I did in this study? The energy savings could reach thousands of barrels of crude oil. What if only 1 percent of the residents in our country's most populated metropolitan areas began to grow their own food and reduce their dependency on food that had been transported from distant places? They could save tens of millions of barrels of crude oil each year and reduce America's dependency on imported oil. If this seems like a lot of people, it isn't.

In fact, this 1 percent would be approximately the same number of people who live in the Birmingham, Alabama metropolitan area. If the abandoned 20 million Victory Gardens of World War II were put back into production and produced as much food as I had in my own backyard, the energy savings would be equivalent to more than 120,000,000 barrels of crude oil each year- enough to generate electricity for 20 million households in the United States. Over the period of a decade, the cumulative benefit is substantial.

An evil twin to the burning of fossil fuels is the release of carbon dioxide emissions to the atmosphere; you cannot have one without the other. Because I grew food in my backyard, I was able to avoid the release of over 1 ton of carbon dioxide emissions to the atmosphere. As with energy savings, the collective benefit from millions of households growing food could reduce carbon dioxide emissions to the atmosphere by millions of tons. By my calculations, if the Victory Gardens were put back into production, the reduction in carbon dioxide emissions would be tens of millions of tons- an amount that is equivalent to shutting down 7 coal-burning power plants.

Government policies and programs spend a great deal of effort and money to reduce energy consumption by increasing fuel efficiencies of everything from home appliances to automobiles to power plants. The newest area of concern is the reduction of carbon dioxide emissions. None of these policies and programs considers the continual consumption of fossil fuels that are expended to transport food into cities from great distances. Considering how much money it takes to modernize a power plant, build renewable energy facilities, increase automobile efficiencies and to take other steps to conserve energy resources, urban agriculture is a very inexpensive and effective alternative. It must be brought to the table and included as one of the most significant areas where energy consumption and carbon dioxide emissions can be reduced.

When an individual thinks about conserving energy resources, the things that most come to mind are purchasing a more fuel-efficient vehicle, driving fewer miles, taking public transportation and turning the lights out when leaving a room. Perhaps one of the most important contributions one could make to energy conservation and carbon dioxide emission reduction is when they are standing in the produce department of their grocery store.

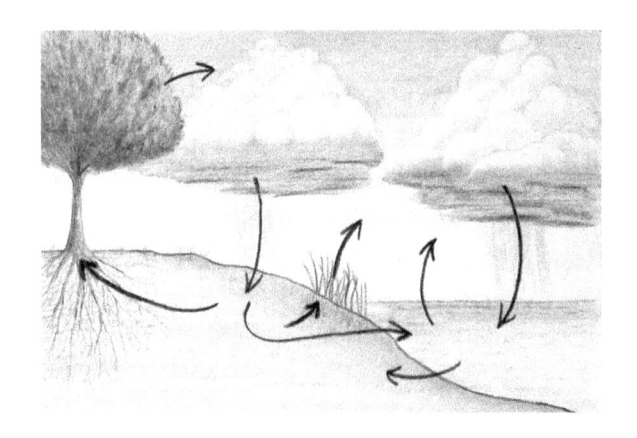

13. WATER, WATER EVERYWHERE AND...

Driving past the verdant green lawns, magnificently manicured hedges and tropical foliage in south Florida, it is clear that a lot of time, effort, expense and water is invested by residents to make their properties conform to some firmly planted idea of the proper urban yard. Peel away the landscaped veneer and you will be surprised at what lies underneath.

The first areas to be settled in southern Florida were sand ridges and high ground. This was out of necessity. Historically, more than half of the state was covered by wetlands and lakes.[55] In south Florida, the number was much higher because the extent of wetlands far exceeded that of perennially dry land; much of the landscape was a virtual water world. It is understandable that older neighborhoods were first constructed on higher ground that did not require complex systems of drainage to allow building, especially when a tropical storm could fill any low space up with life-threatening floodwaters in a matter of hours. It was easier and less risky.

The vast system of drainage canals and ditches in Florida that allows today's large population to live there has caused the destruction of more wetland areas than any other state in the United

States. From the time of European colonization to the 1980s, Florida lost 9.3 million acres or 46 percent of its original total area of wetlands, approximately one acre per resident.[56] In the United States, the average rate of wetland loss between 1780 and the 1980 was approximately 60 acres per hour and the loss of wetlands continues. The destruction of tropical rain forests in other regions of the world has caused a global outcry, yet there is silence with respect to the catastrophic loss of wetlands in our own counties. With few exceptions, these wetlands were drained to support the development of agriculture or human settlement.

Although there is a belief that natural lands are less valuable than farmland or urban land, this is not true. Take wetlands, for example. Wetlands are among the most important natural resources because of the many environmental and economic benefits they provide.[57] In many of the world's regions, wetlands maintain environmental health because they remove pollutants from water supplies and recharge groundwater, which is the source of drinking water for many cities across the country. Wetlands also have tremendous economic value by providing aesthetics that increase property values, providing habitat for fish and wildlife, and supporting lucrative rural businesses involved with fishing, hunting, camping, boating, bird-watching, nature photography, wild food harvesting (e.g. wild rice and other edible plants, frog legs, alligator, turtle, fish, shellfish, waterfowl), hiking and tourism. Extending directly from these activities are the indirect financial benefits to hotels, fishing supply manufacturers, marinas, watercraft manufacturers, restaurants, transportation providers, camera manufacturers, tent makers, hiking supplies manufacturers, outdoor sport clothes manufacturers and so on. As you can see, the linkages between wetlands and commercial markets are numerous and enormous when taken as a sum. The value of wetlands is at least as great as the gross revenues produced by these activities and generated by the industries that support them. It is possible for people to sustainably harvest and live off of the numerous natural products found in wetlands. If you are skeptical, then think back to the Uri people who live off of the wetlands on Lake Titicaca.

Growing lush lawns on land that was historically wetlands may be easy because water naturally tends to pond on the site. But, look underneath the lawns growing on ridges and you will find sand. Dry, nutrient-sterile grayish sand. Desert plants grow well in these sands. In Florida, a unique desert-like plant community called scrub once grew on the sand ridges in the central and southern part of the state. Most scrub plants are particularly adapted to survive the near desert-like conditions found there by conserving water with root storage structures or having spines to prevent being eaten or giving off repulsive volatile oils to deter pests or having leaves that contain lethal toxins or having leaves that prevent water loss through evaporation. In spite of the nutrient-poor soil, scrub is a rich and unique habitat. Approximately 90 species of plants and animals are found exclusively in Florida scrub and nowhere else in the world. Scrub has been growing on the Florida peninsula for at least a million years. Today, it is listed as an endangered forest type; in southeast Florida alone estimated losses range from 95 to 99 percent- first to agriculture then later to urban development.

Underneath many of the most mature and affluent neighborhoods in south Florida are the naturally dry sands upon which the ancient scrub once flourished. Getting these sands to produce the lush tropical landscape expected by today's residents and neighborhood associations requires amounts of manual labor, fertilizer and water beyond that which is financially feasible to those of more modest incomes. Much of the water used by the millions of residents of southeast Florida comes from underground sources that are recharged by the Everglades and the amount of water is staggering. In 2010, the average quantity of freshwater taken from the environment each day was 1.7 billion gallons (more than 70 million gallons per hour) in southeast Florida alone.[58] That amounted to approximately 305 gallons per day per resident. Water withdrawals in southeast Florida are expected to increase by more than 200 million gallons per day by 2030. A significant portion of this water is used to irrigate agriculture. Another significant portion of this is used to irrigate golf course greens and landscaping and lawns, some of which are on land that was once desert-like scrub. It seems unthinkable that south Florida, a region that receives between 4 to 5 feet of rainfall per year, would have water shortages but there are. Today, year-round water use restrictions have been adopted in areas that a decade ago saw them only during droughts. Decades before that, there were no water restrictions at all. With so much development on the low lands that were once wetlands, there are fewer places left to capture and store rainwater. With so many wells and intake pipes taking water, groundwater levels, lakes and wetlands are shrinking. Some blame over-population. But, looking under the surface, there is more to this story.

A colleague of mine, who was working on her masters thesis at the same time I was working on my Ph.D., studied the actual lawn irrigation water use of residents in a couple of suburban West Palm Beach neighborhoods. These neighborhoods had, combined, 165 residential lots and covered a total area of approximately 69 acres (one-tenth square mile). After asking residents about how much water they thought they used for lawn irrigation, she then observed and measured their actual usage. What she found was that residents overwatered their lawns, applying up to 2.9 times the amount that was actually needed.[59] Residents that did not have a private well relied on municipal water for landscape irrigation and applied almost half of their monthly household water usage for watering grass. Over the 16-week study period, over 22 million gallons of water were used to irrigate lawns in these two developments, an average of 8,300 gallons of water per week for each household. Although the results from this study cannot be extended out to all neighborhoods in the region, these numbers are alarming nonetheless. Multiply this much water use by thousands of acres of similar residential development in south Florida and you can understand the enormous volume of water used to grow nothing more than grass. Neighborhoods like these are spread across the United States, many of which are in climates that receive less than one-third of the amount of rainfall that south Florida gets. The extent of grassy lawns in the United States covered an estimated 49,000 square miles in 2005, seven times the area of vegetable-producing fields.[60] This vast area of lawn would more than cover the land area of the District of Columbia plus that of eight states: Connecticut, Delaware, Hawaii, Massachusetts, New Hampshire, New Jersey, Rhode Island and Vermont combined. The extent of natural habitat that has been replaced by turf grass is staggering. Although not all of these lawns are irrigated, many are and the amount of water used to irrigate this much grass is enormous.

High consumption of freshwater supplies is not unique to southern Florida; in fact, south Florida's water woes are but an ordinary example of a problem that has been plaguing many other parts of the world or soon will be. Fortunately, in south Florida there is plentiful rainfall during half of the year to recharge water supplies. But, this is not the case everywhere. Perhaps the most precarious water users are the enormous metropolitan and agricultural areas of California, Arizona and Texas, areas that receive very little rainfall each year. The demand for water is so high, that it comes with great environmental and economic costs, and often requires transportation across long distances. Yet, vast agricultural fields, golf resorts and great manicured lawns sprawl across land that naturally grew scrub and desert, and was too dry to grow a leaf of lettuce or a single blade of turf grass. In essence, these agricultural fields and lawns are on life support, naturally weak to the point that when the tap is turned off, they rapidly wither and die.

In California alone, a vast network of aqueducts provides water for over 30 million people and irrigates nearly 29 million acres of farmland. Between 80 and 85 percent of the water used by California is for agriculture and only about 10 percent is for urban uses.[61] In southern California, 60 percent of their imported water is used to irrigate landscaping and lawns.[62] This water comes from dammed rivers, ecologically important lakes, a national park and overused groundwater supplies. The amount of energy required to move water to coastal urban areas is high. The extent of environmental damage from the collective water withdrawals is astounding. Fortunately, a few government entities and residents see the absurdity and unsustainability of this water system. The Los Angeles Department of Water and Power, the Long Beach Water Department, and Pasadena Water and Power offer residents a way out of their lawns through a program that pays rebates ranging from $1 to $3 per square foot of grass that is replaced with low-water alternatives such as Xeriscape®. From 2009 to 2014, the Los Angeles Department of Water and Power had requests to remove 7.4 million square feet (170 acres) of turfgrass.

Although some water sources are being used in sustainable ways, human development is expanding and poses a threat to these as well. The severe depletion of groundwater supplies, particularly in arid regions, has reached a point of crisis in some areas. One common source of groundwater is aquifers, which are often tapped to irrigate farm fields or supply municipal water utilities. Aquifers are underground pools of water that are contained within soil or rock. The Ogallala Aquifer in the central United States spans eight states and contains ancient water that is being used unsustainably. Portions of the Ogallala Aquifer are exhausted and in other areas, aquifer recharge is only about 10 percent of what is being withdrawn; most of the aquifer's water is used for agriculture and fossil fuel extraction.[63] In places like northern Africa, ancient and unreplenishable groundwater supplies are being exhausted, leaving future generations with an uncertain ability to live. The large-scale unsustainable use of water resources to support an unsustainable agricultural system can only lead to an unsustainable future for our children. But, it this really necessary?

I was concerned that the amount of water needed to grow fruits and vegetables in cities might be excessive, so I tracked water use over the 5 years of my garden study. To do this, I watered by hand, which was painstaking and time consuming. I would have preferred to use sprinklers or drip irrigation, but I wanted to be sure that my numbers were accurate. I once heard criticism from someone who was against the practice of urban agriculture; that person felt that urban water supplies were already stretched and that adding food production into cities would further exacerbate the problem. That was a point worthy of consideration.

The volume of water that I applied to my food garden varied from year to year because of drought and rainfall, but on average I used 9600 gallons per year. This was comparable to the 8,300 gallons of lawn irrigation water used *each week* by a single suburban West Palm Beach household studied by my colleague for her master's thesis. During the 2010-2011 growing season, when South Florida had record dry weather, I used almost 17,000 gallons for the year. Water use during a wet growing season fell to less than 5000 gallons. To put this water usage in perspective, according to the Marin Municipal Water Authority (Marin County, California) approximately 7000 gallons of water evaporate from a medium-sized swimming pool each year with more lost to spash-out.[64] That is comparable to the average amount of water I needed to grow hundreds of pounds of food in my backyard.

If I had installed a lawn instead of a food garden and watered it according to recommended turf grass irrigation guidelines,[59] I would have applied approximately 40,000 more gallons of water per year than what I used to grow my food. In the last two years of the study, I recorded how much rainwater I had captured and used to irrigate the food garden. During this time, I was able to collect between 50 and 70 percent of all of the garden irrigation water I needed even though rainfall followed normal weather patterns. By doubling my rainwater storage capacity, I would be entirely self-supplied by rainfall collected during southeast Florida's dry growing season. This is a level of water efficiency that could never be matched by industrial or large-scale agricultural systems.

The real significance of these findings is that there are enormous benefits that could be realized when thousands of homeowners begin to grow food gardens instead of irrigated lawns. As I mentioned above, the average quantity of freshwater taken from southeast Florida's environment each day was 1.7 billion gallons. If we were to replace some of our irrigated residential backyard lawns with food gardens, the water savings could be as much as 150 million gallons per day, about 10 percent of the region's total water usage! If only 1 out of 10 households in southeast Florida replaced irrigated lawn with food gardens similar to mine, the water savings would equal 23 million gallons per day. In a year, that accumulated water savings would equal enough water to flood all of Manhattan, New York under 4 ft. of water, approximately the same amount of water it receives from rainfall annually. I will talk more about this in the next chapter, but these are not small numbers. Development and implementation of programs to promote and support residential food growing would be a less expensive alternative to the creation of long-term water development projects. It is an option that is never discussed when water conservation is being promoted. Food growing is a better use of water resources than lawn irrigation and reduces the need to grow produce in areas where groundwater supplies are being unsustainably used.

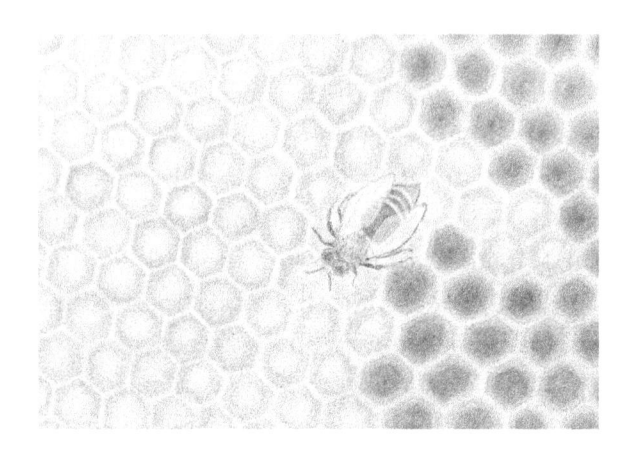

14. OF SAHARAN PROPORTIONS

Growing food in residential backyards and on unbuilt city land carries with it a range of benefits, but perhaps the one most overlooked is financial. On average, households will spend from 10 to 40 percent of their after-tax income on food purchases, with smaller proportions spent by higher-income households.[65] Although home food growing has financial benefits, this is often not a main reason why people grow their own food.[66] No matter the reason, growing food allows the household to retain money it would have otherwise used to purchase groceries, leaving more money to be spent on other things like paying bills or for purchasing non-essential products. This extra unspent money also means that the net value of the household, which is the amount of money earned minus the amount of money needed to pay essential living expenses, increased.

In the same way that water cycles through the environment, money circulates within the community. Spending money on locally produced food can be economically beneficial to the community. This point was eloquently described in a document entitled "Why Local Linkages Matter," which was produced by Sustainable Seattle.[67] Their economic analysis described how money flows through a community and how local purchasing can have substantial local benefits. For every dollar spent on locally produced food, a portion goes to the local grower, to local transportation costs and to the local seller. These may be the same person or any combination of people, but since all are local, that dollar remains within the community and is available to be respent on other items. As long as that dollar is spent on locally-produced goods and services, it can be recirculated many times, benefitting many people.[67] However, when money is spent on food that is brought in from another region, particularly food produced by large-scale commercial agriculture operations, a high percentage of that dollar pays for services that were performed outside of the community. These services include growing the food, farm worker wages, packaging, brokers and long-distance transportation. Everyone who performed services outside of the community gets a part of that spent dollar and that money is lost from the local economy. This loss of money from the local economy can be substantial.

When I recall the neighborhood stores that were still around when I was a child, I understand how they played an important role in the local economy. When my family purchased locally grown food or spent money at the milk house or meat market, most of that money stayed in my community because the business owners were neighborhood families who usually purchased from local sources. When supermarkets put those small stores out of business and began to carry food that had been grown on distant farms, money that would have stayed in my community began to be exported to another part of the continent. That money was lost from my community. As more and more money began to be taken away from the local economy through stores that carried fewer local goods and services, my community became poorer.

Sustainable Seattle's economic analysis demonstrated how urban and near-urban food production and local spending create stronger local markets and build local food economies.[67] The economic impact of urban agriculture is such that even a small shift in spending away from food that has been grown in another region has a large local economic benefit. When food is produced within a community, jobs can be created and local stores will sell more garden seeds, tools and supplies. Producing and purchasing from local sources supports a network of economic activity that makes for economically healthier and more prosperous communities. Spending on local goods and services can contribute two to three times more to a community's income than spending at non-local businesses.

Results from my backyard food growing study showed that I was able to produce approximately $2000 worth of fruits and vegetables each year when priced from food grown by conventional agricultural methods. For organic prices, the value was approximately $3000. Although this is not a significant part of an affluent family's budget, it is significant for low-income households and can amount to a monthly savings between $175 and $250. For some, this can be the same amount of money needed to pay utility bills or yearly property taxes. Over the long-term, that money adds up. Over a thirty-year period, the average duration of a home loan, the savings could equal enough money to purchase a home with cash.

Although the household's monetary benefit is important, the local economic impact can be substantial when there are many food growers within a community. For example, if a city of 10,000 people had 1000 residents (10 percent) who produced food as I did, the cumulative economic benefit to residents would be approximately $2 million to $3 million dollars. I know that cities of this size would welcome that kind of economic stimulus. If this same percentage of food growers were applied to larger cities, the economic impact becomes quite large. As an example, there are more than 1.3 million people living in the West Palm Beach metropolitan area and if only 5 percent of these residents produced the same amount of food I did during this study, the economic impact to these households would total between $130 million and $195 million dollars each year. That is an economic stimulus that few local businesses or federal tax breaks could hope to match.

By expanding this concept out to large metropolitan areas, you can understand how the cumulative financial impacts of urban agriculture can play an important role in a region's economy. Areas like Washington D.C. (5.7 million residents), Philadelphia and Houston (6 million residents), Chicago (9.5 million residents), Los Angeles (13 million residents) and New York (19 million residents) could enjoy hundreds of millions of dollars of economic boost from even modest percentages of urban food gardeners. At the national level, the potential economic impact is huge. If just 1 percent of the people in major metropolitan areas across the United States grew a food garden as I had, the direct economic benefit to their households would exceed 200 billion dollars per year. An important aspect to this economic boost is that it is independent of financial market variability and the state of the economy.

The results from my backyard food growing study get even more interesting when you compare them with commercial agricultural production. Florida is a major agricultural state in the United States, being second only to California in vegetable production. In 2012, Florida's commercial farms harvested fresh market vegetables on 186,700 acres of land with total cash receipts (money earned by the farmer for his produce) of approximately $1.1 billion dollars (an average of $5,892 per acre).[52] My food garden produced approximately $1500 (retail price for conventionally-grown produce) worth of vegetables per year on 1000 square feet of land (equivalent to $65,300 per acre) using organic methods. Comparing the value of produce grown on commercial farms and my home garden must be done carefully, because the former was a wholesale value and the latter was a retail value. But, even if retailers sold vegetables with a 1000 percent markup from the farmer's price (which is an unusually high profit margin), my organic urban food garden would still be more productive (per unit area) than commercial farms. Some agricultural scientists and horticulturalists believe growing food using organic methods, which does not use chemical fertilizers or pesticides, will result in lower food productivity.[9] Results from my backyard research, and other studies, suggest that growing food commercially on large tracts of rural land reduces agricultural productivity.

The economic benefits of local and urban food production suggested by my backyard study show not only what can be gained by expanding the practice of urban agriculture, it also tell us what was lost when communities became dependent on food produced outside their own regions. Yet, with all of the potential benefits from urban agriculture, it still seems like a foreign idea to many people. It shouldn't. Many of our parents and grandparents were among those who benefitted from or participated in the Victory Gardens planted in the 1940s. At that time, there was approximately one Victory Garden for every 7 people in the United States. This was achieved because the Federal government promoted and supported the gardens as a way to conserve resources. If we could tap that same spirit today, we would see a substantial boost in our nation's economy. Unfortunately, national economic policy and government stimulus programs are woefully ignorant of the financial benefits afforded by the collective efforts of numerous small urban food growers. Yet, these gardens can offer great economic rewards. If only $100 of public money were spent to successfully assist one individual in establishing a home food garden, the economic return could be from ten to thirty times the investment.

The economic benefit of urban food gardens, collectively, is an important and unseen part of the local economy. However, with fewer people growing their own food today, as compared to a century ago, some communities are entirely dependent on commercially produced food. As the number of people living in cities continues to rise, the dependency on large-scale and more distant agriculture will only grow. Unfortunately, the availability of affordable and quality fresh fruits and vegetables is already a problem in some communities, particularly in minority and inner city neighborhoods. New terms have been created to describe the different aspects of food access. Those that are being discussed at length in the news today include food deserts, food insecurity, food resilience, food sovereignty and, a new one concept that has emerged recently, food sustainability. As cities continue to grow, problems with access to fresh and healthy food will only become exacerbated unless the current food system is changed.

These food access problems have often been blamed on the financial state of the individual or community. But this is a simplistic conclusion. When working on my dissertation research, I talked with many of the residents of these underserved communities and found that their parents or grandparents once grew food for themselves, but the younger generations would not even recognize food plants. The food growing skills that used to be in their families have been lost. The loss of food growing skills is not restricted to low income neighborhoods, it cuts across all demographic groups and communities. It is no less than a national crisis. The near death of food growing skills has been caused by several factors. The first is our food system's dominance by industrial agriculture, which has made food a market commodity that can only be acquired by those who can afford to buy it. Additional blame must be placed on municipalities that frown upon those who wish to grow their own food. Those who do not see the practice as valuable enough to learn it for themselves or to teach their children must also share the blame.

Although food deserts have been described in different ways, most experts agree that it is a condition where people living in poor urban communities have few or no choices to purchase affordable, healthy food because of a lack of money or a lack of retail outlets. In addition, the price of fresh fruits and vegetables are often higher in poor areas, and selection and quality are usually lower.[68] Food deserts occur in every major metropolitan area and even within the nation's most productive agricultural regions. Residents in food deserts usually have to travel outside of their neighborhoods to purchase fresh and healthy food, which can be particularly difficult for those who are handicapped or elderly, or those with limited transportation options.

Besides food deserts, another problem that affects many low-income residents is food insecurity. People who are food insecure are those that cannot regularly obtain enough nutritional and safe food.[69] Factors that are associated with food insecurity include a limited income, limited education and large household size.[70] Because people who are food insecure are also more likely to have unhealthy diets, they can have a higher risk for health problems.[71] Inadequate access to fresh and nutritious food has been linked to higher rates of diabetes, obesity, cardiovascular disease, certain types of cancers and some types of chronic illnesses.

Food resilience is a relatively new concept and it is based on the idea that your food system, your food sources, should be able to provide even in the face of climate change, occasional agricultural crop failures, natural disasters or other events that might disrupt food access. For example, after hurricanes Frances and Jeanne struck south Florida, grocery stores were damaged and could not open until repairs had been done. Many major roads were impassable, which did not allow the transport of food or supplies to restock store shelves. However, my household would have been food resilient if I had planted my vegetable garden and preserved its harvest from the previous season. I could have had enough fresh and preserved food to eat until the economic food system had opened for business again.

Home food gardens provide households with a certain level of food security and resiliency they would otherwise not have. Even those who have a limited income are within arm's reach of a healthy meal. Having fresh garden vegetables and fruits just steps from your back door or preserved on your pantry shelves ensures a food supply that is not affected by commercial availability or price fluctuations. In 2010, several frosts in the agricultural areas of south Florida killed some winter vegetable crops. Although green beans and other types of produce became expensive luxuries to purchase or vanished from supermarket shelves, I still had them to eat fresh from my garden (I was able to protect some of my plants from the frost) and canned on my pantry shelf.

A man who came to my house one day to remove a particularly

huge honey bee nest that had aggregated on my garden shed (that is a great story for another time[72]) told me about what it was like to grow up in the Ural Mountains of western Russia and Kazakhstan forty years ago. He lived there during the time of the Soviet Union and told me how little food there was to eat. "We all grew our own food, we had to- there was nowhere else to get it from. We only had a 3-month growing season; all we could grow were apples, cherries, potatoes, cabbage, carrots and other cool-weather crops. The grocery store shelves had vodka," he told me, "four, five, six different kinds of vodka, but no food. People died of starvation, mostly elderly people." Later, he moved to a city on the Black Sea and the Soviet Union dissolved. I asked him if people in that city grew their own food. "We couldn't," he said, "there was no space; the homes were on very small lots." Thinking carefully and speaking in his pleasant accent, he continued, "The lots were only one-fourteenth of an acre; there was only room for the house." I thought about my quarter-acre lot and how much food it had produced. "Things got better after the Soviet Union broke up- after that there was food, but it was shipped in by the government from other countries," he recalled. After he wrapped up his work, we sat down and talked more about growing food. The bee man would take my live bees to a farm where they would help grow food. I was happy to see them go and pleased to see them go to a good home. The bee man also grows organic honey to sell and is an advocate for healthy food. This is a man who knew what it was like to go hungry and to have his food supply controlled by others. He left me with this advice, "It is dangerous to have your food controlled by commercial enterprises. They grow for profit, not for your health. It is also dangerous to have your food controlled by your government. But, I don't think that people in America will grow their own food, I don't think they know how to or want to." The bee man had seen the problems that happened when you don't have control of your food supply.

Food sovereignty refers to a community's, region's or nation's control over its own food production and supply. For example, residents of an Alaskan village are unable to grow food for much of the year and depend on food that has been grown elsewhere to survive. Because of this, the community is at the mercy of food market prices and supplies. These Alaskans are not as food sovereign as residents of the state of California, which grows much more food than it consumes. The more a region or country relies on food produced elsewhere, the less food sovereign they are. Because food is a basic human necessity that has become a commodity that, in some places, can only be acquired through a market system, this has caused real social and health concerns.

Food sustainability encompasses the entire range of issues from food production, delivery, access and sovereignty. Food sustainability requires that food is grown using sustainable methods, is available locally and is a response to local food needs. It is a food system that sustains both the population and the environment while protecting natural resources. Locally produced food supports urban sustainability by offering greater regional self-reliance.[21] Sustainably produced food is not necessarily food that was grown using organic fertilizers or methods, although it can be. There are organic fertilizers, organic pest control products and traditional food growing methods that can be applied in ways that are unsustainable or damaging to the environment. Food sustainability results from the application of an ethic rather than the implementation of a method.

Urban agriculture, such as local farms, community gardens and home food gardens, offers an inexpensive means to alleviate some of the problems of food deserts and food insecurity by placing food production in the areas of greatest need. The presence of farmers markets and community food gardens improve community nutrition and diet because of easier access to fresh fruits and vegetables.[73] Growing food, either in a home garden or a community garden, is associated with an increase in fruit and vegetable consumption.[74] There are also benefits to being exposed to food growing while young. School food gardens can give students a more positive attitude toward fresh fruits and vegetables, from grade school through high school.[75] Urban food gardens can also nourish the community in other, more unexpected ways.

Recently, my spouse Eddie and I were traveling through Tennessee and decided to spend a day in Chattanooga, a city in the Appalachian Mountains that is re-inventing itself. The city has a youthful edge- art galleries, coffee shops, craft breweries and a revitalized waterfront district. It is also home to more than 20 community gardens. I decided to visit a couple of them while we were in town. Close to our hotel was The Hart Giving Garden on Main Street. We parked on a side street adjacent to the Hart Gallery and saw raised vegetable beds on a strip of land near the corner of Main Street. Right here, out in the open in downtown Chattanooga, was a community garden!

The garden's dozen or so raised beds were arranged outward from a central obelisk that was faced with art tiles. The walls of the raised beds were decorated with intricate mosaics of glazed tiles, seashells, art glass, beer caps and wine bottle corks. The garden beds contained a variety of herbs, food plants and flowers. The beds could be watered from rain barrels that captured water off of the roof during summer showers. This downtown community garden was unfenced, accessible to anyone who wanted to enjoy its interesting and quirky beauty. In another, less caring community, this garden would have been raided and vandalized unless protective barriers surrounded it. Intrigued by the garden and uncertain of its connection with art, we went into gallery to find out more.

The gallery contained a collection of varied, interesting and provocative artwork, which was arranged in corners dedicated to a specific artist. The sole person in the gallery greeted us, who I assumed to be the owner or salesperson, and I explained to her that I wanted to know more about their community garden. She explained, "The Hart Gallery is a homeless non-traditional art center, a non-profit organization that provides a space for homeless people to do art, but also welcomes the mentally handicapped, political refugees, fixed-income seniors and disabled veterans. The gallery provides them with a meal and art materials two afternoons each week and offers a venue to sell their art so they can supplement their incomes. The homeless also work in the community garden." The gallery was a place of refuge; each week, it gave these artists a few hours of hope in an otherwise bleak world. Looking around me, I was profoundly moved and found myself unable to speak. I thought back to the time when Hurricane Jeanne made my house unlivable and I got along only because others opened their homes up to me. As hard as those times were, these artists had circumstances much worse than I have ever had to live with. The woman continued, "The community garden is maintained by our clients for their benefit. Each tile on the obelisk was created by a local homeless person to tell a story about what a home means to them." The community garden at the Hart Gallery was integrated with art and combined, they gave mental, emotional and physical sustenance to society's most disadvantaged. The Hart Gallery also provided these homeless people with something most associated with a home- a vegetable garden. Thinking about my own home, my garden and my spouse, and what it would be like to live without them, I was on the verge of tears. I believe that this was the most beautiful community garden I had ever seen.

The Hart Gallery garden grew food for a small community of homeless artists. Growing food to supplement one's food supply is one thing, but feeding an entire community from food gardens is an entirely different challenge. During the first year of my backyard food garden study, I produced 167 pounds of vegetables and the amount increased each successive year. In the fifth year of my study, I produced almost 500 pounds of vegetables even as my garden area decreased in size. This increase in productivity may have been because I became more skilled at growing food. I have every reason to believe that this trend would continue since there are still better ways that I can grow. This was a lot of food! Even still, I wanted to find out how closely this could come to feeding my household of two people. I recalled my Aunt Elizabeth's backyard food garden in small town Iowa and how it seemed to be enough to feed her and her husband- I wondered if it could still be done.

To find this out, I consulted the United States Department of Agriculture's Choose My Plate guidelines (www.choosemyplate.gov). There, I found tables listing how many servings of fruits and vegetables people within different sex and age groups would need for a healthy diet. The guidelines described five different types of vegetables that a healthy diet should include: dark green vegetables, beans and peas, starchy vegetables, red and orange vegetables, and other vegetables. Looking at how much of these vegetable types and fruit I had produced in the last years of my study, along with considerations of unused food garden space I could have used to grow types I had not produced enough of, I found that my backyard was capable of growing enough to provide all of the fruit and vegetables needed by my household. This seemed intuitive because I was already purchasing so little from the grocery store. It was nice to know that even though my late aunt did it in an entirely different period in this country's history, it could still be done!

These results were significant for several reasons. First, I was no longer dependent on the commercial food market system I had been relying on since I was a teenager. After 40 years, I had broken free and learned how to feed myself as my ancestors had. In a way, I had returned to my food roots. Second, the food was so much better tasting that I ate more servings and more types of fruits and vegetables. They had flavor that was memorable and desirable. Grocery store produce never excited me in that way. My homegrown food was alive.

I wondered what would happen if my neighbors grew food gardens like mine. How much food could be produced by the cumulative efforts of many urban food gardens? To find out, I used aerial photos to add up the area of residential backyard food growing space within urban Palm Beach County. I only used backyard areas, away from street view, so that the community's aesthetics would be unchanged. These backyard areas were where food could be grown away from street view. I did not include public (e.g., parks) or institutional (e.g., hospitals, schools) green space, which is a lot of land area. Using the fruit and vegetable production numbers I got from my backyard, I estimated the quantities of each that could be grown on all of this urban backyard land.

I also looked at how much produce would be needed each year to feed the people living within this urban area. Could we grow enough fruits and vegetables in our metropolitan area to feed all of our residents? I used the United States census data from Palm Beach County for this estimate. When I compared how much food could be grown with how much was needed to feed the population living here, I found the answer. My heart skipped a beat! The results showed that *it was* possible to grow all of the fruits and vegetables needed by all of the urban residents in Palm Beach County. Because West Palm Beach is part of the South Florida Metropolitan Area, an area with more than 5.5 million residents that has similar development patterns and history throughout, there is every reason to think that these results can be extended out to the entire region. We *could* grow all of the fruits and vegetables needed by our population within our cities and eliminate the need to transport them to our area from across the continent. The economic, environmental and resource conservation implications were enormous, particularly with respect to water conservation. It was estimated that in 2010, America needed 13 million more acres of productive vegetable fields to meet the minimum daily food requirements for its citizens.[76] This could be achieved by putting a little more than one-third of the nation's total area of residential lawn into food production.

The social implications of this revelation were enormous as well. By expanding the practice of urban agriculture, we have the ability to reduce or eliminate hunger, food deserts and food insecurity within the metropolitan area I live in. Because most of our protein and dairy foods are grown within Florida, my region has the ability to become regionally food sovereign. I could also be so bold to say that programs to promote urban agriculture could shrink or eliminate the need for government food assistance programs, charity soup kitchens and food pantries. In 2013, there were 47 million people receiving assistance from the Federal government's Supplemental Nutrition Assistance Program (SNAP) at a monthly per person average cost of $133.[77] For SNAP recipients who have access to food gardening space, either where they live or in a community garden, investing one or two months of their benefits could put them on their way to growing a substantial portion of the food they need for the entire year. The total monthly cost of the SNAP program was $79.9 billion. If only a fraction of this was invested in establishing urban food gardens in low-income neighborhoods, it would provide a long-term solution to a problem that is currently being treated with temporary fixes. This is not some distant dream; the results from this one small backyard study indicate that it is a real possibility.

Are people willing to grow their own food? If not, then the results from my backyard study are nice, but not really something that could be expanded throughout the community. As I pondered this question, I thought about my conversation with my college department chairperson- he asked me why anyone should care. I thought about my conversation with the bee man; he didn't think that city residents would grow their own food. I also thought about other green movements and how, against all odds, they took hold. One that struck me most was recycling. In the mid-1980s, approximately thirty years ago, if you told me that people would willingly separate out tin cans, glass bottles, used plastic containers, paper and cardboard from their home trash and place it out to the curb for roadside pickup, I would have said that you were dreaming. Certainly, no one would voluntarily separate their trash when they get no benefit from it. Nor would I have believed that businesses and government offices would make recycle bins available to workers and voluntarily place large collection bins for recyclable materials in every department. But, here we are today, with successful home and business recycling programs in most metropolitan areas. In 2009, almost one-third of the total waste generated by the United States was being recycled, including more than half of all paper products.[78] This was estimated to be 1.5 pounds per day per person! By any measure, that is success and it is being done entirely by individuals who receive no tangible benefit from it.

The question of whether urban residents were interested in growing their own food was something that I had addressed in my dissertation research.[66] My dissertation research involved surveying almost 300 people and spending hundreds of hours interviewing them about their experiences with home food growing. I asked people who currently do not grow food how they felt about home food gardening. Approximately 5 percent of the people in the study said they didn't like it, less than 10 percent said they would rather do other things and 12 percent said they had no opinion about it. Less than 15 percent of people said that they simply weren't interested in growing food. Overall, the percentage of people with negative feelings about home food growing was small. Over 55 percent of people in the study who were not food growers said that they thought it was a good idea and more than 40 percent said that they considered food gardening themselves. For every person who said that they didn't want to grow food, there were at least three who said that they did. These results show that there are a lot of people who are receptive to the idea and willing to try it, at least in the region where I live. After chatting with people on social media across the world, I have every reason to believe that the desire to grow your own food is universal.

When I asked urban residents who didn't grow food what it would take to get them to start, the responses were clear- they needed education, guidance and assistance. Existing networks of community colleges, agricultural extension programs, community gardens, garden clubs and other related social resources could easily provide education and assistance. Not surprising, one-third of people in my study said they needed access to growing space, a role that can be filled by community gardens. This survey showed that a majority of people were interested in growing food in their communities and that all of the parts of the puzzle were there- we just need linkages to connect them.

One perceived roadblock could be the time, effort and expense that are needed to grow food. Several participants in my community survey echoed that concern. So did the bee man. I am sure that there are many others who would agree. One of them is Theresa, a woman in her senior years who is from Los Angeles. Theresa grew up with vegetable gardens; her parents grew some of their own food and so did her grandparents. Theresa is a woman who knows what it takes to grow her own food and her garden has more than 15 different kinds of herbs, vegetables and fruits. To her, people are growing food less these days because they are working more and their lives are getting busier. It is a challenge to have a career, maintain a home, raise children and to grow food too. She also thought that it might cost a lot of money to set up a garden, money that some families may not have. Many others have expressed the same thoughts to me.

During my backyard study, I tracked the time worked in the garden and the monetary expenses so that I could answer some of the questions that Theresa and others had raised. My average annual expenses were about $350 (including construction materials for raised beds), which I made up by trading excess produce for other goods and services. During the 2012-2013 season, I grew between $12 (conventional agriculture prices) and $20 (organic agriculture prices) worth of produce for every hour I worked. On average, I spent between 2 and 3 hours per week working in my food garden. These numbers included all of the time I spent hand watering the garden beds so I could measure how much water I used. If I had used sprinklers or drip irrigation instead, the amount of time I would have spent would have decreased by almost two-thirds and the dollar per hour return would double or triple. In contrast, I found that the average homeowner in my community survey spent almost 9 hours per month maintaining their lawn and grooming landscape that provided little benefit beyond aesthetics and spent from $50 to $150 per month on maintenance.[66] This is similar to the results of a national study that found the average homeowner spends $1200 per year on lawn care services, supporting a nation-wide $28.9 billion dollar service sector.[79] One could dedicate a share of that landscape maintenance time to growing food or hire the same workers who mow the lawn to maintain the home food garden. This would provide the household with a source of fresh produce just steps from their back door and the money saved from lower food costs would offset the expense of hiring the food garden maintenance service. The time, effort and expense involved in the food garden are the far better investment.

15. THE GREEN STUFF

Gardening is so much more than growing plants. Gardening involves nature, culture and the expectations of the people around you.[80] Gardens come in a wide range of styles and types. Private gardens are each unique, reflecting the gardener's personal values, traits and preferences.[81] Public gardens are communal spaces where people interact on social, cultural and religious levels.[82] All urban gardens are part of the greenspace, that vast area of unbuilt land within cities. Urban greenspace can be flower gardens, food gardens, lawns, landscaped areas, vacant lots, parks and other unpaved spaces. Greenspace can be found on both public lands and private residential lots. Some of it is actually green.

Greenspace plays an important role in the lives of city residents. Gardens, parks and bucolic natural landscapes are used by urban residents to restore a sense of self, separate from other people, remove themselves from daily rituals and observe nature.[83] Food gardens are points of communication with family members and neighbors. Living in greener environments has been associated with improved health and vitality,[84] and contact with plants can be beneficial.[85] Gardens have intrinsic value for the gardener by providing a sense of calm, a place of retreat and a space in which to regain equilibrium; gardens are well known as places where people go for solace[86] and to regain a sense of happiness.[87] A lack of contact with greenspace has been associated with more symptoms of illness and a higher risk of mental illness.[88]

One community garden in Parkland County, a municipal district in central Alberta, Canada, recognized the important psychological benefits of gardens and has written this into its mission statement. The garden strives to be a place for neighbors to interact and to provide a stress reducing, mentally relaxing environment where an individual's skills can be shared with others. By creating a place that makes food and flowers available to local residents, the garden's organizers feel that it will also instill a sense of comfort and ease to the community.

Living in cities physically and psychologically distances urban residents from the ecosystems that sustain them.[21] Urban greenspace plays an important role in communities by allowing people to interact and reconnect with the environment. Without interacting with the environment, people's sense of interconnectedness and dependency on the land vanishes. Gardening is one way for people to reconnect with the land, even in small ways.

I once had a conversation with a man who had been born and raised in a small town in Montana, but moved to an apartment building in a larger city to take a job. Steve was single, living alone and missed how the rural life made him feel. He told me how he grew up with open spaces, ranchlands and vegetable gardens. "I want to grow a vegetable garden, but can't where I live," he told me, "but I will, I will start soon." He told me that growing his own food gave him a sense of independence and made him feel a connection with the land in a very small, but important, way. He used to grow vegetables on his apartment patio and these brought back memories of his time in the country. "When my girlfriend and I were together," he lamented, "I bought her earth boxes to grow vegetables in as a gift for her birthday. She loved them and we really enjoyed growing things in them. Then, she dumped me and took the earth boxes when she left." This story had all of the makings for a really clever country song.[89]

Besides television watching and Internet surfing, landscape maintenance and gardening are among the most common leisure pastimes in America.[90] With little exception, the area dedicated to lawn is much larger than the area dedicated to food gardens, which is a reflection of the value placed on each. With respect to the size of home food gardens, my community survey found that these were approximately 1/8th of the size of the other landscaped or lawn area.[66] This is not unlike the ratio of lawn to vegetable-growing acreage in this country. There are approximately 7 acres of turf grass to every acre of vegetable farm in the United States.[59,60] Homeowners in my survey felt that non-food producing landscape was important mostly because of its aesthetic value and that there would be community backlash if it was not properly maintained. In contrast, food growing was considered to be optional and was overwhelmingly described as an enjoyable activity by homeowners. The results from this survey led me to think that there was plenty of space for growing food on residential lots and, since people were already spending a lot of time and money maintaining grass, many of these residents could easily add food-growing areas into their properties.

There are many reasons why people grow food gardens. These include money savings, better food freshness, better food quality, personal enrichment, a focus for family activities, aesthetics and community connections.[90] People across all income levels and backgrounds have food gardens, but not always for the same reasons. In my dissertation research, I found that food gardening was most practiced by city residents who were in upper income brackets, were college educated, were over the age of 50 or were in long-term relationships.[66] Most people told me that they didn't grow food because they needed it, they could afford to buy it. Instead, the food they grew was a better quality than they could get from the store and they enjoyed the experience of growing their own food. People in low-income communities are more dependent on the food they grow and their food gardens help to raise the homeowner's standard of living.[38] Regardless of whether or not people grew food for economic reasons, they all benefitted from the feelings of self-sufficiency, happiness, contentment and satisfaction that gardening gave to them.

Sometimes, the happiness given from vegetable gardens come in unexpected ways. My friend Toby, who was born and raised in Virginia into a family that always had vegetable gardens, started his first home garden this past season. He has two young children that are now at the age of curiosity, the age where they can help out with the garden and watch the miracle of food growing. "Food growing was a big part of my dad's life. My grandpa had a farm in Virginia and when I was young, I loved going to the farm," Toby told me. He said that food gardening brought back memories of his father and grandfather, memories that are peaceful, pastoral and filled with nostalgia. He stirs with excitement about his vegetable gardening, not because of what it produces for him but what it does for his children. "My son loves to go to the bean plants and pluck bean right off of the vine and eat them," he says. "My children love to eat them fresh, right from the plants. My daughter is picky about vegetables and, at dinnertime, will only eat the ones that come from the garden." Toby's greatest reward from his food garden is the bond that it forms between him, his children, his father and his grandfather. It also physically and psychologically reconnects him and his family to the land. "The food that I grow means a lot more to me than the food that I buy because it is something that I have done for myself." Toby then cautioned, "Unfortunately, familial knowledge about how to grow food is being lost and that's a shame." But, his home garden has proved that it doesn't have to be that way.

Urban gardens can reconnect people with the environment; with planning and planting, these gardens can also reconstruct some of the environment that had been lost to development. As I was planning and planting my backyard gardens, I became curious about what kind of natural vegetation existed here, the place where my home had been built, before the area became a housing development in the

1950s. What did it look like when the Native Americans still lived in this area? If I knew that, perhaps I could replant a little bit of it and return a small part of my backyard to its former self. What I did know was that the soil was dry grayish sand and devoid of nutrients. I was applying large amounts of mulch and compost to my garden beds to get the soil to hold enough moisture to grow food in. I had talked with long-time residents who remembered it as ranch land, grazed by cattle, with pine trees. One house a few streets away appeared to be a barn that had been converted into a large home. Also, there were a few very old pine trees in the neighborhood, which may have been relics from the original forest. The pine forests in Florida all grow on very sandy soil. So, with these clues in hand, I was prepared to discover that this housing development had been built on native pinelands. That would be easy to replant!

To get a definitive answer, I consulted the only authoritative source on the matter- hand-drawn maps and eyewitness accounts from the original surveyors hired by the federal government to lay out the township, range and section tracts across the state. These surveys were generally done between 1860 and 1880, and the field notes were available through the Internet from a state database. Opening up the surveyor's field notes and maps for the place that would one day be my neighborhood, I read through the descriptions and drawings in anticipation. What I read was confusing. Believing that I had made a mistake, I had to check it three times to be sure it was correct; sadly, it was. These maps and surveyor notes unquestionably showed that my entire neighborhood was situated on land that used to be sawgrass marsh- it once looked just like the Everglades! During my time working in the Everglades, I became intimately familiar with sawgrass marsh, what it was like and where it liked to grow. It seemed unbelievable that sawgrass marsh once grew in the same place I was having difficulty growing my vegetable garden. Sawgrass marsh is covered with water from one to three feet deep during much of the year. Today, the water table at my house was about 10 feet lower than that; you could see it in the series of drainage canals in my neighborhood. As this fact sunk in, I realized that I was living in an environmental catastrophe where nothing native to the site remained. The soil was originally Everglades soil, whose natural organic matter had rotted away long ago. It made sense to me why my soil was pure sand, so nutrient poor and, with the water table lowered by as much as 10 feet, why it was so dry. I abandoned hope for replanting any of the original native vegetation.

Humans by nature have a bias toward the way things were when they were young or when they first arrived somewhere- it seems to be a fixed reference point by which all other things are compared with. What we don't realize is that things may have been enormously changed by the time we arrived and that a particular reference point may not be a good one to have. The long-time residents who remembered my neighborhood as ranch land were recalling what they saw, but that was an incomplete picture. By the time the ranch had been established, the sawgrass marsh was already gone and those long-time neighborhood residents had not yet moved here. By the time the ranch land had been sold for development, the land had been changed from wetland to upland and pine trees had invaded. The image of the land, already profoundly changed with no trace of the original plants and wildlife remaining, was the image that became fixed in the minds of the first neighborhood residents as the reference point by which all further change was measured. To them, it was the way the land had always been and the way it should be if it were ever restored. They would have never believed that it was once like the Everglades.

It is like that for my family too. My mother never saw the endless tallgrass prairie that her father had carved a homestead from. To her, Iowa had always been a great expanse of agricultural fields and that was the way it should be. Anyone who did not raise corn or cattle on a piece of land that was suitable for agriculture would have been considered to be foolish. If someone had a piece of land that was still virgin prairie, they would have been considered to be crazy. I too, was raised with that vision of Iowa's vast cornfields. My grandfather, though, had seen the seemingly limitless prairie but he did not understand its wealth. He was a foreigner to the land and there was no one to teach him about what it could have provided. The bison that would have been a sustainable alternative to his imported cattle breeds had been killed off by the time he arrived. The nutritious and abundant food plants of the prairie that grew all around him were plowed under because he did not know what they were or how they could have fed and healed his family. Only the Native Americans and the first European visitors to this region would be able to fully grasp the full magnitude of what had been lost. My generation has no understanding of what once occupied the land their homes stand on today and many of them don't particularly care. They have been separated from the land for so long that they don't realize that they too are living in an ecological catastrophe.

Sometimes, the land has been so changed that it is not possible to reestablish what was there before. In that case, you do what you can to make it better than what it currently is. It is like this with my backyard. Although I could never restore wetlands on my small urban lot, there were other options and my decision to plant native tropical trees and a prairie garden were good ones. They are the center of attention for the birds, butterflies and bees in the neighborhood. If my little bit of "natural" plantings seemed to be so beneficial to urban wildlife, just how much environmental benefit could a city's greenspace provide?

Because urban greenspace is the largest area within cities,[91] improving the ecology of these lands could provide a range of important benefits, such as groundwater recharge, water and energy conservation and carbon dioxide absorption by plants.[42] Greenspace helps to cool cities on hot days.[92] City gardens are also important for their ecological value. One study from Toronto found that there were a surprising number of organisms, including insects, birds and wildlife, living within backyard gardens.[93] A national survey conducted in the United Kingdom found that the country's 15 million gardens were a haven for wildlife and played an important role in the conservation of biodiversity.[94] In cities, wildlife lives within the mosaic of greenspaces, using them as a kind of wildlife corridor through which a number of organisms pass as they travel in, out and through cities.

The topic of wildlife corridors, which are networks of interconnected undeveloped lands, has gained considerable attention in the study of ecology and is often something that rural land managers are concerned with maintaining. Wildlife corridors are critically important for many species. Without them, patches of plants or animals would become isolated and unable to breed with outside groups, making the separated groups vulnerable to extinction or inbreeding. Wildlife corridors are also important for migrating species such as birds. Great swaths of coastal land in Florida have been developed, eliminating large expanses of natural lands that lie within one of the major bird migration routes in North America. This same problem has happened along other major bird migration routes, such as the Mississippi River valley, which contains vast agricultural lands, and the West Coast of the United States. Even though developed areas can be made more wildlife-friendly, unfortunately, most ecologists only consider wildlife corridors to be a rural issue.

Along with wildlife corridors, the focus on environmental restoration has also been relegated to rural areas. This is unfortunate. The potential benefits of urban ecological restoration are enormous. Over the past decades, landscaping trends have focused more on cultivating native plants, which can protect environmental quality, reduce the need for irrigation and reduce maintenance.[95] Although native plant landscaping and food gardening are different in scope and purpose, they both can support sustainability goals. Urban native plant landscaping can provide wildlife habitat, which can be important havens for organisms that help control agricultural pests in urban food gardens. In contrast, urban food gardens can be used by wildlife. Urban food production reduces the need to grow food in rural areas and can play a passive role in protecting rural natural lands. For every acre of food-producing urban land, one less acre of rural agricultural land is needed, reducing the need to convert natural land to agriculture.

In Florida today, the expansion of agriculture and urban development into rural areas has fragmented the prime habitats of the Florida black bear and the Florida panther. Other affected species include the crested caracara and the Everglades snail kite. There are endangered scrub plant species too, which suffered heavy losses to agriculture and development. The same issues are being played out across states and countries worldwide. With an ever-growing human population, the continual loss of natural land for agriculture and expansion of development cannot go on forever. We cannot continue to expand our human footprint into rural areas and protect biodiversity at the same time.

Urban agriculture can be a part of the solution. It can do more than grow food; it can also be beneficial to both rural and urban ecology. I have seen this in my own backyard. Within my food gardens and prairie gardens, I identified 31 types of plants (cultivated and wild, including the weeds) that are used by 39 local species of butterflies as host plants. I have logged over 30 species of birds in my backyard, 40 percent of which are migratory and spend the winter in my garden or rest there while traveling through from another distant land. This is a start. Rural agriculture and urban development have cleared expansive areas of native habitat. A mosaic of urban food gardens can play a role in reducing the need for rural agriculture and urban greenspace can restore some ecological benefits in areas where it has been eradicated. Although this idea may seem foreign to some, it is only a return to how things used to be.

During the second year of my food growing study, I looked at the empty spaces next to the food garden and little prairie garden and thought about what I should do about them. These spaces were not appropriate for growing food so they would have other uses. Whatever I would do to these empty areas needed to be something that required little maintenance, so I expanded my options beyond the conventional strips of turf grass. I know I could not restore the wetlands that had been on the site prior to settlement, but there were other options. Two thoughts immediately came to mind. The first would be a tree canopy over the northeast side of the property, around the shed, that would be perfect for shading the house during the hot summer months. That would lower my air conditioning bills too. Some kind of wildflower garden on the southeast side of the property would be perfect for wildlife that preferred open areas and a full expansion of my little prairie garden seemed to be the right thing to do. There, I could watch flowers grow, the bees and butterflies come to search for nectar, and the birds forage for food.

With the final empty space in my backyard planned, I visited native plant nurseries and scouted stores for the types of plants that were in harmony with my plans. The area surrounding the shed had a loquat tree that occasionally bore fruit that was eaten by ever-watching wildlife and me. I decided to keep it because it was a food producer and wasn't an invasive species. The remaining area around the shed was planted with species that are commonly found in Florida's tropical forests, but in an arrangement suitable for home landscaping. Native tree and shrub species included those that produced fruit eaten by birds. Other important native species included those that are food plants for rare and native butterflies. Once planted, these butterflies took up permanent residence and it is common to find a roosting colony of them under the loquat tree at dusk.

The little prairie garden I had planted earlier was expanded to fill out all of the remaining available space. This was not to be a flower garden to be admired by humans, but used by birds, butterflies, bees, wasps, ladybugs, grasshoppers, crickets, frogs and other organisms that can help control some of my garden pests. It included a generous list of native plantings, but did not focus purely on native species. I decided to include millet and sunflowers in my prairie plantings, allowing the plants to flower and set seed for the birds to feast on naturally. This was a better choice than setting out the same food in a bird feeder, which saved the expense of purchasing birdseed that had been grown in another part of the continent and transported here.

I think that using birdseed in my prairie garden throws people off. Local native plant purists would argue that I should be using native plants only. They have a point. To attract wildlife, I decided to include some non-native, non-invasive species that were beneficial, along with native plants. I have a bird feeder, which I used to keep well stocked. I noticed several things while watching the behavior of those that used it. The blue jays ate only the sunflower seeds. The grackles loved something, I was never quite sure what, but they tossed beakfulls of seed from the feeder onto the ground in search of a single morsel. Below, the hungry doves cooed in delight while pecking at the seed raining down upon them. Some of the birdseed was never consumed; instead it sprouted and grew into millet and sunflowers. I noticed that the birds returned to feast on the millet and sunflowers after they had bloomed and set seed. This gave me an idea and rather than set birdseed out, I planted it instead. The bird feeder remains in the prairie today, but it is empty. It is better for the birds to forage for food in the prairie garden; there they learn how to provide for themselves, rather than to expect a handout.

As the prairie plantings matured, the collection began to flower in successive waves, creating a changing palette of color and interest. Some of these were relatives of the native prairie plants I knew as a child in Iowa. It meant a lot to me to be surrounded by them again. Butterflies, ladybugs and other insects appeared and settled into their new habitat. Birds, both year-round and migratory species, came to the prairie and adjacent food garden each morning and evening to forage and roost. I would sit in the prairie patio and watch the changing scene. At night, while watching the stars and being serenaded with the sounds of crickets and tree frogs, screech owls would arrive for the night watch.

As my prairie garden grew, it became a place for connecting with wildlife in ways that I would otherwise not have the opportunity to do within the city (sometimes in ways that I never intended[96]). That wildlife is also connected with the urban ecology in profound and important ways. Most wildlife, by nature, is mobile. If there is good habitat in one area, then wildlife can reproduce and spread to surrounding areas. If a habitat is degraded or polluted, wildlife will be unable to reproduce or will have poor health. Within my backyard gardens, I have observed over eight types of agriculturally beneficial insects, six types of beneficial animals, 17 species of butterflies and 31 species of birds. I'm certain this list is incomplete and a more serious study would certainly yield higher numbers.

Of great interest are the birds. I have an old oak, which is dead on one side and would have been cut down long ago by an owner other than myself. The tree is the neighborhood magnet for birds. It has hosted many nests over the years and is subjected to intense grooming by warblers and gnatcatchers while they spend time here in the winter. One morning, while watering the garden, the oak was host to a blue-gray gnatcatcher, a red-bellied woodpecker, a pair of cardinals, and a hummingbird- all at the same time. At one point, the hummingbird swooped down to sip from my hose and lapped droplets that drifted away from the main stream and fell onto leaves. It also zoomed over to other plants to sip the heavy dew from the leaves. I was ecstatic! What a wonderful thing to have seen! The wonder was replaced by panic when I realized that if I had been spraying toxic chemicals in my garden to control pests, the dew that this tiny hummingbird lapped up would have been poisonous.

One late January afternoon, while watering a row of red cedar trees that I planted in the hopes of attracting the elusive cedar waxwings (and to screen the view into the neighbor's backyard), I thought about these birds. These red cedar trees bear fruit that are eaten by the waxwings. I grew up with red cedar, which grew readily in meadows and clung precariously to narrow crevices in the tall and ancient limestone bluffs along the upper Mississippi River. Red cedar is one of those trees that most typifies the rugged bluffs of the Midwest. I had read about the cedar waxwings and saw pictures of them in books, but had never seen one in person. They were, to me, one of the most elusive, beautiful and oddest birds! Their sleek profile and subtle colors were unlike any other. Living in Florida, I held little hope of ever seeing one; they are not permanent residents here but only pass through during their annual migration to warm climates. As sunset overtook the sky and orange clouds streamed overhead, I was finishing up my watering and thinking about the cedars and how I hoped to attract cedar waxwings one day. I was roused from my thoughts by an unfamiliar cheeping sound above me in the old oak tree. I looked up and saw a flock of cedar waxwings, which had come to roost in the tree. There were at least two-dozen of them.

At a community garden in the City of Markham, which is near Toronto in the Canadian province of Ontario, is a community garden tucked amongst five story office buildings in the urban setting. The garden is relatively new, having been formed in 2012. Its goals are to turn an underused urban lot into a beautiful, productive piece of land that educates families about fresh, healthy foods and ecologically sound practices. They were serious about the ecologically sound practices part. At the grand opening in June 2014, some members were greeted by an unidentified bird that fanned its tail out and squawked when anyone approached. One member snapped a picture and posted it on the garden's Facebook page. It was identified as a killdeer, a migratory bird that spends its summers in the temperate north and winters in Central America. Upon a closer look, the members discovered that the bird stayed in Bed #2 all day (near the sugar baby watermelon seedlings) and was protecting a nest that had 4 eggs! The garden's members banded together, adopted the bird family and protected both the mother and nest. In July, the chicks hatched. The garden erected a temporary fence around the garden bed that had the nest and posted a sign informing people about the bird. In a suspenseful turn of events, a 2 day-old chick took a stroll with its mother one afternoon and fell into a sewer. The mother bird became upset and squawked hysterically. Some of the gardeners heard the mother bird and investigated. Soon, they found the baby chick in the sewer, but could not rescue it because of the heavy metal grating over the sewer opening. Gardeners and residents who lived near the garden banded together and, with the help of a construction worker who pried opened the sewer grating, saved the chick. One day, that rescued chick may stop to rest in my prairie garden as it migrates to and from its winter home.

Of the bird species that I have recorded from my gardens, approximately 40 percent are migratory. This is a lot. It is also important. What actions I take and the decisions I make about my backyard can have impacts that ripple out beyond my property, beyond my neighborhood, out to other areas of the continent. If I use environmentally safe and responsible practices, migratory birds will have a safe haven for the part of the year when they reside here or are passing through this region. Irresponsible use of pesticides could threaten the migratory birds' lives and they would not return to northern forests and meadows the following summer. Because birds play an important role in the lives of many other species, losing these migratory birds would impact northern ecosystems by their absence.

The issue is not just responsible use of pesticides and other potentially harmful chemicals. It is also a decision to plant a wildlife-friendly landscape and care for it in environmentally friendly ways. My food garden benefits wildlife. Because many of the animals and insects that have found a safe haven in my gardens are also those that are important for controlling agricultural pests, the tropical trees and prairie garden are ecologically integrated with the food garden. Any separations that exist are only in the human mind. This is the same with rural agriculture and rural environments. Anything put into the countryside, be it rangeland or farm field, is integrated into the rural ecology and how those fields are managed have significant, far-reaching and sometimes hidden impacts elsewhere.

The model for modern commercial agriculture is to clear away all vestiges of the local environment, plant very few types of crop plants and rely heavily on chemical fertilizers and pesticides to grow much more than could possibly be grown under natural conditions. Many farmers do not see the farm field as something that is integrated with the local environment; instead it is seen as a special area where different laws and rules apply; this is not true. In conventional vegetable fields, agricultural pests are viewed as threats rather than natural extensions of the local ecology. The solution is to attempt large-scale eradication of these pests with chemicals, often with devastating environmental consequences. But, the laws of ecology state that when you have a blank slate, things will move in to colonize it. The very act of large-scale eradication of pests only creates more opportunity for pests to move in.

The model for modern urban development is similar to that of commercial agriculture. Usually, all vestiges of the local environment are cleared away (except for a token tree or two) and land is replanted with very few species of plants. In many cases, these new plantings rely on irrigation, chemical fertilizers and pesticides. Many urban residents do not see the city landscape as something that is integrated with the environment; the urban landscape is seen as a special area that is detached from the natural world, a place where different laws and rules apply. This also is untrue.

Management of my backyard garden, and of agriculture that is based on sustainable and environmentally safe methods, is based on the understanding that our food gardens are interconnected with nature. Homeowners with food gardens, community gardens and urban farms have control over a very small piece of land, relatively speaking. Although urban residents may be able to eradicate a certain pest from their property, that pest will likely live in a nearby vacant lot or neighbor's landscaping and will soon return. For this reason, most pests must be considered a part of the normal flora and fauna of the urban environment. Fortunately, there are also organisms that have the ability to control some of those pests.

Because the same birds, butterflies, bees, wasps, ladybugs, grasshoppers, crickets, frogs and other organisms live in my vegetable beds and prairie garden, these gardens share the same pests and pest-controlling predators. As long as these gardens are maintained in environmentally friendly ways, the natural garden ecology can lend a hand in keeping pests under enough control to ensure that my food yield is minimally impacted. Of course, not all pests are controlled all the time and other methods may be needed from time to time. But, this is a much more desirable situation than attempting to eliminate pests from your food gardens through the wholesale use of pesticides, which will also drive away the very things that are able to assist you with control.

In colleges and universities, there is a critical need for focusing the disciplines of environmental, ecological and agricultural sciences on the challenges of urban food production. Agricultural ecology, or agroecology, is an area of study that integrates these disciplines but is traditionally concerned with rural agriculture. The benefit of this more natural approach to urban agriculture is that food gardens can help to improve the impoverished environment around them, if designed and managed properly. From a practical perspective, one cannot hope to completely reconstruct natural rural habitats within cities. However, urban agriculture can play a part in restoring some of the environmental benefits that were lost to development while feeding the city's residents.

16. JUST ONE BACKYARD

I did not come to agriculture or food gardening through the garden gate. I have never belonged to a garden club. Nor did I come to food growing through the halls of land-grant agricultural universities. These approaches to agriculture are founded in the science of horticulture, of which I have never had a class. Horticulture seeks to understand the optimum growing conditions of a plant and is focused on how the environment can be manipulated, reshaped and engineered to achieve those conditions. Often, those optimal growing conditions come with negative environmental and ecological impacts that are not known to or may not concern the person who is growing the plant. For example, the horticultural perspective recommends that certain agricultural crops should be grown in places where the entire native plant community has been cleared away; this way, a more ideal condition for the crop plants can be created. In its most extreme form, horticulture gave us the tropical rainforest contained within the glass confines of the Garfield Park Conservatory in a temperate climate suburb of Chicago. Horticultural sciences also guided the development of our modern industrial agricultural system.

I came to agriculture through backyard food gardens. I came to agriculture through an immigrant-homesteaded farm, through the woods and prairies, and through a career founded in environmental and ecological research. Ecologists seek to understand the natural conditions of a site and study the interactions between the organisms that live there, including plants and other things. To ecologists, food plants are a part of the web of life and not the center of the web of life. Food plants, in the ecological perspective, occur in all natural ecosystems and can be sustainably harvested up to certain limits. If one wants to grow food plants on a site, then only those that are adapted to the natural conditions of the site are best to use. That way, the environmental integrity (including the goods and services produced by the environment that humanity depends upon) is preserved.

The enormous contrast between the perspectives of horticulturalists and ecologists is why there has been a recent surge in the public's interest in food safety and the environmental impacts of industrial agriculture. At the beginning of the 20th century, when natural lands were plentiful, a few hundred thousand acres of industrial agriculture were not a problem. Chemical fertilizers and pesticides were almost unknown to most farmers, irrigation was seldom practiced, most farms were family owned and most food was consumed within the region it had been produced. The natural environment could mitigate the pollution and other impacts of industrial agriculture then. But by the end of the 20th century, the extent of industrial agriculture in many regions was so great that the natural environment was no longer able to completely absorb its impacts. This conclusion came from ecologists and not horticulturalists. It is time for these disciplines to come together and work on a solution that can sustain a healthy environment and food system. Sustainable agriculture is rooted in both scientific disciplines.

I began this book talking about the subject of sustainability and how scientists have come to a broad agreement on its definition, but popular culture is still struggling with its meaning. This struggle often leads to misunderstandings about what is sustainable agriculture, even among members of garden clubs, community gardens and food growing movements. These misunderstandings often arise because each is looking at only a single aspect of sustainability. For example (and these are real examples), I once had a conversation with a rancher who lived in the country, near forested parks and preserves. To him, a person who was surrounded by nothing but undeveloped lands, the woodlands were wasted land because they were not being used to grow food. In his mind, only land that produced commercial products was valuable and the more sustainable thing to do would be to clear all of this natural land and plant it in crops. That way, the land would generate food for humanity, which he felt would be a much more sustainable use of the land. He did not include environmental or ecological issues in his determination of what was sustainable nor considered the impacts of these actions on other areas outside of his region. I had a similar conversation with another man who lived in a small town surrounded by semi-arid undeveloped prairie as far as his eye could see. He was an advocate for intensified growing methods that produced a single type of crop and felt that urban agriculture could never be sustainable. This man's concept of sustainable agriculture was based on maximizing what could be produced from an area of land but, as it was with the rancher, the environmental and ecological issues were not important considerations. A third perspective came from a resident of a major metropolitan area; she believed that planting a food garden was a sustainable practice. This woman grew vegetables using raised beds made from wood cut from unsustainably-managed forests, chemical fertilizers and water from a municipal source, but did not consider the environmental impacts associated with the products she used to grow her food. This big city resident, who rarely saw forests or prairie, would be horrified at the sustainability definitions offered by the other two people. These three people carried very different ideas about sustainability, which had been shaped by their perspectives. For the men who lived in the country, the world was mostly natural lands and wasted space. Losing some of that to agricultural development was considered to be beneficial and sustainable. To the city resident, the world was mostly urban development. Each based their assessment of sustainability on a narrow set of criteria that were given different levels of importance. With so much at stake, sustainability must be measured by a more comprehensive set of criteria that apply everywhere at the same level of importance.

Having read all that I have said up to this point, you may have the impression that I believe that industrial agriculture should be abolished. That is neither true nor practical. Industrial agriculture has an important role to play in feeding the world's population. However, the current industrial agricultural model is unsustainable and is having profound negative impacts on the environment and humanity. The world's food system is too heavily supported by unsustainable agricultural practices and this needs to change. If we are to feed the world today and in the future, industrial agriculture must be remade into a form that is sustainable and urban agriculture must become a primary food producer.

Up to now, I have tended to focus on the negative impacts of industrial agriculture. This is only part of the story and it is not fair to dwell only on the negative aspects of these practices. What is misunderstood or being left out by critics is the context in which industrial agriculture was born and promoted. Industrial agriculture was established to benefit mankind and to address threatening problems that could have had catastrophic consequences. In some ways, it was successful. We must respect that.

In most cases, the wholesale destruction of our great native ecosystems was not brought about by the farming families that live on those pieces of land today and they should not be vilified. Development of the vast industrial agricultural areas on the near-extinct American prairie, the northern Everglades, California's Central Valley and the semi-arid regions of the Southwest were the result of government actions. Government-funded transportation systems, wetland drainage projects and water delivery systems opened up these lands to agriculture. Financial incentives were offered to citizens who would be willing to farm in these rural areas. Many of the farmers on these lands today are the children of the original settlers of these lands and they are carrying on long-held traditions. Unfortunately, after observing the effects of a century of industrial agricultural practices, changes must be made because they are unsustainable both environmentally and financially. The key is to work with farmers and landowners to solve the problems and not to isolate them with insults. Viable solutions must come about by recognizing that only sustainable farming methods can be used if agriculture is to be a long-term venture.

Industrial agriculture has made valuable contributions to humanity during the past century. It was a response to the fast growth of cities during the 20th century and was a catalyst for the creation of efficient production, distribution and supply linkages. It has also been partly responsible for the creation of the great, densely packed metropolitan areas of New York, Chicago, Dallas-Ft. Worth, Los Angeles and other areas whose residents' lives depend on food that has been transported into their cities from great distances. Industrial agriculture was developed to find more efficient ways of growing food during a time in our history when the population was growing rapidly; it was a solution that was more agreeable than hunger and starvation. One event that fanned the flames of industrial agriculture was the Great Depression. No one in the United States was left untouched by it and everyone who lived through it has never forgotten. For those who saw families that were destitute and without food to eat, industrial agriculture was seen as a way to ensure that food production would be plentiful. So was the development of chemical fertilizers and pesticides.

The expansion of commercial agriculture into rural areas was encouraged so that rural landowners, far from the employment opportunities offered by cities, could earn a living from their land. Large-scale rural agriculture grew food on inexpensive land, which drove down costs and provided a way for cities to allocate more living space for their ever-expanding populations. Technological advances that created chemical fertilizers, chemical pesticides and genetically-modified (GM) crop plants were hailed as necessary advances to increase crop yields so that more food could be grown on fewer acres. These are reasonable and important goals.

However, now that we have experience with these products and the industrialized agricultural system, we need to assess them. How well have they performed? What are the negative consequences of using them? What are their broader costs? Are they necessary? Can we produce comparable quantities of food by using other methods? What other options exist that avoid some of the problems associated with these high-tech innovations? The people involved in these discussions must include agriculturalists, ecologists, environmental scientists, natural resource managers, sustainability researchers, economists and nutritionists. This assessment is needed because the practices and products that are ultimately used to produce humanity's food supply must be sustainable or they cannot be a permanent part of food production. It is the nature of unsustainable practices to become obsolete. They are simply bad business practices over the long-term.

It is important to recognize that many farming families are reconsidering their agricultural practices and are changing the way they do business. These families recognize that they need to be responsible land stewards if they are to pass their land onto future generations. They have also come to recognize that what they do on their land can have negative impacts elsewhere. Some ranches and large landowners have voluntarily entered into cooperative agreements with government agencies to help manage endangered and threatened species, something that would have been unimaginable only two decades ago. Many tools exist to achieve both environmental protection and sustainable agricultural production; some of these tools include purchasing development rights, establishing conservation easements, the setting aside of conservation lands, landowner-management of ecologically-sensitive lands and improving agricultural methods using guidance from sustainable agriculture experts. Fortunately, efforts to create a more sustainable food production system have reached beyond the farm field. Fertilizer companies are recognizing the growing concerns about fertilizer runoff and are developing products that are more environmentally friendly. Some have created new organic fertilizer and pest control products that are from sustainable sources. These are important changes and consumers need to become vocal and financial supporters of these new directions.

In the end, there are a limited number of things that can be done to mitigate the negative impacts of unsustainable agricultural practices. In spite of all of the fixes that have been contrived to deal with the problems associated with an unsustainable use of a resource, the natural environment (and the goods and services it provides) is always damaged or destroyed. The current industrial agricultural system is an unsustainable system that does not have enough fixes to mitigate the list of problems it creates. Nor can it because it is based upon methods that destroy the land's natural ecological functions. At some point, we are going to run out of natural land and in some places we already have. As I mentioned before, it is the nature of unsustainable practices to become obsolete.

Urban and near-urban agriculture is not perfect and can also be practiced in ways that are destructive and unsustainable. City residents who want to increase yields from small gardens can irresponsibly broadcast chemical fertilizers and pesticides, polluting their land, runoff from their property and the groundwater underneath them. They can also use water indiscriminately, wasting it by irrigating when it is not necessary. Many people have raised beds constructed with wood taken from unsustainable sources, which will rot and need to be replaced every few years. Imagine the number of trees that would need to be cut down to create raised beds for millions of urban food gardens. I know of some who grow vegetables only in plastic containers and manufactured bags that need to be replaced every year to two. The petroleum and energy needed to manufacture and transport these wood, plastic and manufactured materials to your home garden center may offset any environmental benefits gained by urban food growing. Although the impacts from a few urban food gardeners using these practices are nothing to worry about, the cumulative impacts of millions of people are. Just as the cumulative benefits of many can solve problems, the cumulative impact of many can cause them. The greatest problems facing mankind today have arisen from the collective actions of millions of people, people who are well-meaning and who believe that their individual contribution is too little to worry about. A very small unsustainable practice, when magnified by millions, becomes a real threat.

Urban agriculture has been viewed as being low-class and old-fashioned. Just listen to the resistance it receives from the boards of neighborhood associations and gated communities if there is any doubt. It is important to listen to the complaints of those who do not wish to have urban agriculture in their neighborhoods because we need dialogue between those who want it and those who do not. We have to understand the resistance to agriculture within our communities and respectfully address those concerns instead of setting up shouting matches across property lines. People on both sides of the fence have something to gain by acknowledging common goals, understanding differences and coming to agreements on solutions.

Discussions about the benefits and negative impacts of our agricultural systems must include constructive dialogue, not polarized accusations and inaccurate propaganda. We all want the same things- to feed humanity in ways that leave the earth unpolluted, the environment healthy and resources intact for the next generations. This requires an open platform that includes all stakeholders and a variety of perspectives. It requires participants in these discussions to be informed on the facts and to let go of fears and prejudices. Delays caused by infighting only make the problems persist longer than they need to. By combining the manufacturing, research and promotional clout of large companies with the sustainability vision, passion and methods of organic farmers, we can feed humanity efficiently and protect the environment we all depend on. Why should any of these entities wish to participate in these kinds of discussions? Because farms that grow food sustainably are economically sustainable and create an agricultural heritage that will continue for an uncounted number of generations. Businesses that support sustainable agriculture are ensuring a sustainable economic future for themselves.

My food growing study must be thought of in its broader context. This study is the result of one person's curiosity and was carried out in just one backyard. One can never say that the same results would be found everywhere else...they won't. In some places, productivity will be higher and in other places, it will be lower. Although local conditions vary by region, there are certain aspects of this study that are universal. Perhaps the greatest use of this study is to provoke discussion and stimulate more interest in the topics presented here. It will take numerous studies by many students and researchers to go beyond this work and to understand what it means for their particular area. But, this study has shown the numerous and far-reaching benefits of sustainably growing food in cities. It can be used as a vision of where we need to go and a roadmap of how to get there. It also tells us what we can gain by expanding urban agriculture and how much we have lost by abandoning its practice. There are significant challenges with urban agriculture. In some regions, there are insufficient water resources and in others, extreme weather conditions. Some areas will always have limited means for growing food, but there is much work that can be done by citizens who are determined to make it work, entrepreneurs who want to be a part of the solution and agricultural scientists who want to solve problems with creative solutions.

There is a human side to urban food growing that is not found in industrial agriculture. Urban agriculture is influenced by individuals, their experiences and their circumstances. But, food growing is not for everyone. I talked with the pastor of an Episcopal church one day and he confided in me that, although there were members of his congregation that were vocal advocates for community food gardens, he had no personal interest in it. He explained that he came from an upper-class New England family that could trace their roots back to this country's earliest European settlers, but they were politicians and community leaders and not food growers. He knew of no one in his entire family- siblings, parents, grandparents or great-grandparents- who ever had a vegetable garden. It was not something they valued. There is something so honest about this pastor's story that you have to respect it and the fact that there are just some people who are not interested in growing food. But, I do not believe that people who are born into families with no food-growing heritage are automatically cold to the idea of having a garden for themselves.

I met a man who lived in downtown Chicago, in a high-rise condo in The Loop, who came from such a family. He was affluent, a career professional and in his later 50s. Not a single person in his family, that he could think of, ever had a food garden. He certainly did not grow up with one. He had no land to grow food nor did he have any experience with a food garden. In spite of his background, he had a container garden on his patio that grew vegetables and herbs. Growing his own food, he told me, made him feel happy and independent. He told me that he had been seeking out farmers markets and loves the experience of knowing the people who are growing the food he eats. Because urban agriculture brings a level of human interaction and connection that is absent in industrial agriculture, it must be approached using both the hard sciences and the humanities.

If I were to sum up the results of my backyard research into a few phrases, it would be that urban and near-urban agriculture is a better alternative to the current industrial agricultural system. Today, rural agriculture is the core food-producing sector for our population; until the beginning of the 1900s, urban and near-urban agriculture were the major food producers. By restoring urban and near-urban lands as our core food producing areas, we can reduce so many of the negative consequences of intensive rural farming that we are experiencing today, including unsustainable use of water resources, the consumption of large amounts of fossil fuels, excessive carbon dioxide emissions to the atmosphere and the extensive use of agricultural chemicals that harm the environment. Urban agricultural production does not need GM crops, the continual breeding of new hybrids or the development of new chemical pesticides. We just don't need them; in fact, we already have everything we need. If you think this cannot be done, then study the Victory Gardens of the past or Cuban agriculture today.

The current commercial agricultural system is heavily supported and subsidized by the United States Department of Agriculture, land grant universities[1] and large multinational agribusinesses.[7] Federal subsidies to farmers each year are nearly $20 billion.[97] Unfortunately, urban agriculture is not considered to be important enough to be subsidized, funded, researched and supported as large-scale commercial farming has been. Agricultural universities and their research have taken us deeper into high-intensity farming in more distant locations, instead of teaching us how to sustainably grow food where we need it most and where most people live- in our cities. If you don't agree, then compare the agricultural solutions that have come from billions of dollars of investment in crop research with the results from my single self-funded backyard study carried out by one person. Acknowledgement of this reality is not intended to denigrate these institutions, rather a recognition of the need for a realignment of priorities, a more balanced consideration of the full range of problems associated with the current large-scale agricultural systems and a plea for a focus on practical solutions.

The return to urban and near-urban agriculture cannot happen quickly and must include a change in government programs and policies. Agriculture policies must include urban agriculture and extend beyond the commercial aspect of food growing. Energy policies must recognize the potential for conservation through the promotion of urban agriculture in our cities. The Environmental Protection Agency must consider the significant role that urban agriculture can play in reducing pollution and carbon dioxide emissions. Lastly, Federal and state food assistance programs would be much more effective if they focused less on providing food handouts and more on providing the essential tools for people to grow food for themselves. This shift in government programs and policies will save taxpayer money, assist the respective agencies in meeting their objectives and move our society toward food sustainability.

17. WHAT HAS BEEN LOST

I stood in the parking lot high on the hill overlooking the restored tallgrass prairie at Mines of Spain Recreation Area, south of Dubuque, Iowa. On this glorious spring day, the air was pleasantly cool and the wildflowers seemed to be clustered into brilliant patches that flowed across the undulating landscape in contiguous ribbons. You could see the wind make waves as it swept over the verdant sea of prairie grasses. All was silent except for the wandering rustle of the breeze. These 1,380 acres of Mississippi River bluffs, restored woodlands and restored tallgrass prairie are a living miracle. This land once sustained bison herds and provided food for Native American families, but the bison were slaughtered, the native people were forced to leave and the first European settlers plowed under the vacant land in the 1800s. Corn was grown on this land for generations until an idea took hold and changed its future into an image of its past. The cornfields and cattle pasture have been restored to the natural habitat that originally grew here. The wildlife has returned too, the bobcat, coyote, fox, otter, badger, beaver and many, many others. Migratory birds, traveling along their ancestral and ancient migration route along the Mississippi River valley, are here too. But the bear and bison are absent. The bear will likely never roam here again, but perhaps the bison will one day. Humanity has not been harmed by the return of this land to its former self, not a single person has gone hungry because corn is no longer grown here. Conversely, humanity has been enriched by the restoration of this property- by the uptake and permanent storage of carbon dioxide from the atmosphere; by reducing the amount of pollution that runs into the Mississippi River, a national treasure, and ultimately into the Gulf of Mexico, an international natural resource. Humanity has been enriched by this valuable natural habitat that is a safe breeding ground for fish, game and non-game wildlife. This is also a place where people come, in all seasons of the year, to be immersed in nature. They come for solitude, they come to see expansive views of one of the world's great rivers, they come to explore, they come to hike, they come to build the strength of their bodies, they come to ski, they come to learn, they come to touch their roots, connect with their own heritage and to reconnect with the land. These intangible benefits are far more valuable than a few acres of corn.

I walked down a trail and became enveloped by the tallgrass prairie. Tall, dead stalks from last-year's flowers stood bleaching in the sun as the new season's growth clustered around their feet like newly hatched chicks under their mother hen's wings. The cycle of renewal had begun again. I stopped at a trail crossroads where there was a grand vista across the Mississippi River, towards the stoic and ancient limestone bluffs on the other side. With the restored prairie all around me, I closed my eyes and listened. In contrast to the deep quite, there were urgent peeps and cheeps from migrating birds as they foraged for food. There were the imperative buzzings of bumblebees and clicks of crickets. The gentle, soothing spring breeze was wonderful beyond words and made me want nothing more than what I had at that moment- open skies, crisp air and peace. My mind drifted along on soft, buoyant currents of memory and soon paused to remember another prairie I once visited. That was a relic piece of native tallgrass prairie, only 240 acres, in northern Iowa in a park called Hayden Prairie State Preserve. That piece of land also had a remarkable story. Outside of the hilly western-most part of the state, Hayden Prairie is the largest parcel of tallgrass prairie remaining in Iowa. The preserve came about because of the efforts of Ada Hayden, an Iowa farm girl who earned a Ph.D. in biology in 1918 from Iowa State University, one of the first women in the United States to earn a doctorate degree at that time. She became alarmed at the rapid disappearance of Iowa's tallgrass prairie and devoted her life to its preservation. By 1940, plows had destroyed all but a few small patches of prairie. She convinced Iowa to give her $100 for gas money to drive around the state and document any remaining prairie lands. The state agreed. She discovered the intact 240-acre parcel, the largest she was able to find, and lobbied for its protection. In 1945, Iowa purchased the parcel for only $42 per acre and, after Ada Hayden's death in 1950, designated is as Hayden Prairie in her honor.

Hayden Prairie, one of the largest remaining parcels of virgin Iowa prairie, is about the same size as a single retail shopping mall in south Florida. Hayden Prairie is small compared to the restored prairie at the Mines of Spain. I think about the history of these two prairie lands and about how very small they are as compared to the vast extent of prairie that was plowed under for agriculture. That lost great prairie, teeming with wildlife, game animals, food plants and healing plants. Was it really worth losing? Are we better for it? Was the native prairie less valuable than what has replaced it?

When the first Europeans arrived in North America, there were an estimated 60 million bison on the Great Plains and eastern woodlands. To put this into perspective, the number of cattle being raised in the United States in 2012 was nearly 90 million.[60] But, bison grow larger than cattle, to well over a ton,[19] so the amount of meat produced by today's cattle industry may be no more than the amount that could have been sustainably produced from the original native bison herd. Americans today eat beef, not because it is a healthier food choice than bison (it is not), nor because cattle ranching is gentler to the land than bison (it is not), but because bison were associated with the Native Americans and destroying the bison was seen as a way to drive the Native Americans off of the land they had inhabited for thousands of years.[17] When considering the restored prairie and what was lost, there are two unanswered questions that remain with me- the questions are simple and profound.

The first question is whether we are better off with today's agricultural system than we would have been if the bison and prairie had not been destroyed. The answer is multifaceted; one must consider the total costs of our agricultural system and the total output. The broad range of costs includes government price supports and financial incentives, species and habitat loss, pollution, impaired human health caused by pollution, unsustainable use of resources and the financial costs of operations. Output can include the amount of food produced and employment opportunities. If the great American prairie was still intact and sustainably managed, the negative impacts of species and habitat loss, pollution, impaired human health issues and unsustainable use of resources would vanish. What could be produced is a much wider variety of meat products (bison and other game animals), employment opportunities comparable to those we have today, wild plant foods, natural plant products (such as fibers, herbs, flowers, essential oils, medicinal compounds), recreational activities and ecotourism. When considering the entirety of costs and products derived from these lands, and considering these over a long time period, I believe that humanity (and the landowners themselves) would have been better off with the original prairie.

The second question is- can we recover some of what we have lost? Not just in America's heartland, but elsewhere. A negative response seems to be a cultural, rather than an economic, financial or environmental, issue.

Sometimes change does not come quickly, but change always comes. The most important thing about change is how it is guided. One day, while driving in the seldom-traversed backcountry of central Florida along Micco Bluff, I saw unmistakable signs of change. At that time, I was working as an environmental scientist for a state water management district and was going into the field to

What Has Been Lost

examine wetlands on property that the agency owned along the Kissimmee River. The Kissimmee River was once a meandering stream that flowed through a vast mosaic of marshy wetlands over a course of 103 miles, carrying water from the Kissimmee River to Lake Okeechobee. The water carried by the river had been collected from a watershed of over 3,000 square miles, draining excess rainfall from areas as far away as Orlando, and would eventually make its way to the Everglades, southwest of Miami. The floodplain marshes filtered and cleansed water that flowed through them and stored excess stormwater during high rainfall periods. These marshes were also an ecological wonder. Like the Everglades to the south, the Kissimmee marshes were a rich and productive habitat for storks, herons, egrets and more than a hundred other bird species. Alligators, crayfish, shrimp and fish hid within in its gentle-flowing water. Then, man intervened.

From 1962 to 1970, the main channel of the Kissimmee River was dredged to create a 56-mile long canal, desiccating 40,000 acres of floodplain marshes and driving away wildlife. Before the channelization project was completed, a movement to reverse the damage had been kindled. Congress authorized a new effort to restore parts of the Kissimmee River in 1992 and today, the restoration effort is nearly complete. I have been fortunate to work and travel within the restored area of the Kissimmee River by all-terrain vehicle (ATV), boat, airboat and helicopter. This restoration, the largest ecosystem restoration project in the world, is an enormous success. With the floodplain marshes rising phoenix-like, the wildlife has returned. During the rainy season, the floodplain is a water world that looks much like its sibling, the Everglades to the south. Great flocks of white pelicans rise up from abandoned oxbows when startled. Roseate spoonbills and wood storks forage among the grassy flats. During the dry season, migratory birds take cover in the swamp willow and alligators sun themselves on sandbars. But, wildlife is not the only beneficiary of this restoration. Floodplain marshes remove excess nutrients, cleansing water before it reaches the fragile

Everglades. Some of this water is collected by downstream municipalities and supplied to city residents for drinking water. Carbon is absorbed from the atmosphere and buried in the floodplain soils, mitigating some of the impacts from burning fossil fuels. The wild game is abundant, sport fishes have returned and a hiking trail rings the floodplain fringe, supporting a local recreation-based economy. There is ecotourism, too. Scientists come from all over the world to observe and learn about how ecological restoration benefits both the environment and humanity.

As I drove along Micco Bluff, the Kissimmee floodplain to my left, I noticed the signs of change. These were literally signs- signs posted on landowners' properties! They read "This Farm CARES." The CARES part of the sign originated from the Florida Farm Bureau's CARES program, which stands for County Alliance for Responsible Environmental Stewardship. The CARES program recognizes farmers and ranchers who voluntarily take action to protect the environment by adopting land stewardship practices that protect natural resources. The principles of the CARES program are a fundamental part of the new Everglades Headwaters National Wildlife Refuge and Conservation Area. Long at odds with each other, this new National Wildlife Refuge is build upon a partnership between private landowners (mostly ranchers and farmers), government entities (federal and state) and conservation organizations (The Nature Conservancy, National Wildlife Refuge Association). Recognizing a common interest and goal in protecting the Everglades ecosystem (which includes the Kissimmee River) and the area's agricultural heritage, the refuge seeks to preserve both the region's natural resources and the rural way of life experienced by generations of local landowners. If fully implemented, the Wildlife Refuge and Conservation Area will span approximately 150,000 acres with up to 100,000 acres protected through conservation easements purchased from willing sellers. Through this cooperative effort, both environmental and agricultural sustainability is possible. When I see these signs, I believe that the impaired Everglades ecosystem will survive.

I think back on the decimated great North American prairie ecosystem. Could it also be revived? Could a network of willing and caring landowners partner with government agencies and conservation groups to recreate some of what has been lost? I imagine a network of prairie corridors that interconnect parks and preserves and private ranch lands and sustainably managed farms, spanning from the Appalachian Mountains to the Rocky Mountains, from Mexico to Canada. It is not an unreasonable dream. Ground roots efforts have already created thousands of miles of recreational trail corridors that span these same regions using the same cooperative approach. It is time we consider a new system of continental wildlife corridors, not for human recreation but for environmental restoration. These restored lands would once again host the prairie chicken, majestic bison herds and the now-rare prairie plants. I imagine this restored ecosystem as a means to preserve our natural heritage, as well as the best of America's sustainable ranching and agricultural practices. These restored lands will also restore the environmental goods and services that were lost when the land was cleared. With the Kissimmee River Restoration Project and the Everglades Headwaters National Wildlife Refuge and Conservation Area as guides and inspiration, I believe it to be entirely possible.

But, there is more that needs to be done within our cities. It is unfair for urban residents, whose own properties are ecological deserts, to demand change only to rural land management practices. Missing from our urban communities is an organized and coordinated effort to grow food and create a more sustainable urban environment. Could our neighborhoods and municipalities adopt the CARES principles? If our communities took steps towards responsible land stewardship by taking action to protect the environment and protect natural resources, the effects would be far-reaching. One way would be to encouraging residents to plant landscape in ways that act as wildlife habitat, especially along existing easements and buffer zones along property lines. Communities could also create food-producing districts where urban agriculture would be encouraged on existing greenspace. Urban environmental and agricultural reserves of interconnected private and public greenspaces offer far more benefit than a few scattered backyard or community food gardens. These kinds of initiatives can offset the environmental degradation and loss of local agricultural land that occurred as a result of urbanization. Implementation of these environmental and food producing areas on private land can be through voluntary participation, cooperative agreements and through the purchasing of easements. Management of these areas can be through volunteers, community representatives or by private companies (some of which already tend to our landscaping and lawns).

Cultural change is a fundamental part of life and the whims of a generation or two should not become long-term guiding principles, social goals or immutable practices. Some of the people I talked with at community gardens had parents and grandparents who felt like the few New Yorkers I once knew at the fruit and vegetable stand I worked at when I first came to Florida. Those natives of the big-city Northeast ridiculed rural, food-growing people then. They considered home growing food to be something for those who lived in poverty, for those who had not been successful and something to be banished from their communities. Many of their children and grandchildren have embraced the food gardens their parents and grandparents disapproved of.

Eddie talks about his dream of living on a farm in the Iowa countryside and someday wants to milk a cow...when he gets over his fear of them. In our backyard food garden, he helps plant vegetables, which is something he has never done before. This season, he could not wait to harvest beets for pickling because they are among his favorite foods. Anyone who comes to the house must taste them, but he quickly hides the unopened jars from sight out of fear that, during a moment of generosity, I may offer a jar to the leaving guests (a tradition I acquired from my Aunt Elizabeth). This isn't mass-produced food, this is homegrown and handcrafted food; this is food

What Has Been Lost

with a heritage, with emotional investment and soul. Industrial agriculture cannot produce a product that can compete with it. People come to see our backyard gardens and Eddie still tells them that he hates vegetables. Fortunately, that is only partially true now. But, that is progress! One day, if we ever do get a farm, his grandchildren will come to visit and experience sustainable agriculture for the first time. They will see how their ancestors grew their own food for thousands of years. They too were born and raised in big cities with no connection to the land. Their visits to the farm will, no doubt, remain with them throughout their lives as warm memories that may inspire them to grow food for themselves one day.

When time permits, during trips back to my hometown, I look up my cousin who still owns the old homestead where my mother was born. He is an encyclopedia of knowledge, particularly about the land itself, its history and what is required to care for it so that it can be passed to his children and grandchildren in a viable state. Although he probably has not heard of the term "sustainable farming" until recently, it is how this land has been managed since it first came into the family. My first trip back to see that land after four decades was moving. I told my cousin about my memory of picking apples in the orchard out in a far meadow. He told me the trees were still there and offered to take me out to see them. The one-room cabin where my Uncle John, my namesake, lived in is still standing, but decaying. The windows and doors are gone. The meager belongings of my uncle lay strewn about with weeds growing up between them. The lot around the cabin is fenced off so that no cattle can graze it and no plow can disturb it. Remnant native prairie stubbornly clings to the land around the cabin, as it had when my uncle lived there. Those wild grasses and wildflowers are the descendants of the vast prairie that existed here before my grandfather tilled the soil. The fenced enclosure where my parents planted the family vegetable garden is still there, exactly as I remembered it as a child. No visible trace of my parent's vegetable garden remains...the prairie has reclaimed it too.

Unlike the bear, bison and Native Americans who lived on the land my grandfather settled, not all of the region's original inhabitants are gone. The children of the original prairie, the grasses and wildflowers and wildlife, persist in tiny remnants such as roadside swales and along railroad tracks. It has become my lifetime dream to purchase a plot of Iowa farmland and return it to its natural state, to return these orphaned species back to the soil of their ancestors. I envision that piece of land with restored prairie and savanna and woodlands, a complete ecosystem with bison. I envision this to be a place of learning about what was originally here, how it has changed and how the land can be used in the future to benefit both humans and wildlife. The Native American people have much knowledge to contribute to that effort for they are as much a part of this land's heritage as my grandfather was. Not a single human being will suffer hunger or malnutrition because of this restoration...including that of the landowner. By growing food in cities, this plot of land will no longer be needed to supply the food needs of an urban household thousands of miles away. If we moved most of our fruit and vegetable production into our cities, just how much of the great American prairie or other decimated ecosystems could be restored? That may well depend upon what we do in our own urban backyards.

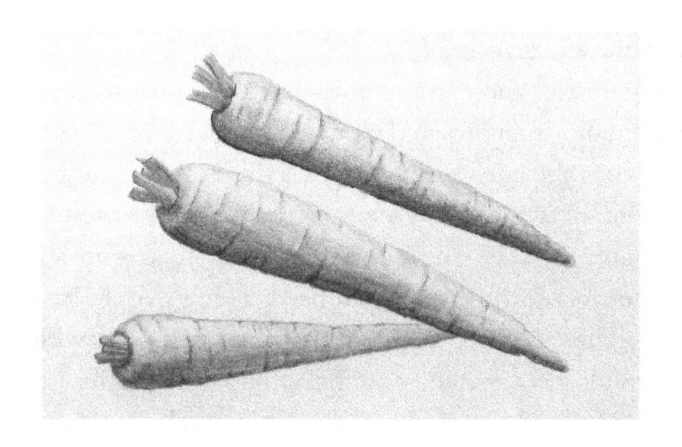

18. BACK ON THE FARM

*I*n late November 2011, the garden looked robust and held the promise of a large harvest. One evening, while enjoying a craft beer at a local hang-out, I became involved in a conversation with the owner of the establishment, a craft brewer herself, and a new friend who did food and wine pairing parties with her boyfriend, a wine connoisseur. I proposed the idea that we pool our crafts and do an event, a true garden-to-table event held in my backyard food gardens! We would start by giving participants a tour of the garden and a talk about urban food growing, then have them harvest some vegetables, which would then be passed onto our chef (my new friend) to prepare. We would serve them a four-course meal centered on organic fruits and vegetables from my garden along with finely crafted beer or wine. The guests would enjoy their meal while seated at elegantly apportioned tables in full view of the garden that was feeding them. The idea took wings, buoyed on the enthusiasm and love for our individual crafts.

Eddie came up with a name for the event- A Taste Of The Garden. The first one took place on a brilliant, cloudless and pleasantly cool (cool for Florida, anyway) January afternoon. Twenty-four guests and five hosts took a tour of the grounds, listened to a talk on how I was growing food and how much I was producing. The tour started in the front yard with a presentation about environmentally friendly and low-maintenance landscaping, then proceeded into the backyard utility area where I stored mulch and the compost bin. After a talk about composting, we then turned the corner around the shed and guests were presented with a panoramic view of the overflowing vegetable beds. Some people gasped. They were not prepared to see such expansive garden beds with so many different kinds of vegetables and fruiting trees. After touring the gardens, the guests harvested baskets of vegetables for their meal and were seated for a short question and answer session. Then, the food was served. First course was a very fresh garden salad, followed by a soup and main course. The meal was topped off with a handcrafted white chocolate port wine that was served with dessert- a black walnut brittle (wild black walnuts I had brought back from Iowa) and a scoop of homemade ice cream made with mangoes from my tree. It was intoxicating. As the guests departed, each was given a small pot of leaf lettuces to grow at home and to have a lasting connection with the time we spent together. As the final guests lingered in the garden, the sun began to drift toward the horizon. Orange clouds streaked through the deep blue sky overhead. I heard an unfamiliar chirping sound coming from above. Looking up, we saw a flock of two-dozen cedar waxwing birds roosting in the oak tree above our heads. How wonderful it was to have made so many people happy with the food produced by my hands and to have made so many traveling birds happy with my oak tree!

Following the success of the first event, we scheduled another one the next season in February 2013. It too was very successful. The interest in backyard food growing was intense and people wanted to know how they could get started growing food for themselves. I could sense a groundswell of interest beginning to rise!

The Taste of the Garden event's third year, 2014, went far beyond my ability to predict. The event was originally set for early February, but my schedule and that of the chef were upended and we had to move it to early March. In early February, I was sitting at home typing at my computer when my cell phone rang. The gentleman on the other end of the call introduced himself as a reporter from the Palm Beach Post and he wanted to do an article on my upcoming garden event for the Foods Section of the newspaper. He wanted to know if I would be available for an interview. Of course! We talked for perhaps twenty minutes and I told him about my research, my findings and the event. He was clearly interested and was patient with me as I tried to explain some of the science behind the importance of urban agriculture. After the call ended, I was pleased and thrilled. Wow, I was going to be in the local newspaper! But, how did he find out about the event? I was never sure.

The article was published on Wednesday, February 26th. At 6:30 a.m., my e-mail box started to fill with requests to come to the garden event, which was only four days away! At 8:15, my cell phone started ringing. By 9 am, we had sold out the event in spite of the fact that we had increased attendance from 20 to 30. By 11 am, I had a waiting list of people long enough to fill a second day. By the next day, I had filled a third day with a waiting list long enough to fill a fourth day. I also had calls to host special groups; one was approximately 15 people, another 40 and the largest with some 200 members. I spent three and a half days doing little more than fielding phone calls, answering e-mails and coordinating schedules to accommodate as many people as I could. Besides the food event, I also hosted classes and visits from others who just wanted to see the gardens. Between early January and late March, I had personally given tours of my backyard to more than 200 people. To say that there was public interest in home food gardening would be understating the obvious in the most extreme way.

For some guests, the visit to my backyard brought back memories of vegetable gardens they used to have and that they missed having. For others, visiting the garden was special because it brought back memories of loved ones who used to have big gardens, like a favorite relative or a grandparent they visited as a child. One woman brought photographs of past gardens that she was still very proud of and missed. Several visitors were drawn by the desire to have healthy food and to be reassured that it was safe. Some brought their children, who had never seen a food garden before or the plants that bore the food that they had been eating their entire lives. Others came to learn how to grow food and to free themselves from the unacceptable options provided by their grocery stores. Some came for the peace that gardens gave to them. There were as many reasons to see the garden as there were people who came, but all were motivated by a hunger to see it and to touch it in a personal way. To me, this food garden was both unremarkable and remarkable...unremarkable because so many people back home had gardens like this when I was growing up and remarkable for the fact that so many people seemed to have never seen anything like it.

Some months later, at 12:02 a.m., I heard my cell phone beep. I had just received a text message from Boz. It said that the fence was finally going up around his urban farm and he attached a picture to prove it! Progress!! The water was expected to be connected and ready for use any day. Soon, the empty lot will begin its transformation into a rich vegetable and fruit garden that will shrink the neighborhood's food desert and unravel its food insecurity. A commuter train is planned for the railroad tracks that pass along the east side of the urban farm's property. Once again, passenger trains will pass by residents tending rows of fruits and vegetables, recalling the era over a century ago when this story began.

When I was seven-years-old, I discovered what I thought was a vegetable mine in my backyard. What it turned out to be was a place where my mother had stored a cache of carrots from the summer's garden to feed to her family during the winter months. Some 45 years later, I discovered a vegetable mine in my own backyard, one that I would cultivate myself through the experiences and heritage from my ancestors.

Humanity is at a crossroad with respect to its food systems. What will the next generation of farmers, the children who inherit the family farms, do to play a role in the future of their own, their neighbor's and our world's food supply and natural environment? What will urban residents do to take control of their own food supply, by demanding the right to food growing space and support from their government? What will environmentalists do to draw the line for protection of the natural habitats, healthy ecosystems and natural resources upon which all life on earth depend? And, most importantly, how will these polarized groups set aside their differences and work together to solve the current food system's failures and avoid the impending global food crisis? We have all of the pieces of the puzzle that are needed to create sustainable food systems that encompass all of these issues, we just need to put them together. It isn't a matter of choice, it is a matter of survival.

AFTERWORD

As I was finishing the last paragraphs of this book, a news story broke about carbon dioxide levels in the earth's atmosphere surpassing 400 ppm for the first time since measurements began and perhaps for the first time in 800,000 years.[98] In addition, new record high temperatures are being set each year and there is every reason to believe this trend will continue. If we do not adopt sustainable food growing practices, we will ultimately face a collapsing commercial agricultural system that will leave entire regions of the world without food and the ability to grow it for themselves.

As cycles go, I am now an adjunct professor teaching at the school where I first began taking college classes in January 1980. The students today seem to be much more in tune with the world and are determined to make a difference. I am certain that the younger generations will rise to the challenge and create change, as my generation once did. I am also saddened when I describe to them the changes I have seen and what it used to be like before this city became part of a major metropolitan area. When I moved to Palm Beach County in 1979, there were almost 575,000 people living here. Today, that number is approaching 1.4 million. The pristine beaches that once had natural scrubby dunes and nesting shorebirds are now overbuilt with towering condominiums. The dark night skies have been replaced with an orange haze that makes it difficult to see all but the brightest stars. A constant rumble of traffic has replaced the quiet whisper of pines. There seems to be no end to the cityscape. I used to be able to drive to the edge of town in five minutes and today it takes forty. The extra time is not because I have moved to a different neighborhood (I haven't), it is because the city is so much larger. Most of the strawberry and vegetable fields just west of town have been converted to strip malls and high-density housing developments, which are now being built right up against the edge of the remaining Everglades. Almost all remaining natural lands are in parks and preserves, and some areas will be fully built-out in a few decades. Farm fields quickly fall to large-scale developments. I have come to miss what this place was like when I moved here 35 years ago; the nearly 1 million new residents don't know.

When I began this backyard research, I envisioned publishing these results as a series of articles in science journals. But, that would have also meant that the whole story couldn't be told, especially the human side of the story. Also, it would have relegated the results of this study to science journals that sat unread on university bookshelves and in electronic databases. I felt that average people, those who love to garden, would be better served by offering the entire story in the form of a book. I will offer all of my data and findings up for review.

On the lighter side, one of the more overlooked and underappreciated achievements of this backyard food garden study was my ability to measure something that has been considered to be unmeasurable. No, I am not referring to all of the facts and figures about money or energy or water. The something I am referring to does not appear anywhere in the main book; it is so special that I have saved it for last- for the Afterword…for this specific paragraph. This particular something is perhaps the thing I am most proud of and it is something that all of us understand to be impossible. But, I have demonstrated that the impossible is indeed possible, at least with respect to this something. We have all heard that you cannot compare apples to oranges. Well, I have proven that it can be done. Through my research, I have found that one New York State grown apple is equivalent to 19.8 Florida grown oranges. For apples grown in the West Coast of the United States, the number is much higher; there are 41.7 Florida oranges per Washington State apple. Of course, if you live in Washington State, the numbers for apples and oranges would be reversed because apples are grown locally in Washington State and oranges are not. The numbers given are calculated from the "ecological footprint" of local versus long-distance transported food.

Now that this book has been written, I realize that this is not the end of the story but the beginning. This story focused on sustainable *urban* agriculture, but another story must follow- a story about sustainable *rural* agriculture. That story will be about the how large agricultural landowners are changing the way they manage their lands and the resources on them. That story must talk about the conversion of unsustainable industrial agriculture into a sustainable system, one that is in harmony with the local ecology that it resides in. Because it can be practiced indefinitely without degrading or exhausting the resource upon which it depends, it offers financial sustainability to the landowners (and their children) who practice it. It is a story that is just beginning but no less exciting than the promise of sustainable urban agriculture.

ACKNOWLEDGMENTS

I am deeply appreciative for those who provided substantial review comments on draft versions of this book: John Paine (John Paine Editorial Services), Joel VanArman, Daphne Lambright (Biotechnical Support Services) and Eddie Ramos-Zahina. Others who provided comments and suggestions included Winnie Said and an anonymous reviewer.

All photographs and illustrations were by John Zahina-Ramos. Cover was by John Zahina-Ramos.

I am appreciative to those who opened up their gardens for me to see and who energized me through their passion for their craft. Thanks to those who took time to talk with me about their vegetable gardens, their lack of a vegetable garden and the food growing heritage in their families. Some of their stories can be found in the pages of this book. Because I assured confidentiality, these individuals' real names have been replaced with reasonable facsimiles.

FOOTNOTES

1. United Nations, Department of Economic and Social Affairs, Population Division (2014). *World Urbanization Prospects: The 2014 Revision, Highlights (ST/ESA/SER.A/352)*. New York, NY: United Nations. For more information, visit http://esa.un.org/unpd/wup/ (link active as of January 1, 2015).

Other interesting and concerning facts from this document are:
- In 1950, 30 percent of the world's population lived in urban areas; in 2014 that increased to 54 percent.
- In 2014, the most urbanized regions in the world were Northern America (82 percent of residents live in urban areas), Latin America and the Caribbean (80 percent) and Europe (73 percent).
- Population growth through 2050 is projected to add an additional 2.5 billion people to the world's population, mostly in Asia and Africa.
- About half of the world's population lives in cities of 500,000 or greater.
- As urbanization increases, sustainable development challenges will be increasingly focused on cities in lower-income countries.

2. Secretariat of the Convention on Biological Diversity (2012). *Cities and Biodiversity Outlook, Action and Policy.* Montreal, Quebec, Canada: SCBD. For more information, visit http://www.cbd.int/doc/publications/cbo-booklet-2012-en.pdf (link active as of January 1, 2015).

Some interesting facts from this document are:
- Our planet is undergoing the largest and fastest period of urban expansion in its history.
- The area of land that will be impacted by urbanization over the next four decades is predicted to be approximately the size of the continent of Africa.
- Urban growth will have a significant and profound impact on

biodiversity, natural habitats and the ecosystem services that humanity relies on.
- Urban expansion over the next decades will come at the expense of natural resources and consume prime agricultural land with impacts to biodiversity.
- Rapid urban expansion is occurring or will occur in areas that are hotspots of biological diversity and have limited ability to protect the resource.
- Urbanized areas across the planet are already experiencing shortages in natural resources (including water) and environmental degradation.

3. Peterson, A. (2000). Alternatives, Traditions, and Diversity in Agriculture. *Agriculture and Human values, 17*(1), 95-106.

This work summarized and reviewed several recent books on the topic of agriculture, including some that examined the linkages between cultural and biological diversity in traditional agriculture. The article also discusses "alternative agricultural practices," many of which had been part of normal agricultural practices in other cultures at other times in history.

4. Marsden, T., J. Murdoch, P. Lowe, R. Munton & A. Flynn (1993). *Constructing the Countryside*. London, England: University College London Press.

5. Roberts, C.E. (1992). *Textural Analysis of Urban Thematic Mapper Data*. Doctoral dissertation, Pennsylvania State University.

This dissertation research is an interesting read about the development of agriculture in the Lower Midwest and Southwest regions of the United States.

6. Ilbery, B., Q. Chiotti & T. Rickard (1997). *Agricultural Restructuring and Sustainability: A Geographical Perspective*. Egham, England: Centre for Agricultural Bioscience International.

7. Lyson, T.A. & A. Guptill (2004). Commodity Agriculture, Civic Agriculture and the Future of U.S. Farming. *Rural Sociology, 69*(3),

370-385.

This science journal article describes the two very different types of agriculture found in the United States: commodity (commercial) agriculture and civic agriculture. I describe civic agriculture later in this book. This article aptly describes how commodity agriculture is focused on producing as much as possible (to maximize profit) and how civic agriculture includes a more robust range of considerations.

8. Pimentel, D., P. Hepperly, J. Hanson, D. Douds & R. Seidel (2005). Environmental, Energetic, and Economic Comparisons of Organic and Conventional Farming Systems. *BioScience, 55*(7), 573-582.

This study is part of the Rodale Institute's landmark Farming Systems Trial research, which examines sustainable agricultural methods. The research compares agricultural productivity and important environmental parameters (soil carbon, soil moisture holding capacity, soil fertility, etc.) resulting from sustainable and industrial farming methods. This impressive body of work will, no doubt, be the basis of future large-scale sustainable agricultural systems. Visit http://rodaleinstitute.org/our-work/farming-systems-trial/farming-systems-trial-publications/ (link active as of January 1, 2015).

9. Smil, V. (2011). Nitrogen Cycle and World Food Production. *World Agriculture 2*, 9-13.

This article describes the role of synthetic nitrogen in commercial agricultural production throughout the 20th century, as well as the problems that have arisen from its use.

10. Information from the United Nations website at http://www.un.int/nauru/countryprofile.html (link active as of January 1, 2015).

11. There are several very good studies that have examined the negative impacts of industrial agriculture. Some of these are:

Hepperly, P., D. Douds & R. Seidel (2006). *The Rodale Institute Farming Systems Trial 1981 to 2005: Long Term Analysis of Organic and Conventional Maize and Soybean Cropping Systems.* Long-term Field

Experiments in Organic Farming. Verlag Dr. Köster, Berlin.

Pimentel, D., P. Hepperly, J. Hanson, D. Douds & R. Seidel (2005). Environmental, Energetic, and Economic Comparisons of Organic and Conventional Farming Systems. *BioScience 55* (7), 573-582.

Reganold, J.P., L.F. Elliott & Y.L. Unger (1987). Long-Term Effects of Conventional and Organic Farming on Soil Erosion. *Nature 330*(6146), 370-372. More information can be found at http://naldc.nal.usda.gov/catalog/19192 (link active as of January 1, 2015).

12. Bengtsson, J., J. Ahnström & A.-C. Weibull (2005). The Effects of Organic Agriculture on Biodiversity and Abundance: A Meta-Analysis. *Journal of Applied Ecology 42*(2), 261–269.

This interesting study reviews of all of the previously-published research (before December 2002, the time when this study was initiated) into the effects of organic farming on the number of species and the abundance of species in agricultural landscapes. The main problem facing commercial agriculture is whether food can be produced while preserving biodiversity. In this study, the question was whether organic agriculture was associated with a greater number of organisms (insects, birds, wildlife, etc.) than conventional (industrial) agriculture. The positive thing about studies like this (meta-analysis) is that one can understand the overall benefit in spite of variability, which can bias the results of a single study.

13. Windham, J.S. (2007). Putting Your Money Where Your Mouth Is: Perverse Food Subsidies, Social Responsibility and America's 2007 Farm Bill. *Environs: Environmental Law and Policy Journal, 31*, 1.

Hoffpauir, J. (2009). Environmental Impact of Commodity Subsidies: NEPA and the Farm Bill. *The Fordham Environmental Law Review, 20*, 233.

14. There are several sources for this information, a couple of which I have listed below:

National Oceanic and Atmospheric Administration (2009). *Dead Zone: Hypoxia in the Gulf of Mexico* (PDF). Fact sheet from the NOAA website can be viewed at http://www.noaa.gov/factsheets/

new%20version/dead_zones.pdf (link active as of January 1, 2015).

From the United States Geological Survey- http://www.usgs.gov/blogs/features/usgs_top_story/dead-zone-the-source-of-the-gulf-of-mexicos-hypoxia/ (link active as of January 1, 2015).

From the Louisiana Universities Marine Consortium; document may be viewed at http://gulfhypoxia.net (link active as of January 1, 2015).

15. Peters, K.A. (2010). Creating a Sustainable Urban Agriculture Revolution. *Journal of Environmental Law and Litigation, 25,* 203.

16. Pothukuchi, K. (2004). Community Food Assessment: A First Step in Planning for Community Food Security. *Journal of Planning Education and Research, 23,* 356-377.

17. Hanson, E.I. (2007). *Memory and Vision: Arts, Cultures, and Lives of Plains Indian People.* Cody, WY: Buffalo Bill Historical Center.

18. Foran, M. (1982). *Calgary, Canada's Frontier Metropolis: An Illustrated History.* Chatsworth, CA:Windsor Publications.

19. Cushman, R.C. & S.R. Jones (2004). *The North American Prairie.* Peterson Field Guide. Boston, MA: Houghton Mifflin Harcourt. I refer to their ideas along with some of my own throughout this paragraph.

20. There are many books written about the Dust Bowl days; the below reference is only one of several that can be recommended.

Hakim, J. (1995). *A History of Us: War, Peace and All That Jazz.* New York: Oxford University Press.

21. Below are some of the landmark studies that defined sustainability and the concepts of sustainable cities.

Rees, W.E. (1992). Ecological Footprints and Appropriated Carrying Capacity: What Urban Economics Leaves Out. *Environment and Urbanization, 4*(2), 121-130.

Rees, W.E. & M. Wackernagel (1996). Urban Ecological

Footprints: Why Cities Cannot Be Sustainable- and Why They Are a Key To Sustainability. *Environmental Impact Assessment Review, 16*, 223-248.

Costanza, R., R. d'Arge, R. De Groot, S. Farber, M. Grasso, B. Hannon, K. Limburg, S. Naeem, R.V. O'Neill, J. Paruelo, R.G. Raskin, P. Sutton & M. Van Den Belt (1997). The Value of the World's Ecosystem Services and Natural Capital. *Nature, 387*(6630), 253-260.

22. Below are a couple of books on the topic of sustainable development and agriculture, drawing from different cultures and regions of the world. I refer to their ideas along with some of my own throughout this paragraph.

Orr, D.W. (2002). *The Nature of Design; Ecology, Culture and Human Intention.* New York, NY: Oxford University Press.

Edwards, A.R. & B. McKibbin (2010). *Thriving Beyond Sustainability; Pathways to a Resilient Society.* Gabriola Island, BC, Canada: New Society Publishers.

23. Many authors over the past several decades have defined urban sprawl in different ways, but all tend to support the idea that it has different characteristics than the original urban core. Below are a several examples of journal articles that have defined the characteristics of urban sprawl and ex-urban development (development outside of the urban area). I refer to their ideas along with some of my own throughout this paragraph.

Mills, D.E. (1981). Growth Speculation and Sprawl in a Monocentric City. *Journal of Urban Economics, 10*, 210-226.

Peiser, R.B. (1989). Density and Urban Sprawl. *Land Economics, 65*(3), 193-204.

Heimlich, R. & W. Anderson (2001). Development At and Beyond the Urban Fringe: Impacts on Agriculture. *Agricultural Outlook*, 15-18.

24. Berke, P.R., J. MacDonald, N. White, M. Holmes, D. Line, K. Oury & R. Ryznar (2003). Greening Development to Protect Watersheds: Does New Urbanism Make a Difference? *Journal of the American Planning Association, 69*(4), 397-413.

25. Downs, A. (2005). Smart Growth; Why We Discuss It More Than We Do It. *Journal of the American Planning Association 71*(4), 367-380.

26. Martin, R. & T. Marsden (1999). Food for Urban Spaces: The Development of Urban Food Production in England and Wales. *International Planning Studies, 4*(3), 389-411.

27. The following studies describe Cuba's agriculture; I refer to ideas from these studies throughout this paragraph.
 Warwick, H. (1999). Cuba's Organic Revolution. *Ecologist, 29*(8), 457-460.
 Altieri, M.A, N.C. Companioni, K. Canizares, C. Murphy, P. Rosset, M. Bourque & C.I. Nicholls (1999). The Greening of the "Barrios": Urban Agriculture for Food Security in Cuba. *Agriculture and Human Values, 16*, 131-140.
 Bahnson, F. (2010). Organic by Necessity: Agriculture in Havana. *The Christian Century, 127*(18), 11-12.

28. Ghosh, S. (2010). Sustainability Potential of Suburban Gardens: Review and New Directions. *Australasian Journal of Environmental Management, 17*(3), 165-175.

29. Okvat, H.A. & A.J. Zautra (2011). Community Gardening: A Parsimonious Path to Individual, Community and Environmental Resilience. *American Journal of Community Psychology, 47,* 374-387.

30. Carter, M.R. (1984). Identification of the Inverse Relationship Between Farm Size and Productivity: An Empirical Analysis of Peasant Agricultural Production. *Oxford Economic Papers, New Series, 36*(1), 131-145.

31. The following studies discuss the productivity of small-scale and large-scale farms. Also refer to references in footnote #44.
 Barrett, C.B. (1993). *On Price Risk and the Inverse Farm Size-Productivity Relationship*. University of Wisconsin-Madison Department of Agricultural Economics Staff Paper Series, No. 369, December

1993.

Assunção, J.J. & M. Ghatak (2003). Can Observed Heterogeneity in Farmer Ability Explain the Inverse Relationship Between Farm Size and Productivity. *Economic Letters, 80*, 189-194.

32. Refer to references in footnotes #42 and #45 (Assunção & Ghatak, 2003).

33. Gordon, P. & H.W. Richardson (1997). Are Compact Cities a Desirable Planning Goal? *Journal of the American Planning Association, 63*, 95-106.

34. Aubrey, C., J. Ramamonjisoa, M.-H. Dabat, J. Rakotoarisoa, J. Rakotondraibe & L. Rabeharisoa (2012). Urban Agriculture and Land Use in Cities: An Approach with the Multi-Functionality and Sustainability Concepts in the Case of Antananarivo (Madagascar). *Land Use Policy, 29*, 429-439.

35. Old World Wisconsin website at http://oldworldwisconsin.wisconsinhistory.org (link active as of January 1, 2015).

36. Byers, K. (2009). *The Psycho-Social Benefits of Backyard and Community Gardening Among Immigrants*. Masters thesis, University of Georgia.

37. Fivush, R., J.G. Bohanek & M. Duke (2005). *The Intergenerational Self: Subjective Perspective and Family History. Individual and collective self-continuity*. Mahwah, NJ: Erlbaum.

38. Along with the study cited in footnote # 29 (Byers, 2009), the following studies also recorded some of the ways that gardens are important to people:

Wilhelm, G. (1975). Dooryard Gardens and Gardening in the Black Community of Brushy, Texas. *Geographical Review, 65*(1), 73-92.

Møller, V. (2005). Attitudes to Food Gardening from a Generational Perspective. *Journal of Integrated Relationships, 3*(2), 63-80.

39. Lyson, T.A. (2004). *Civic Agriculture: Reconnecting Farm, Food, and Community.* Lebanon, NH: University Press of New England.

40. Refer to the Wikipedia article on Victory Gardens for a summary of the effort at http://en.wikipedia.org/wiki/Victory_garden (link active as of January 1, 2015).

41. Bissett, T.L. (1976). Community Gardening in America. *Brooklyn Botanical Garden Record, 35*, 4.

42. Two noteworthy studies on this topic are:
 Garnett, T. (1996). Harvesting the Cities. *Town and Country Planning, 65*(10), 264-266.
 Martin, R. & T. Marsden (1999). Food for Urban Spaces: The Development of Urban Food Production in England and Wales. *International Planning Studies, 4*(3), 389-411.

43. Broadway, M. (2009). Growing Urban Agriculture in North American Cities: The Example of Milwaukee. *Focus on Geography, 52*(3-4), 23-30. I refer to ideas from this study throughout this paragraph.

44. Corrigan, M.P. (2011). Growing What You Eat: Developing Community Gardens in Baltimore, Maryland. *Applied Geography, 31*, 1232-1241. I refer to ideas from this study throughout this paragraph.

45. Lu, H., et al. (2009). Earliest Domestication of Common Millet (Panicum miliaceum) in East Asia Extended to 10,000 Years Ago. *Proceedings of the National Academy of Sciences of the United States of America 106*(18): 7367–72.

46. Palm Beach Post (2011). *Rain in Forecast, but Area to Stay Thirsty.* Article published March 27, 2011.

47. Refer to the following webpages for data from the U.S. Census Bureau and the U.S. Environmental Protection Agency:

http://www.census.gov/compendia/statab/cats/population.html and http://www.epa.gov/osw/nonhaz/municipal/index.htm_(links active as of January 1, 2015).

48. Environmental Protection Agency webpage entitled *Overview of Greenhouse Gasses*; document can be viewed at http://www.epa.gov/climatechange/ghgemissions/gases/ch4.html (link active as of January 1, 2015).

49. Aphale, P., M. Balot, L. Dupont, R. Gaylord-Miles, L. Grier, T. Huffman, E. Kosmala & K. Schwab (2014). *Expanding the Organic Waste Recovery Program in Orange County: A Feasibility Study*. University of North Carolina Institute for the Environment report. Document can be viewed at http://www.ie.unc.edu/for_students/courses/capstone/14/organics_final_report.pdf (link active as of January 1, 2015).

50. New York City Department of Sanitation webpage entitled *About NYC Organics Collection*; document can be viewed at http://www.nyc.gov/html/nycwasteless/html/compost/collections_ocp.shtml (link active as of January 1, 2015).

51. Massachusetts Department of Environmental Protection's webpage describing their commercial organics waste ban; document can be viewed at http://www.recyclingworksma.com/commercial-organics-waste-ban/ (link active as of January 1, 2015).

52. United Stated Department of Agriculture's 2007 Agricultural Census, Data from Palm Beach County. Refer to Vol. 1, Chapter 2: County Level Data, Table 30. Document may be viewed at http://agcensus.usda.gov/Publications/2007/Full_Report/Volume_1,_Chapter_2_County_Level/Florida/_(link active as of January 1, 2015).

Summary of Florida vegetable production data and values can be found at: http://www.freshfromflorida.com/Divisions-Offices/Marketing-and-Development/Education/For-Researchers/Florida-Agriculture-Overview-and-Statistics (link active as of January 1,

2015).

53. Smit, J. & J. Nasr (1992). Urban Agriculture for Sustainable Cities: Using Wastes and Idle Land and Water Bodies as Resources. *Environment and Urbanization,* 4(2), 141-152.

54. U.S. Department of Energy webpage entitled *Frequently Asked Questions: How Much Electricity Does an American Home Use?* Document can be viewed at http://www.eia.gov/tools/faqs/faq.cfm ?id=97&t=3 (link active as of January 1, 2015).

55. Shaw, S.P. & C.G. Fredine (1956). *Wetlands of the United States, Their Extent and Their Value for Waterfowl and Other Wildlife.* U.S. Fish and Wildlife Service Circular No. 39. Document can be viewed at http://www.npwrc.usgs.gov/resource/wetlands/uswetlan/ (link active as of January 1, 2015).

56. Dahl, T.E. (1990). *Wetlands Loss Since the Revolution.* U.S. Fish and Wildlife Service, National Wetlands Inventory, St. Petersburg, Florida. Document may be viewed at http://www.fws.gov/wetlands/Documents/Wetlands-Loss-Since-the-Revolution.pdf (link active as of January 1, 2015). Information from this source provided throughout the paragraph.

57. Florida Department of Environmental Protection (undated document). *Florida State of the Environment- Wetlands: A Guide to Living With Florida's Wetlands.* Document may be viewed at http://www.dep.state.fl.us/water/wetlands/docs/erp/fsewet.pdf (link active as of January 1, 2015). Information from this source provided throughout the paragraph.

58. South Florida Water Management District (2010). *2010 Lower East Coast Regional Water Supply Plan.* South Florida Water Management District, West Palm Beach, Florida. Document may be viewed at http://www.sfwmd.gov (link active as of January 1, 2015). Information from this source provided throughout the paragraph.

59. Below are two interesting pieces of research dedicated to quantifying the extent of lawns in the United States and how much water two neighborhoods in south Florida used for irrigation.

Lindsey, R. (2005). *Looking for Lawns.* NASA Earth Observatory article. Document may be viewed at http://earthobservatory.nasa.gov/Features/Lawn/ (link active as of January 1, 2015).

Survis, F.D. and T.L. Root (2012). Evaluating the Effectiveness of Water Restrictions: A Case Study From Southeast Florida. *Journal of Environmental Management*, 112:377-383.

Survis, F.D. (2010). Residential Lawn Water Use and Lawn Irrigation Practices. Masters Thesis, Florida Atlantic University.

60. For data on the extent of certain types of agricultural crops in the United States, refer to the United States Department of Agriculture's agricultural survey data at http://agcensus.usda.gov/Publications/2012/Full_Report/Volume_1,_Chapter_1_US/st99_1_038_038.pdf (link active as of January 1, 2015).

There is also data related to the cattle industry; please refer to USDA (2014). 2012 Census of agriculture. United States summary and state data. Vol. 1. Geographic area series. Part 51. AC-12-A-51. 695 pp.

61. For a comprehensive discussion about water use in California and links to reliable sources of data, refer to the Wikipedia article entitled *Water in California.* The article can be viewed at http://en.wikipedia.org/wiki/Water_in_California (link active as of January 1, 2015).

62. Crotta, C. (2014). *Drawing a Line on the Lawn Amid Water Conservation and Drought.* Los Angeles Times article published on April 18, 2014 in the L.A. at Home section. The article can be viewed at http://www.latimes.com/home/la-hm-lawns-20140419-story.html#page=1 (link active as of January 1, 2015). Information from this source provided throughout the paragraph.

63. For a comprehensive discussion about the Ogallala Aquifer and links to reliable sources of data, refer to the Wikipedia article entitled

Ogallala Aquifer. The article can be viewed at http://en.wikipedia.org/wiki/Ogallala_Aquifer (link active as of January 1, 2015).

64. *Swimming Pool Tips*, Marin (California) Municipal Water District website. The information can be viewed at http://www.marinwater.org/159/Swimming-Pool-Tips (link active as of January 1, 2015).

65. Senauer, B., E. Asp & J. Kinsey (1991). *The food industry: An overview and implications of consumer trends, in food trends and the changing consumer*. St. Paul, MN: Eagan Press.

66. Zahina-Ramos, J. (2013). *Attitudes and Perspectives About Backyard Food Gardening: A Case Study in South Florida*. Doctoral dissertation, Florida Atlantic University. Document can be viewed at http://www.fau.edu/library/ (link active as of January 1, 2015).

67. Many of the concepts in this and the following paragraph are from- Sonntag, V. (2008). *Why Local Linkages Matter; Findings from the Local Food Economy Study*. Seattle, WA: Sustainable Seattle.

68. There are several studies that address the issues of fresh food availability, price and location of markets. The following are good examples:
Koh, E.T. & V. Caples (1979). Frequency of Selection of Food Groups by Low-Income Families in Southwestern Mississippi. *Journal of the American Dietetic Association, 74*(6), 660-664.
Lang, T. & G. Rayner (2002). Why Health is the Key to the Future of Food and Farming. *Issues, 202*, 222. Document can be viewed at http://www.ohpe.ca/node/2956 (link active as of January 1, 2015).
Hendrickson, D., C. Smith & N. Eikenberry (2006). Fruit and Vegetable Access in Four Low-Income Food Deserts Communities in Minnesota. *Agriculture and Human Values, 23*, 371-383.

69. Anderson, S.A. (1990). Core Indicators of Nutritional State for Difficult-to-Sample Populations. *The Journal of Nutrition*, 120.

70. Below are several good studies on food insecurity:

Rose, D. (1999). Economic Determinants and Dietary Consequences of Food Insecurity in the United States. *The Journal of Nutrition, 129*(2), 517S-520S.

Nord, M. & C.P. Brent (2002). *Food Insecurity in Higher Income Households.* Washington, D.C.: United States Department of Agriculture.

Eikenberry, N. & C. Smith (2005). Attitudes, Beliefs, and Prevalence of Dumpster Diving as a Means to Obtain Food by Midwestern, Low-Income, Urban Dwellers. *Agriculture and Human Values, 22*(2), 187-202.

71. The follow studies has shown linkages between health problems and inadequate access to healthy food:

Resnicow, K., T. Wang, W.N. Dudley, A. Jackson, J.A.S. Ahluwalia, T. Baranowski & R.L. Braithwaite (2001). Risk Factor Distribution Among Sociodemographically Diverse African American Adults. *Journal of Urban Health, 78*(1), 125-140.

Many studies have been conducted on the relationship between health problems and inadequate access to fresh and nutritious food. Some of these include references in footnote #27 and others have been listed below:

McCormack, L.A., M.N. Laska, N.I. Larson & M. Story (2010). Review of the Nutritional Implications of Farmer's Markets and Community Gardens: A Call for Evaluation and Research Efforts. *Journal of the American Dietetic Association, 110*, 399-408.

Corrigan, M.P. (2011). Growing What You Eat: Developing Community Gardens in Baltimore, Maryland. *Applied Geography, 31*, 1232-1241.

72. Rather that make you wait for another time, I decided to tell the bee story here…

One August morning, I was picking up dead palm tree fronds that had fallen to the ground during a heavy wind. I have a palm tree next to my backyard shed (where I store my gardening equipment) and as I passed it, I noticed a dead frond beginning to slip from the tree. As I approached the palm tree, being only about six feet from it, my eye travelled from the base of the dead frond towards its other end, which seemed to be lodged in something near the upper part of the shed. I reached out my hand to grab the dead frond to yank it from the tree. As my eye reached the upper end of the frond, I froze in fear and then stepped back in shock. At the tip of the dead palm frond was the largest bees nest I have ever seen.

My mind raced with questions, the first being "how long had that been there", the second being "how could I have missed seeing it before" and the third being "how many times have I walked passed this buzzing hive of thousands of bees and risked my life?" It wasn't the idea of a bee hive that most concerned me, it was the fact that we had Africanized bees here, a hybrid between our native bees and an overly aggressive invasive species that has the potential to attack and kill a human with hundreds of bee stings.

I backed off from the shed and went into the house to let my nerves recover. After I regained my composure, I searched the Yellow Pages for a bee removal expert to take them away. I found someone who was local, used a no-kill approach and did not use pesticides. I called and a man answered the phone with a pleasant Russian accent. We chatted briefly about the bees and he asked me to tell him how large the hive was. I told him I thought it was about 1 ft. by 1 ft., but in my panic I wasn't exactly sure. He quoted me a price of $250. I agreed and he took my address. After I got off the phone, I went to the back window of the house for another look…hmmmm, the hive was more than twice that size! Not wanting to surprise the man, I called him back and, to avoid language confusion, I slowly told him I had made a mistake and the hive was actually more than 2 ft. by 2 ft. in size. He let out several curse words in surprise and said that this was a different matter altogether. The price, understandably, went up by $100. I agreed to the price again and two hours later, he was in my driveway preparing a smoking can and utensils to remove the hive.

He was a man of gentle demeanor with a deep respect for the bees. His respect was not grounded in fear, but in admiration. To him, they were wondrous creatures. He did not want to kill them, but take them away where they could continue to do their work in a safer place. He approached the shed, climbed a ladder and examined the hive. After wafting clouds of smoke over the bees to calm them, he began to work. He took a metal scraper and slowly dislodged parts of the hive from the shed wall, removing plate after plate of comb and examining them for honey. He did all of this without protective gloves or netting. This surprised me. Since childhood, I had always been taught to fear bees, even the lone bee that works to collect nectar from a garden flower. I wasn't allergic to bees (fear of bees by those who are allergic to their stings is understandable), so there was no rational reason for me to be so frightened of them.

The bee man scooped empty wax comb and bees into a container. A few parts of the comb contained honey, which I took and placed in a dish. The whole process surprised me because it challenged misconceptions I had held all of my life. I picked up a piece of the empty comb and looked at it carefully. It was beautiful in its simplicity and was eloquently constructed. I was captivated. The comb was fragile, being made only of beeswax, a very high quality natural product that is prized by humans. I picked up a piece of comb that contained honey and looked at it too. It was no less wondrous. The craftsmanship was beyond that of human hands. As the bee man came to the center of the hive, he paused to put on protective gear as a precaution. I left him to finish his work and wandered off to my garden to weed the beds.

As I worked in the garden some 30 ft. away, around a corner of the shed, six bees shot from the hive and rushed towards me. They had a hysterical buzzing that made it clear that they were going to attack and I knew the bee man was not their target. They went straight for me and landed on my hat. I slapped them frantically with my gloved hand to kill them, but they persisted. I was able to kill several of them, but several escaped. I returned to my work. A few minutes later, three bees returned and went for my face. I was able to kill one of them, but the other two stung me on my cheeks before I could kill them. These few bees had escaped the tranquilizing smoke poured over the hive by the bee man and they realized that their home was under attack. They seemed to be under orders to strike until dead. I went into the house and watched from behind the safety of glass panes.

After the bee man finished his work, we sat at my dining room table and talked about his life in the Soviet Union, before he came to the United States. He had a fascinating story to tell! Time passed quickly and, although we both felt like we could talk for hours, it was time for each of us to move on with our day. As the bee man pulled out of the driveway, I went to the tray of honeycomb and pushed it into a pint mason jar. At $350, this was the most expensive honey I have ever had. I pinched off a corner of the dark comb and put it in my mouth, licking the honey from my fingers. As I chewed the honeycomb, the flavor was robust and deep, richer than any I ever had before. This was my first homegrown honey, made from the flowers in my garden and my neighbors' gardens. That made me feel proud! It was nourishing. It was sweet, but not in the same way that the empty calories of a candy bar are sweet. There were also honeycomb cells that contained bee pollen, which is nutritious and can be rich in protein. Those too were a delicious and rare treat. I began to treasure this jar of honeycomb.

When I talked with other beekeepers about my experience, they all told me that it was a rare occurrence. It is unusual for bees to take up residence and create such a large hive on a residential property, but it does happen. For whatever reason, I didn't notice his hive for many months and it could have been dealt with quickly had I found it sooner. Seeing the fierce determination of the attacking bees and realizing the hive's collective power was a frightening and humbling experience. The feeling I now have for bees is like that I have for thunderstorms. Thunderstorms are beautiful and awe inspiring. I watch them in wonder. They are also dangerous and deadly when you do not respect them. That is how nature is. Bees, thunderstorms and nature don't exist for our entertainment nor do they exist for our servitude. They exist for themselves, as we do. If we respect bees and thunderstorm and nature, we can enjoy the things that they can bring into our lives- things like rainfall to grow our food plants, bees to pollination our flowers and honey to eat.

73. Besides the studies listed in footnote #72, also refer to:

Steptoe, A., T.M. Pollard & J. Wardle (1995). Development of a Measure of the Motives Underlying the Selection of Food: The Food Choice Questionnaire. *Appetite, 25,* 267-284.

Worsley, T., K. Baghurst & G. Skrzypiec (1995). *Meat Consumption and Young People. Final Report to the Meat Research Corporation.* Adelaide, SA, Australia: CSIRO Division of Human Nutrition.

Nijmeijer, M., W. Worsley & B. Astill (2004). An Exploration of the Relationships Between Food Lifestyle and Vegetable Consumption. *British Food Journal, 106*(7), 520-533.

74. Alaimo, K., E. Packnett, R.A. Miles & D.J. Kruger (2008). Fruit and Vegetable Intake Among Urban Community Gardeners. *Journal of Nutrition Education and Behavior, 40*(2), 94-101.

75. A number of studies of school vegetable gardens and the attitudes of school students towards fruits and vegetables have been conducted. Below are some good examples:

Lautenschlager, L. & C. Smith (2006). Beliefs, Knowledge and Values Held by Inner-City Youth About Gardening, Nutrition and Cooking. *Agriculture and Human Values, 24*, 245-258.

Linebergert, S.E. & J.M. Zajicek (2000). School Gardens: Can a Hands-on Teaching Tool Affect Students' Attitudes and Behaviors Regarding Fruit and Vegetables? *HortTechnology, 10*(3), 593-597.

Skelly, S.M. & J.C. Bradley (2000). The Importance of School Gardens as Perceived by Florida Elementary School Teachers. *HortTechnology, 10*(1), 229-231.

Koch, S., T.M. Waliczek & J.M. Zajicek (2006). The Effect of a Summer Garden Program on the Nutritional Knowledge, Attitudes, and Behaviors of Children. *HortTechnology, 16*(4), 620-625.

McAleese, J.D. & L.L. Rankin (2007). Garden-Based Nutrition Education Affects Fruit and Vegetable Consumption in Sixth-Grade Adolescents. *Journal of the American Dietetic Association, 107*(4), 622-665.

Blair, D. (2009). The Child in the Garden: An Evaluative Review of the Benefits of School Garden. *Journal of Environmental Education, 40*(2), 15-38.

Beecha, B.M., R. Ricea, L. Myers, C. Johnson & T.A. Nicklasa (1999). Knowledge, Attitudes, and Practices Related to Fruit and Vegetable Consumption of High School Students. *Journal of Adolescent Health, 24*(4), 244–250.

76. American Farmland Trust press release, July 7, 2010. Text can be accessed at http://farmland.org/news/pressreleases/13-Million-More-Acres.asp (link active as of January 1, 2015).

77. For information about the costs of the Supplemental Nutrition Assistance Program, visit their website at http://www.fns.usda.gov/snap/supplemental-nutrition-assistance-program-snap   http://www.fns.usda.gov/pd/SNAPsummary.htm

(links active as of January 1, 2015).

78. Sustainablog web information page, *Recycling by the Numbers: The Good, Bad and Ugly of Statistics and Comparisons.* Webpage can be accessed at http://sustainablog.org/2008/08/recycling-by-the-numbers-the-good-bad-and-ugly-of-statistics-and-comparisons/ (link active as of January 1, 2015).

79. Results from a Harris Interactive® national survey on consumer spending on lawncare services. Results and contact information can be accessed at https://www.loveyourlandscape.com/LYL/Research_Page_-_Harris_Documents/National-Survey-on-Consumer-Spending-on-Landscape-Services.aspx (link active as of January 1, 2015).

80. Kiesling, F.M. & C.M. Manning (2010). How Green is Your Thumb? Environmental Gardening Identity and Ecological Gardening Practices. *Journal of Environmental Psychology, 30,* 315-327.

81. Lewis, P. (1993). The Making of Vernacular Taste: The Case of Sunset and Southern Living. In J. D. Hunt & J. Wolschke-Bulmahn (Eds.), *The Vernacular Garden.* Washington, DC: Dumbarton Oaks.

82. Many studies have been conducted that recorded the importance and meaning of gardens to gardeners; below are a few examples:
Francis, M. & R.T. Hester, Jr. (1990). *The Meaning of Gardens.* Cambridge, MA: The Massachusetts Institute of Technology Press.
Kimber, C. (2004). Gardens and Dwelling: People in Vernacular Gardens. *Geographical Review, 94*(3), 263-283.
Sinclair, D. (2005). *The Spirituality of Gardening.* Kelowna, BC, Canada: Northstone Publishers.

83. Below are two good studies on the value of open space to people:
Rubinstein, N.J. (1997). The Psychological Value of Open Space. In L. W. Hamilton (Ed.), *The Benefits of Open Space* (Chapter 4). Morristown, NJ: The Great Swamp Watershed Association.

McConnel, V. & M. Walls (2005). *The Value of Open Space: Evidence from Studies of Nonmarket Benefits*. Washington D.C.: Resources for the Future.

84. There have been a number of studies on the importance of greenspace to people's well-being. Some of these are:
De Vries, S., R.A. Verheij, P.P. Groenewegen & P. Spreeuwenberg (2003). Natural Environments-Healthy Environments? An Exploratory Analysis of the Relationship Between Greenspace and Health. *Environment and planning A, 35*(10), 1717-1732.
Nielsen, T.S. & K.B. Hansen (2007). Do Green Areas Affect Health? Results from a Danish Survey on the Use of Green Areas and Health Indicators. *Health & Place, 13*(4), 839-850.
Ryan, R.M., N. Weinstein, J. Bernstein, K.W. Brown, L. Mistretta & M. Gagne (2010). Vitalizing Effects of Being Outdoors and in Nature. *Journal of Environmental Psychology, 30*(2), 159-168.
Freeman, C., K.J.M. Dickinson, S. Porter & Y. van Heezik (2012). "My Garden is an Expression of Me": Exploring Householder's Relationships With Their Gardens. *Journal of Environmental Psychology, 32*, 135-143.

85. Several studies have examined the linkage between gardens and plants with psychological well-being. Some of these are:
Unruh, A.M., N. Smith & C. Scammell (2000). The Occupation of Gardening in Life-Threatening Illness: A Qualitative Pilot Project. *Canadian Journal of Occupational Therapy, 67*(1), 70.
Tse, M.M.Y. (2010). Therapeutic Effects of an Indoor Gardening Programme for Older People Living in Nursing Homes. *Journal of Clinical Nursing, 19*(7-8), 949-958.

86. Francis, C. & C. Marcus (1991). Places People Take Their Problems [Thematic Session Affective Relations Between 'Person-Object-Place']. In J. Urbina-Soria, P. Ortega-Andeane, & R. Bechtel (Eds.), *Healthy environments* [Proceedings of EDRA 22/1991]. Oklahoma City, OK: EDRA.

87. Bliatout, B.T. (1986). Guideline for Mental Health Professionals to Help Hmong Clients Seek Traditional Healing Treatment. In G.L.

Hendricks, B.T. Downing, and A.S. Deinard (Eds.), *The Hmong in Transition*. Minneapolis, MN: University of Minnesota Press.

88. De Vries, S., R.A. Verheij, P.P. Groenewegen & P. Spreeuwenberg (2003). Natural Environments-Healthy Environments? An Exploratory Analysis of the Relationship Between Greenspace and Health. *Environment and planning A, 35*(10), 1717-1732.

89. I couldn't resist. Here as a country song I penned for this story:

The Love We Sowed
(Lyrics and music by John Zahina-Ramos)

Where did our love go
On that dark Montana night?
When you stood up and tore down
That one thing that was right.
You put out your fire
And drove on down the road
Takin' with you the earth boxes
That grew the love we sowed.

I began to cry.
How could I ever go on?
I'll never know just what
I'll do since you've gone.
The empty open plains
And seldom-traveled roads
Will never fill this heart
That's been left so hollow.

It's lonely on the rangeland
Can't seem to find my joy.
I need to get away somewhere,
Like Iowa or Illinois.
One day I'll move along
And find my peace of mind.
I'll plant some new earth boxes,
Leave your memories behind.

I'll forget to cry
At the mention of your name.
My heart will safely rest
In the arms of a new flame.
The empty open plains
And long-forgotten roads
My lover and I will travel on
'through the late day shadows.

90. Hall, D. (1996). A Garden of One's Own: The Ritual Consolations of the Backyard Garden. *Journal of American Culture, 19*(3), 9-13.

91. Please refer to the following studies:
Randall, T.A., C.J. Churchill & B.W. Baetz (2003). A GIS-Based Decision Support System for Neighbourhood Greening. *Environment and Planning, 30*, 541-563.
Gaston, K.J., P.H. Warren, K. Thompson & R.M. Smith (2005). Urban Domestic Gardens (IV): The Extent of the Resource and Associated Features. *Biodiversity and Conservation, 14*, 3327-3349.

92. Stone, Jr., B. & M.O. Rodgers (2001). How the Design of Cities Influences the Urban Heat Island Effect. *Journal of the American Planning Association, 67*(2), 186-198.

93. Sperling, C.D. & C.J. Lortie (2010). The Importance of Urban Backgardens on Plant and Invertebrate Recruitment: A field Microcosm Experiment. *Urban Ecologist, 13*, 223-235.

94. Ryall, C. & P. Hatherell (2003). A Survey of Strategies Adopted by UK Wildlife Trusts in Promotion of Gardening for Wildlife. *The Environmentalist, 23*, 81-87.

95. Diekelmann, J. & R.M. Schuster (2002). *Natural Landscaping: Designing With Native Plant Communities.* Madison, WI: University of Wisconsin Press.

96. I have to tell you a true story about attracting wildlife to my backyard. Although we often talk about concepts and principles, about things we *should* do because there is a greater good for doing it, it is sometimes not everything you envision...

Several years ago, when I was dreaming grand schemes for my largely Saharan backyard, I envisioned a small pond filled with happy little fish and effusive wetland plants just next to a formal patio. This would be a little oasis- a striking visual focal point, I was creatively assured; the place where people would be naturally moved to congregate, to reflect and ponder upon the little Edenistic ecosystem within. It would be free form, of course, with a shape suggested by Nature. Tumbled stones would recall the shores of desolate lakefront beaches or charming babbling brooks. I would gather together a noble collection of native aquatic plants and animals, recreating part of what was lost as the neighborhood developed. Pride welled up at the thought of how this small, but significant, water feature would become a center of local wildlife diversity. I almost saw the tired and thirsty migratory birds stopping gratefully to sip from its clear waters before continuing their arduous journeys to faraway lands. Frogs would come too, tree frogs and the cute little oak toads. I love their calls and anticipated their nocturnal serenade of thanks to me through my bedroom window.

I purchased a pond liner and carefully dug the hole where the miracle was to unfold. The design must be ecologically sound. There was a shallow shelf for wetland plants and a deeper place where the tiny fishes could be safe from the sharp eye of the hungry predatory bird. There was the littoral zone where important biogeochemical processes would occur, I recalled from my ecology course in college. I collected plants that live in the deeper water for snails to graze on and marsh plants for the pond's rocky edge. Over a couple of weeks, new additions were brought into the fold and the pond began to work like a well-crafted machine. It flourished. It was beautiful, as beautiful as any fantasy *could* be.

One day, I came home from work to find the plants upended. Some had been broken off at the roots. Stones lay in heaps. The fish seemed traumatized. Had a storm struck? I carefully surveyed the damage and replaced survivors into their niches. They could recover if given a generous amount of time, but I couldn't understand what had caused this. Birds searching for food? Crows, or maybe the grackles? Hmmm...they had been suspected in other mysterious happenings.

The next morning, I found damage that was much worse than the first attack. The water was fouled and turbid. Plants were shredded and some were chewed down to the roots. Few fish could be found in the dark water. Stones were shoved into the pond and it looked like the kind of wreckage that may be brought about by a teenager's party when the parents are away on vacation.

What kind of vile beast could have done this? It must be intelligent, and crafty; otherwise, how could it have known the pond was there. Had it been clandestinely observing my life from just beyond the hedge? If so, how long had I been watched? Was it driven to this pond by a force beyond reason and why did it want to destroy it? The Swamp Ape, perhaps? They have not been reported from this area. I also eliminated Yeti- Yeti are not found in this part of the world (there is no snow or winter). I knew that the only way to solve this mystery was to set up my own counter-surveillance.

That night, I waited for the beast's return. I watched though a window nearest the pond, peering cautiously from behind drawn curtains and looking out into the darkness for some movement or rustle that might signal the intruder's arrival. After an indescribable, and excruciatingly, uneventful duration of time, I dozed off into a foggy slumber. Oh, how tedious and boring and terribly inconvenient surveillance can be! At some unknown hour of the night, I was awakened by a chipper, chatty sound coming through the window. It was somewhat high pitched, trilled, oddly jubilant and child-like. Hmmm, a teenagers party?? Splash! Splash! Laughter!! More splashing....at that moment, I was assured that no Swamp Ape or Yeti could be responsible. Wanton abandonment is not something that they are known to express.

Through the curtains I saw two raccoons wrestling in the middle of the pond. Several others were on the sidelines cooing with bliss. Another was shimmying down the large oak tree to join the party. When I yelled at them, they gave me a blank stare, then ran for the safety of the neighbor's yard. The party was over!

The next night, they returned to frolic in the pond. Then again, the next. No screens or barriers I could erect could keep them away. Then things got really nasty...

For those who are not familiar with the habits of raccoons, they have a peculiar desire to defecate in the same place, a place referred to as a "communal latrine". They also love to defecate in water. Homeowners without screens or fences around their swimming pools quickly discover this. As the raccoons returned to my fallen Eden each night, the water became more fetid and murky, and so did my dreams for reconstructing a little ecosystem of happy fish and wetland plants...dreams that were done in by the arrival of chipper and playful wildlife.

The following weekend, the pond came out. I drained the putrefied water and pulled the liner out to dry on the sand mound next to the hole where fish once swam in their idyllic oasis. I raked the rocks into a pile and tossed the remaining wetland plants into the compost bin. That was the end of it.

But, it wasn't the end of it. The raccoons returned each night to play, but with the pond gone, they turned their attention towards what remained. Among the stones, they played and played, then left their mark by defecating on the liner before leaving at dawn. I hosed the liner off in the morning, but they came again the next night. I moved the liner to another place, but they followed it. Frustrated, I pulled the liner over a shrub and hosed it down yet again. There, now they couldn't get to it.

Undeterred, the raccoons defecated on the small corners of liner that touched the ground. I even slung the liner over a branch of the old oak tree, but they are excellent tree climbers too. At last, I rolled up the liner, placed it in a heavy-duty garbage bag and set it out for pickup. I suspect that the raccoons chased the liner down the street as it traveled to the landfill.

It has been many months since the raccoons have come to visit my yard at night. Sometimes, when I am awake in the dark hours of the early morning, I listen for them but only hear silence- and the chirping of crickets, the occasional sleepless bird and, thankfully, the tree frogs. (*Note: For many years, my neighbor has had a water feature like the one I installed and has never had a problem! I later found that I could have avoided this whole incident by installing an inexpensive motion-sensor sprinkler.*)

97. For a comprehensive discussion about agricultural subsidies in the United States and links to reliable sources of data, refer to the Wikipedia article entitled *Agricultural Subsidy*. The article can be accessed at http://en.wikipedia.org/wiki/Agricultural_subsidy (link active as of January 1, 2015).

98. Revell, T. (2014). *April Carbon Dioxide Levels Above Landmark 400 ppm Threshold for Entire Month.* Article published at Blue & Green Tomorrow, May 4th, 2014. Article can be accessed at http://blueandgreentomorrow.com/2014/05/04/april-carbon-dioxide-levels-above-landmark-400ppm-threshold-for-entire-month/ (link active as of January 1, 2015).

ABOUT THE AUTHOR

Dr. John Zahina-Ramos holds a M.S. degree in the biological sciences (focused on ecology) and a Ph.D. in geosciences. His dissertation research surveyed urban residents' attitudes and perspectives about home food growing. John is an adjunct professor and is the president of Casa Jardin Co., a consulting company whose services are focused on urban agriculture and environmental issues. He founded the Just One Backyard web resource (www.justonebackyard.com) to promote the practice of sustainable food growing, particularly in cities.

John worked for the Duke University School of the Environment from 1991-1997, supporting a wide range of ecological studies in the Everglades. From 1997-2014 he was an environmental scientist with the South Florida Water Management District, working on projects dedicated to Everglades restoration, Kissimmee River restoration, sustainable water use and natural resources protection. He has authored numerous peer-reviewed publications, technical documents, book chapters and conference presentations on the topics of soils, ecological modeling, historic vegetation mapping, the impacts of water withdrawals on wetlands, food sustainability, the benefits of urban agriculture and the potential productivity of urban agriculture.

CPSIA information can be obtained
at www.ICGtesting.com
Printed in the USA
LVHW011121221222
735766LV00009B/517

9 781505 834826